CREATIVE
SPIRIT

CREATIVE SPIRIT

Toward a Better World

Alexander Blackburn

Creative Arts Book Company
Berkeley • California

FOR
David, Philip,
and Kathy

CREATIVE SPIRIT is published by Donald S. Ellis
and distributed by Creative Arts Book Company

For information contact:
Creative Arts Book Company
833 Bancroft Way
Berkeley, California 94710
(800)-848-7789

ISBN 0-88739-315-2
Library of Congress Catalog Number 99-66710

Printed in the United States of America

Eros is not a god in the sense of being above man, but the power that binds all things and all men together, the power *informing* all things...Eros is the god or demiurge, Plato continues, who constitutes man's creative spirit. Eros is the drive which impels man not only toward union with another person in sexual or other forms of love, but incites in man the yearning for knowledge and drives him passionately to seek union with the truth. Through eros, we not only become poets and inventors but also achieve ethical goodness. Love, in the form of eros, is the power which generates, and this generation is 'a kind of eternity or immortality' — which is to say that such creativity is as close as men ever get to becoming immortal.

Rollo May, *Love & Will*,
in commentary on
The Symposium

Other Works by Alexander Blackburn

The Lamp Beside the Golden Door
   (novel)

Suddenly a Mortal Splendor
   (novel)

The Cold War of Kitty Pentecost
   (novel)

A Sunrise Brighter Still: The Visionary Novels
   of Frank Waters

The Myth of the Pícaro

The Interior Country: Stories of the Modern West
   (anthology)

Higher Elevations: Stories from the West
   (anthology)

ACKNOWLEDGEMENTS

"A Writer's Quest for Knowledge." *The Colorado Quarterly*, 24 (Summer 1975): 67-81.

"Experience, Imagination, and Revolt." *Writers' Forum*, 13(1987):1-7.

"On Teaching Creative Writing." *Riverrun*, 5 (Spring 1976): 24-34.

"Character as Style." In *Frank Waters: Man and Mystic*, edited by Vine Deloria, Jr. (Athens: Swallow Press/Ohio University Press, 1993), 106-121. Reprinted with the permission of Ohio University Press/Swallow Press, Athens, Ohio.

"Myth and the Picaresque Novel." *New Mexico Humanities Review*, 5:1 (Spring 1982): 23-35.

"The *Pícaro* in American Literature." *In Dictionary of Literary Themes and Motifs*, Vol. 2 (Westport: Greenwood Press, 1988): 983-991. Reprinted by permission of Greenwood Publishing Group, Inc., Westport, Connecticut.

"Higher Elevations." In *Higher Elevations: Stories from the West, A Writers' Forum Anthology*, edited by Alexander Blackburn and C. Kenneth Pellow (Athens: Swallow Press/Ohio University Press, 1993), xi-xv. Reprinted with the permission of Ohio University Press/Swallow Press, Athens, Ohio.

"The Interior Country." In *The Interior Country: Stories of the Modern West*, edited by Alexander Blackburn with Craig Lesley and Jill Landem (Athens: Swallow Press/Ohio University Press, 1987), ix-xvii. Reprinted with the permission of Ohio University Press/Swallow Press, Athens, Ohio.

"A Western Renaissance." *Western American Literature*, 29:1 (May

CONTENTS

Preface 1

I. Writing 3

   A Writer's Quest for Knowledge 5

   Experience, Imagination, and Revolt....................21

   The Long Habit of Living....................................31

   On Teaching Creative Writing.............................53

   Character as Style 67

II. Pícaro..83

   Myth and the Picaresque Novel..........................85

   The *Pícaro* in American Literature 103

III. West 115

   Higher Elevations 117

   The Interior Country 125

   A Western Renaissance 135

IV. Novelists 151

   Faulkner and Continuance of the
      Southern Renaissance..............................153

   On Reading Frank Waters.................................171

   Waters and Modern Fiction 181

V. Atomic Age 195

   Archetypal Promise from Apocalyptic Premise 197

   The Self as a Force for Human Survival.......................225

   Peace Stars..243

   A Theodicy of Human Love 261

Notes...269

CREATIVE
SPIRIT

PREFACE The topics of these essays might at first glance seem too diverse for the presentation of a single, unifying theme. Reflecting some of my interests as a novelist, an editor, a critic, and an educator, the essays take up such subjects as creative writing, the picaresque novel, the American West, the Southern Renaissance, the art and philosophy of Frank Waters, issues of war and peace, and revolutionary discoveries in neuropsychology. Then, too, there are variations in tone and range. Depending upon occasion, some essays originated as public lectures and others as literary investigations, though none, I would hope, of an overly specialized kind. But, whatever the topic or occasion, all of the essays gradually develop the theme of the creative spirit in literature and life. Their underlying, passionate preoccupation is what it means to be a man of letters in the Atomic Age, an era when our very existence has hanging over it a sword of Damocles.

The creative spirit, as I conceive it, is that power of the human mind that is aligned with and has possibilities to express Creation. It is an ontological power having to do with essences and a cosmogonic power related to evolution. The creative spirit accordingly manifests the quality of unpredictable, unprecedented experience; of spontaneity, adventure, and adaptability. In literature, this essential power has been known as the imagination, its correlation with the mythic mode of consciousness and with the archetypes of the collective unconscious being a recent enhancement of definition.

The creative spirit shatters and reinterprets the fixed and already known, the predetermined codes. It opposes all the forms and forces of disorder and division, all that diminishes the freedom, the dignity, indeed, the authority of the individual human being. From the perspective of the creative spirit, the biologically unique individual is the mythogenetic center of meaningfulness and thereby in revolt against automatisms, ideologies, and tribal authorities. This perspective yields order and seeks to heal divisions of man and nature, man and God, and man against himself. For, to the creative spirit, man and nature are interconnected; man has his Being within a timeless mystery; his mind is not limited to rational consciousness; and no man is an island, solid, separate, and alone. The creative spirit discerns the tragedy of the modern world, especially in Europe and the United States, in materialism, rationalism, and the cult of individualism. And so the creative spirit would give us moral orientation in the direction of a valid world culture, restoring the notion of our common humanity and holding out the vision of transcending world crisis through a process of creative enlargement of consciousness.

This free and accommodating power has, of course, always been associated with fictions that make sense of life. Literature, mythology, and mysticism are among its most celebrated achievements. Yet science, too, is creative in its initiating phases, and science is constructing a vision of reality that is remarkably similar to that known for thousands of years to introspective philosophy: namely that the universe is unfolding according to a hidden dynamic order in which human consciousness participates. The recent discoveries in neuropsychology, that the human consciousness controls and directs behavior, are obviously of enormous interest in any consideration of our nihilistic and destructive age, and of our power to redeem it. In other words, contemporary science is empirically validating that what I call the creative spirit is a function—perhaps *the* essential function—of the mind.

My indebtedness to others is, I trust, sufficiently acknowledged in notes, if not in the text. My especial mentors, those from whom I have learned and am still learning how to live in what has been called a new world of the mind, were William Blackburn, Joseph Campbell, and Frank Waters.

I. Writing

A WRITER'S QUEST FOR KNOWLEDGE

A few miles south of Oxford, the Thames meanders through meadows, caresses the long green hair of willows, slips past pubs and thatched cottages whose smoke makes S-signs in wet air, and eventually flows past an old, picturesque village called Sutton Courteney. Here is post-card pastoralism indeed: golden Cotswold stone houses, gardens aflame, a Norman church with the flag of the Cross of St. George flying from its tower and with a small cemetery, grass-grown and shaded by yew trees. Buried in Sutton Courteney cemetery is a man who died in 1950 and who was both highly cultivated and humble. This was a man who repudiated much of the England of his day and at the same time celebrated native virtues, the old-fashioned rectitude and decency for which his own life served as an excellent expression. Some have called him a "social saint" and a "revolutionary personality," but he was, first and foremost, a writer who was an artist and, as an artist, one of the great prophets of our time.[1]

His name was Eric Arthur Blair. Until he was twenty-four, his life was in all its visible details a training for membership in the administrative middle class of imperialist Britain. His family, on both sides, had lived and worked in India and Burma, in the army, administration, and trade. It was in the pattern for him to attend Eton College, then join the Indian Imperial Police, and serve in Burma. Suddenly, however, in 1927 he resigned from the police and, in effect, from the England and world of Eric Blair, and during the next nine years set about consciously creating a new set of social relationships and a new social identity. He developed as a writer through the years of the Depression and of fascism of the Left as well as of the Right. At every point, in these years he exposed himself to these facts in their most direct form. He became unemployed and penniless, partly because of the early difficulties of being a writer but also deliberately, as a way of cutting his connections with an unacceptable establishment. He went to Spain to fight fascism.

Blair's courage and persistence in repeated exposure to the hardest facts of his time are by any standard remarkable. Imperialism, racism, totalitarianism, and whatever else he saw as diminishing the freedom and dignity of a human being, he opposed. Writing under a pseudonym that was his created identity, he developed until, in the 1940s, he had composed two masterful prophetic novels, *Animal Farm* and *1984*. Eric Arthur Blair had become the writer whom the world knows as George Orwell.[2]

This conversion is, I think, a crucial instance of what it can mean to be a writer. What Blair did in recreating himself as Orwell was, by any account, difficult and admirable. But was it necessary, necessary to the actual writing? I think not. It is true that the Orwellian *persona* comes across to us as that of a revolutionary, and accordingly we are free to regard Orwell as a hero, which he is to diverse elements in Anglo-American life. Unlike a Ghandhi or a Che Guevara, however, Orwell was essentially a writer—that is, someone who expresses experience in words. Although Orwell to some extent shaped the content of this writing, it was Eric Blair, after all, who had wanted to be a writer since boyhood and who wrote. Orwell's awareness of the enormous injustice and misery of the world centered his artistic vision; but pity and compassion had been experienced all along and thus did not necessitate a political formulation.

One of the mistaken notions that people have about writers is that they, to be authentic, have to have lived the experiences that are the subject matter of their works. But to experience the truth of the human heart, one does not need to have experienced battle or the charge of a rhinoceros or nights on a barroom floor. Such a program, if logically followed, would eliminate most writers through exhaustion and death. Stephen Crane is a classic example of the writer who chased after dangerous experience until he met an early death. The curious thing is, Crane's *The Red Badge of Courage*, one of the best novels ever written about war, was composed out of imagination before its author had ever seen a war. Similarly, although Crane actually survived the sinking of a ship and the ordeal of the sea that followed, his great short story, "The Open Boat," gains its impact from words that convey the feeling of being alone in an indifferent universe—a feeling that all of us share at some time or other without having to be shipwrecked. Then there is the example of Ernest Hemingway. I suppose of all American moderns Hemingway has been the most idolized. He chased after wars and game; he thought his power as a writer had something to do with his potency as a male, and so he wrote about soldiers, hunters, fighters—both bull and prize. And he extolled one virtue, courage, and one day he put a bullet through his head. The Hemingway the public did not see was a tragic personality. He disguised this fact by limiting the range of what he wrote, by selecting and cultivating one kind of experience. To me, it seems conceivable that the areas of life-experience that he ignored or neglected finally engulfed him.

But to return to George Orwell. The sort of experience that made him the writer he was is compellingly revealed in an early essay called "A Hanging" (1931). I do not know if it is *the* experience which prompted Blair to leave the Imperial Police and convert himself into Orwell, but the precision of insight, the kind of *knowledge* he gained from experience, leaves little doubt that he had found himself. The British authorities are about to execute an Indian. Here, from *Shooting an Elephant and Other Essays*, is the critical passage:

> It was about forty yards to the gallows. I watched the bare brown back of the prisoner marching in front of me. He walked clumsily with his bound arms, but quite steadily, with that bobbing gait of the Indian who never straightens his knees. At each step his muscles slid neatly into place, the lock of hair on his scalp danced up and down, his feet printed themselves on the wet gravel. And once, in spite of the men who gripped him by each shoulder, he stepped slightly aside to avoid a puddle on the path.

It is curious, but till that moment I had never realized what it means to destroy a healthy, conscious man. When I saw the prisoner step aside to avoid the puddle I saw the mystery, the unspeakable wrongness, of cutting a life short when it is in full tide. This man was not dying, he was alive just as we are alive. All the organs of his body were working—bowels digesting food, skin renewing itself, nails growing, tissues forming—all toiling away in solemn foolery. His nails would still be growing when he stood on the drop, when he was falling through the air with a tenth of a second to live. His eyes saw the yellow gravel and the gray walls, and his brain still remembered, foresaw, reasoned—reasoned even about puddles. He and we were a party of men walking together, seeing, hearing, feeling, understanding the same world; and in two minutes, with a sudden snap, one of us would be gone—one mind less, one world less.[3]

The prisoner's stepping around the puddle is called, technically, a telling detail, and what it tells is that there are a mystery and order of life that are meaningful and that in this instance are being coldly and brutally ignored. *Till that moment I had never realized*, writes Orwell: it is a moment of revelation, a moment of enlarged consciousness of existence, a moment when the creative spirit makes contact with another's full humanity, a moment when our rational mind listens, in terror and pity and awe, to an inner voice of our being. Literature, sacred and profane, is full of such moments. Since St. Augustine wrote the first autobiography, we have had frequent testimonials to the power of this moment of spiritual insight. *Till that moment I had never realized*: the meaning of time has changed, there is a before and an after, there is the past that is now revealed as having led, by a mystical yet inevitable process, up to the moment, and there is the present looking back and evaluating that past, the consciousness finally open to what it means to live. It is the sort of experience that gives a writer insight into the form and pressure of his time.

I venture to say that no one will become a writer, at least beyond a certain superficial level, who has not attained to some vision of order, who has not experienced something that answers to our deep human need for meaning. It is strange that in our society we do not readily acknowledge that the need for meaning can be as strong as our needs for food and sex. We must know inwardly that without something such as literature that meets our need for meaning, we may in fact die—as, for example, may die the person outlawed by his tribe, it being repository of all the available meanings, and the person thrust outside seeing himself as having lost all significance, with it the will to live. To survive, then, we may need meaning. Literature is one of the means by which we gain insight into our significance as human beings. In literature we find reassertion of the power and aristocracy of the spirit.

Thus far what I have been driving at is that a writer plays a vital role in society because s/he has had some experience of meaning or order which compels her or him to seek its expression in words. But before going further, let me admit at once that the term *writer* is a generalization. Poets and novelists are writers, but so too are journalists, advertising copyists, preachers, politicians, and teachers. In a literate society everybody is a writer. There is, therefore, no justification for thinking that all writers are rare and talented, colorful personalities endowed beyond the claim of the majority. Some people are better writers than others, just as some people are better human beings than others. One can assess the quality of a person's writing only by comparing it with the work of others, past and contemporary. Yet, in our society, where the word *writer* has its showbiz equivalent in *star*, any person described as a writer is supposed to possess not one talent that he has developed to a point of excellence but a special personality giving him a right to our hero worship. We forget to distinguish between George Orwell, who had a fascinating life-style, and Eric Blair, who did the writing. An obsession with *being* a writer can make a sad spectacle.

A philistine force works against clear understanding of what some writers may be trying to do. I do not underestimate the profit motive. In a commercially run society such as ours, one has feelings of anxiety when not making money. When something is good, it *should* be selling, and, conversely, if something does not sell, it must be bad. Yet many have written without reward in their lifetime, and not a few have suffered directly or indirectly for their literary efforts. Although Shakespeare made enough money to buy a coat-of-arms and some real estate, Dante died in exile, Marlowe was murdered, Villon was hanged as a thief, Southwell was tortured and disembowelled, Raleigh was beheaded, and Keats died convinced that his life was writ on water. Shelley drowned. Kafka did not live to see his works in print. The Hungarian poet Radnoti was enslaved by the Nazis, shot, and dumped in a mass grave. Some of the greatest American writers were largely unrecognized in their time. Poe's stories made little impact in America, but in France, where they were translated by Baudelaire, they altered the shape of modern literature. Herman Melville's *Moby Dick* sold less than a hundred copies in his lifetime, though he lived for forty years after that classic's publication. The Dream of Success is probably best ignored by writers.

I am not, mind you, against writers making money. If I were, I suppose I would have to favor the alternative, which is to have all writers unionized and paid by the state. I, for one, think that too risky. Russia's greatest living writer, Solzhenitzen, was expelled from the writer's union before being exiled. Philistinism obviously is preferable to ideological barbarism enforced by a blind, stupid bureaucracy, and the reason is clear: people need access to what artists have to communicate as true, be the truth ever so critical of received ideas or ever so subversive of institutions' authority. A strong truth is bracing to the minds and hearts of men. It stirs the blood like mountain air. To have it denied is to be choked and stifled in an ocean of bland and fatuous twaddle. But though American writers are relatively free, philistinism still encourages them to relax their vigilance with respect to intellectual honesty. A writer as good as Hemingway could sometimes slip into the money-making phraseology of a Mickey Spillane or Harold Robbins, as for instance in *For Whom the Bell Tolls* when he comments on a sexual union by writing, "The earth moved."

Writing, I believe, may best be approached, not with a view of being a writer—to get power, profit, and pleasure—but as a human activity, perhaps no more, but certainly no less important to our survival than other human activities and, like them, varying in quality according to talent, work, and aspiration. One of the most difficult of human activities, writing may induce pleasure in the writer who writes well and may become a profitable source of income because writers meet consumer demands for fantasy, for sensationalism, and, sometimes, for truth. But considered as an activity of art, writing is not primarily for pleasure or profit, but has a great purpose, described by Tolstoy as "a means of union among men, joining them together in the same feelings, and indispensable for the life and progress toward well-being of individuals and of humanity."[4]

———≈———

To explain a writer's quest, let me draw an analogy between a writer's character and that of the Greek hero Odysseus, or Ulysses, as that fictive being has come down to us through the ages.[5]

Homer's Odysseus, you will recall, spent ten years in the Trojan War and another ten years of wandering before that. With the help of gods and men, he returned to his homeland, slaughtered his enemies, and became reunited with his wife Penelope. Perhaps there is something faintly comical about a man who struggles for two decades to get home to his wife,

especially after adventures with a couple of bewitching goddesses, Calypso and Circe, along the way. But Homer's
Odysseus is no respectable bourgeois: he lives by his wits and
has no qualms about putting a hundred people to death. And he
is the original chauvinist pig. Penelope is part of *his* identity,
their marriage but one means whereby Odysseus becomes a
name to be recognized. Recognition of his identity, that is what
this Odysseus wants above all. What's in a name? According to
George E. Dimock, Homer's hero has a name which means in
Greek, "to cause pain and to be willing to do so."[6] Thus the
name Odysseus implies subjectively and objectively what it is
to persecute. To be Odysseus, in Homer's sense, is to adopt the
attitude of the hunter of dangerous game, deliberately to
expose oneself for the purpose of recognition, of being somebody with a complete identity and thus to snatch a victory from
death, itself. By the same token, Odysseus' greatest enemy is
the power that destroys identity—and those goddesses almost
destroyed his. Again, according to Professor Dimock, in Greek
the word Calypso suggests the perfect security and satisfaction
of the womb. To be Calypso is to engulf you in a paradise where
(1) you do not seek the meaning of life and (2) you do not strive
for recognition or waken others to a sense of their own existence or establish their identities in harmony with the nature
of things. To sum up, Homer's Odysseus is a character who
struggles to create something out of nothing—a fulfilled being
or identity—and who must continuously beware of being calyp-
soed into a Brave New World of waste and apathy. As such, he
may already be taken to suggest the artist.

But there is more to be added before the analogy with the
artist becomes appropriate. Dante, in the thirteenth century at
the dawning of the modern consciousness, also gives us a portrait of Odysseus (with his latinized name, Ulysses), and
Dante's version is significantly different from Homer's. In *The
Inferno*, Ulysses is the very personification of the restless wanderer and intrepid explorer of the unknown. Dante depicts
Ulysses as having deserted Penelope and taken a last fatal voy-

age in defiance of an edict of God declaring: Thou shalt not cross the Atlantic Ocean. Ulysses crosses it anyway, and thus his thirst for knowledge lands him in a sticky place in hell. Now of course it's remarkable that a poet should dream of a fictitious voyage that Columbus was to make real several centuries later. But the point is this: Dante, in the character of Ulysses, prophetically portrays the spirit of modern man, the spirit free and affirmative that is ever in quest of knowledge, that is seeking the meaning of life in experience. In other words, he had hit upon the myth of Faust. Good Christian that he was, Dante had to back off from the spirit of individualism and science, but he was a humanist, too. And what is the *Divine Comedy* if not a subjective epic, the journey of a soul in search of wisdom and grace by means of imaginative confrontation with the realities of his time?

> Who even dead, yet hath his mind entire!
> This sound came in the dark
> First must thou go the road
> to hell
> And to the bower of Ceres' daughter Proserpine,
> Through overhanging dark, to see Tiresias,
> Eyeless that was, a shade, that is in hell
> So full of knowing that the beefy men know less
> than he,
> Ere thou come to thy road's end.
> Knowledge the shade of a shade,
> Yet must thou sail after knowledge
> Knowing less than drugged beasts.

That passage—echoing Homer and Dante—is from Canto XLVII of *The Cantos* of Ezra Pound. *The Cantos* are not impenetrable: their organizing principle is once more a spiritual odyssey with the artist now a modern Odysseus sailing after knowledge. Where he sails, where he must seek, is hell, for now the whole world is hell, a cultural waste-land. His quest is for redemptive vision.[7]

For at least a century, thinkers have been aware of cultural failure. The whole edifice of meaning that we know as Christianity, that multi-faceted myth that gave, and still gives to some, an idea of order with respect to personal conduct, social organization, and spiritual history, has, for many, fallen apart. The magic of the Word has dissolved into thin air. The symbolism of the language by which we knew ourselves and our destiny seems weak, no longer touching us. Men of prophetic soul such as Melville despaired to see the gods going home, yet knew in their hearts they would have to find another Holy Land. Melville found his in the myths of Asia and Oceania, back where many myths, including the Christian, started. Unlike Melville, humanists such as Wallace Stevens rejoiced that man is free of the gods at last. And some writers stayed within the Christian tradition: T.S. Eliot embraced orthodoxy, his poetry recovering the sweet sounds of a saint. William Faulkner and D.H. Lawrence reworked Christian symbolism, placing particular emotional emphasis upon pity, compassion, and sacrifice, and upon the theme of resurrection. Whatever ground has been lost and found, the task of the writer in modern times has become immensely difficult. He or she can no longer rely upon a community of meaning. The stories and poems that he or she makes have to generate their own meaning. Surely in all the literary epochs there has been no time when a writer's quest for knowledge has assumed such importance, yet at the same time been so beleaguered by chaotic appearances, theories, and ideologies, as ours. Yet our psychic survival could partly depend upon this quest.

In their efforts to describe and evaluate modern literature, critics and writers seem agreed upon a number of related observations. The first is that, since the later Middle Ages, there has been an accelerating decline in the other-worldly point of view. Thus a writer is virtually denied the old belief-systems and their social expression as a fixed standard of conduct. And hence many modern writers express in their works a sense of loss, especially of the intimate relation between man and man.

Outraged by the complexity, incoherence, and violence of modern times, they may look back to a time of social order when life was not the realization of Macbeth's nightmare, "a tale told by an idiot full of sound and fury, signifying nothing." A second observation of critics is that the literary generations of the twentieth century are best distinguished in their manner of responding to the fact of death—that is, in their manner of somehow getting beyond it. As R.W.B. Lewis has written, "[The] first fact of modern historic life is the death that presses in on it from all sides: death in battle, death in prison, death in the pit of the soul and the very heart of culture.... Yet," Lewis continues, "the true artist is constantly seeking ways to confound death."[8] Typically, many novelists begin their fiction in an atmosphere of such death. They express hostility to the reality they represent, their observers being solitary individuals on the fringe, outside the prevailing, decaying culture and yet striving to open up some relationship with the world. Thus a vital question that a writer may put to himself is this: how can he transcend a disintegrating culture? Put another way—and the question profoundly affects the formal design of literary works, hence their seeming difficulty and eccentricity for many readers—how can we find grounds for living in life, itself, and give emphasis to what is felt as meaningful? From this, a third observation about modern literature follows, namely, that technique is employed, not as a perverse means of exalting art-for-art's sake at the expense of communication, but as *the* authentic way of seeing our condition, as the channel *into* an affirmative illumination of life.

All three of these observations point up a writer's quest for knowledge. The loss of the other-worldly point of view means that a writer must be prepared to define the experience of the present age imaginatively and to make of the very difficulty of definition one of the enriching values of his art. His solace must be that he is emancipated from the whole past complex of stock responses to and literary arrangements of experience. Secondly, so many of the forms and pressures of our time have a deadening effect. Television, for example. Recently I heard a boy ask his mother, "Shall we have fun tonight, or watch TV?" That's it. Much in our society is not fun. Our world, to some, is like a gigantic insane asylum, a world that stupefies, sickens, and infuriates. A writer has much difficulty in trying to understand, then describe, and then make credible much of reality. But despite the deadly and deadening appearances of society, a writer must still seek, within imagination, some life-significant symbolism. And a writer, like as not, will employ techniques that demand that the reader share in his quest—take with him an imaginary Odyssean voyage into the world, until we *see*, together, where we are.

The climactic passage of Joyce's *A Portrait of the Artist as a Young Man* comes at the moment shortly after the hero, Stephen Dedalus, has finally rebeled against all the symbols of authority: home, Ireland, and the Church. Excited by the realization that he is called to be a writer, Stephen is walking along the strand when he has an experience of ecstatic vision, aesthetic and religious, profane and sacred, all at the same time.

> He was alone. He was unheeded, happy and near to the wild heart of life. He was alone and young and wilful and wildhearted, alone amid a waste of wild air and brackish waters and the seaharvest of shells and tangle and veiled grey sunlight and gayclad lightclad figures, of children and girls and voices childish and girlish in the air.
>
> A girl stood before him in midstream, alone and still, gazing out to sea. She seemed like one whom magic had changed into the likeness of a strange and beautiful seabird. Her long slender bare legs were delicate as a crane's and pure save where an emerald trail of seaweed had fashioned itself as a sign upon the flesh. Her thighs, fuller and softhued as ivory, were bared almost to the hips where the white fringes of her drawers were like feathering of soft white down. Her slateblue skirts were kilted boldly about her waist

and dovetailed behind her. Her bosom was as a bird's, soft and slight, slight and soft as the breast of some dark-plumaged dove. But her long hair was girlish: and girlish, and touched with the wonder of mortal beauty, her face.

She was alone and still, gazing out to sea; and when she felt his presence and the worship of his eyes her eyes turned to him in quiet sufferance of his gaze, without shame or wantonness. Long, long she suffered his gaze and then quietly withdrew her eyes from his and bent them towards the stream, gently stirring the water with her foot hither and thither. The first faint noise of gently moving water broke the silence, low and faint and whispering, faint as the bells of sleep; hither and thither, hither and thither; and a faint flame trembled on her cheek.

—Heavenly God! cried Stephen's soul, in an outburst of profane joy.

He turned away from her suddenly and set off across the strand. His cheeks were aflame; his body was aglow; his limbs were trembling. On and on and on and on he strode, far out over the sand, singing wildly to the sea, crying to greet the advent of the life that had cried to him.

Her image had passed into his soul forever and no word had broken the holy silence of his ecstasy. Her eyes had called him and his soul had leaped at the call. To live, to err, to fall, to triumph, to recreate life out of life! A wild angel had appeared to him, the angel of mortal youth and beauty, an envoy from the fair courts of life, to throw open before him in an instant of ecstasy the gates of all the ways of error and glory. On and on and on and on![9]

Before Stephen's eyes—before our eyes—a simple girl is transformed into a goddess, image incarnate of the beauty and joy of life. She is life itself, representing Experience, the eternal opposite to Authority.

And she is what a writer seeks and sings.

The Odyssean voyage toward knowledge is, I think, for a writer a journey toward an affirmation of life. To clarify this point, I began by distinguishing between Eric Blair, a writer, and George Orwell, a *persona* and revolutionist. Where a revolutionist seeks to inspire mass movements and expresses a pity for the downtrodden and injured that has been hatched out of his hatred for the powers that be, an artist, in my opinion, has that kind of love toward mankind that makes him able to endure the general condition of evil and suffering, regardless of any relations these may have to his own life. Whereas an artist reveals, often at great personal cost, a profound skepticism of collective human efforts, a revolutionist preaches and glorifies such efforts, often at his own peril, for in discrediting a specific ruling order for specific grievances, he may give rise to far greater tyrannies. A revolutionist, though he speak of freedom, is committed; an artist, like the true scholar, may be said to adopt the Socratic ideal of detachment before possible worlds of the truth. An artist resists the call to identify completely with the everyday social process and thereby to confront all that is wrong in our midst.[10] His is the call of life, as it was for Eric Blair at the hanging and as it is for Joyce's Stephen Dedalus. An artist's freedom is to be free of falsity of all kinds, to be free to affirm authentic experience. Nothing kills that freedom so much as the Calypso-Circe promise of a Brave New World or a 1984 where few would dare to question the meaning of life.

And that is why we should heed what our good writers say to us. Here is the conclusion of Robert Lowell's "Waking Early Sunday Morning," in which the poet envisions a world without discipline or meaning, a world in which we remain aware of our moral potentiality, but must accustom ourselves to the permanent loss of joy:

No weekends for the gods now. Wars
flicker, earth licks its open sores,
fresh breakage, fresh promotions, chance

assassinations, no advance.
Only man thinning out his kind
sounds through the Sabbath noon, the blind
swipe of the pruner and his knife
busy about the tree of life . . .

Pity the planet, all joy gone
from this sweet volcanic cone:
peace to our children when they fall
in small war on the heels of small
war—until the end of time
to police the earth, a ghost
orbiting forever lost
in our monotonous sublime.[11]

But surely not all the loopholes for the soul are closed. True,
our symbolic language is not the potent force it once was.
Peace, in our time, may mean war. The metaphor *rock of ages*,
a hymn about the comforting strength of Christendom, now
refers to the Mosler Safe that survived the atomic bombing of
Hiroshima. And we are deluged with meaningless abstractions
such as *extra vehicular activity*. No doubt, too, the pleasant con-
notations of an image such as *bug-whine*—the word conjures up
for me the grandeur and solitude of warm evenings in the
Carolinas—are being destroyed because of a slang association
of *bug* with a spying device. So a writer has his work cut out for
him once he realizes, like Eric Blair, that mankind is one. On
his quest for knowledge he goes, like Stephen Dedalus, alone
and often unheeded, clearing from his path the tangled shrubbery of dead language and of false feeling, hoping to recover
and express in words an experience of joyful pulsing from the
wild heart of life. On and on and on!

EXPERIENCE, IMAGINATION, AND REVOLT

Write about experience. Write about what you know. How often we are told this, first perhaps by a teacher, later by our own inner voice. The advice is by no means clear. Are we, like Hemingway, to chase after wars and wild game, to pay homage to bullfighters, before we have the experience to write about them? If so, how are we going to explain Emily Dickinson, who wrote thousands of poised and intricate poems without venturing far from her father's house in Amherst? True, we must sometimes get away from our Amherst in order to focus feelings and refresh the sense of wonder. We might, like Thomas Wolfe, conclude that we can't go home again. On the other hand, we might, like William Faulkner, conclude that the little postage stamp of earth called home provides enough experience to inspire a lifetime of writing. Either way, experience is something we already possess, though it may be hidden from consciousness, like the roots of sleep.

Beginning writers, in particular, are wary of probing and quarrying-out the deep and possibly painful experiences that might threaten an already tentative self-identity with such mysteries as sex and death unless emotion is contained in art and is no longer identifiable as the writer's self. Lacking confidence in art, beginning writers are prone to turn away from self-discovery and indulge in something vaguely called "self-expression," a kind of detour around emotion and in the direction of intergalactic space, of frontier towns where everyone is quick on the draw, or of the family life of Minnie Mouse. Of course, we all share a compulsion to get away from reality and to soar on wings of fantasy to a world elsewhere. As I shall explain later, the American imagination thrives on creation of new worlds. But there comes a time when your spaceship develops an oil leak, when your cowboy has such a bad case of flatulence that even the vilest galoot in Yellow Sky won't get close enough to fight him, and when Minnie Mouse gets coked to the whiskers on dope. Continued avoidance of real experience means you are apt to fly, not to outer space, but to pieces.

Wallace Stegner has written that writers born in the West face a special problem. They are "born square ...a sort of majority product, a belated and provincial one at that, formed by majority attitudes and faiths."[1] Although western-born writers are healthy animals in what until very recently was an essentially pre-industrial, pre-urban society, they are nonetheless lured from the land they know and persuaded that literature is concerned with what they don't know, the lives of exiles, junkies, and hustlers, of victims of holocausts, of poverty and the class struggle. Poor westerner, he finds dignity and hope in living. Still, it seems, he must learn to suffer quiet desperation in order to be "literary," perhaps imitate Mary McCarthy and write scathingly sophisticated accounts of the rot in Denmark when she was born in Seattle.

But the real problem is not the lack or inadequacy of experience; it is, rather, the delayed arrival of revelation. Like the bourgeois gentleman who was astonished to discover he'd been speaking prose all his life, a writer has to open his eyes to the immediate and obvious. There is a scene in Faulkner's *Absalom, Absalom!* when young Thomas Sutpen has been rebuffed at a plantation owner's door and flees to a cave where he reviews the whole of his life. It was "like when you pass through a room fast and look at all of the objects in it and you turn and go back through the room again and look at all the objects from the other side and you find out you had never seen them before."[2] In other words, a writer has to learn to see stars in daylight; they are there in the firmament, obscured by the glare of the sun, but sooner or later you can *feel* their presence. Humanity, too, needs to be seen "from the other side." Recall Joseph Conrad's *Heart of Darkness*. After finding Kurtz in Africa, Marlowe realizes that this European who has reverted to savagery is still, at the last gasp, human—unspeakably free but capable of understanding his own damnation, hence a creature worthy of compassion. Marlowe's quest for self-knowledge is a journey beyond the environments of civilization and into the "heart" of humanity's capacities for good and evil. A writer's quest is a similar awakening to the glory and horror of being, a recognition of one's self in the human image in both a specific and a universal sense. Whereas specific experiences are infinitely varied, universal experiences are those that bleed to a prick and occur in a visible world. Compassion, pity, humility, fortitude, grief, endurance: these are some of them, and you will find them anywhere, even in sunny California.

Because writing is self-discovery, not self-expression, we need to pay attention to experience up close and then seek to surpass in our real experience that portion of it that is merely given. This is the point where imagination comes into play: imagination can approach a particular object to reveal it in its fullness, the net of analogies in which each object reaches out to another object.

Some experiences are more bound up than others with the feelings and meanings that enshrine the spirit. These are the experiences of the heart's blood, the ones that have absorbed our attention, often from an early age, the ones that have bestowed on us our awareness, the ones inside of which we have grown. They are spiritual shrines where the gods abide, those images so imbued with strong emotions as to have the power to crack us open and to fuel the long endeavor of art. Probably in your childhood years you stood still and looked about in awe and terror at the mystery of being until you had your fill of time and place. Then when you went through the rite of passage into youth and were figuratively reborn into the life of struggle and fulfillment, the world, in Wordsworth's phrase, was "too much with us." You looked back upon childhood as if from afar, as if, again in Wordsworth's phrase, "there hath past away a glory from the earth." Still there in your mind's eye, however, are the enshrined images awaiting your acknowledgement. As James Joyce discovered in exile, Dublin had never been lost. You had little idea before just how myste-

rious is the mystery of yourself, and now you must be prepared, like Faulkner's Sutpen, "to go back through the room
again and look at all the objects from the other side." It is going
to be difficult, but you have to be faithful to the wounds of life
and not be discouraged from your task by a sense of your
nakedness before social, economic, and religious authorities of
the tribe. You are breaking away from the tribe's daylight world,
submerging in the sea of images, beginning your pilgrimage to
the shrines where the truth of your experience lies. And out of
this submergence, this pilgrimage, you may surface with the
poems and stories that teach the lesson of life renewed. Oddly,
you will be told by the tribe—you may even tell yourself—that
you're wasting your time away from the "real" world, that
"truth" is just "information," something to be retrieved from a
database and put to use. But it is the tribe that lives in the world
of illusions, lost on the surface of reality, emotions suppressed,
with reason itself unable to recognize the impracticality—
indeed the insanity—of the pursuit of wealth and power.

The feelings of time and place that spirit enshrines return
to us in memory and dream, the images transformed in pattern
and significance and pliant enough to be moulded to new, unifying shape. The power of the image lies in its capacity to beget
other images, to expand from the Big Bang of deep feeling to
the creation of unsuspected stars. The containment of this
power is art. What begins as a strong emotion-charged image-
particle is gradually externalized into form, so that the poem or
the story finally assumes a life of its own, irrespective of autobiographical origins. How do you know when the poem or story
is finished? When you're able to see it from all sides. When it is
no longer "you." When your "you" is, as John Donne said centuries ago, "involved with mankind." The one "for whom the
bell tolls." When mortal time is no longer quite the old winged
chariot hurrying near, but an element arrested in the mystery
of here-and-now. That's when.

One of the greatest of American novels, Faulkner's *The
Sound and the Fury* originated from an image of a little girl who

is climbing a tree and whose brothers observe her muddy underwear. When the grandmother, whom Faulkner and his three brothers called Damuddy, died the children were sent away from home so that the house could be fumigated. To Faulkner's memory of this event he added an imaginary sister, "the daughter of his mind," Caddy, who had first appeared in a story called "Twilight" before reappearing as the pivotal character of this novel. "I loved her so much," he said, that "I couldn't decide to give her life just for the duration of a short story. She deserved more than that. So my novel was created, almost in spite of myself." In Faulkner's novel we observe four children come of age amidst the decay and dissolution of their family. His sense of it began, Faulkner recalled, with "a brother and a sister splashing one another in the brook" when they have been sent away to play during the funeral of a grandmother they call Damuddy. As Caddy clambers up a tree to observe the funeral inside the house, her brothers see her muddy drawers from below. From this sequence Faulkner got several things: his sense of the brook that was sweeping Caddy away from her brothers; his sense that the girl who had the courage to climb the tree and ponder the mystery of death would also find the courage to face change and loss; and his sense that her brothers, who had waited below, would respond to loss differently, with incomprehension, despair, and rage. At this stage, Caddy, the figure of imagination added to remembered experience, had not emerged as a character. However, she seemed to offer the comfort and tenderness elsewhere unavailable from the family, and her brothers' needs for these, frustrated by their parents, could be met by her. Thus, Faulkner said, "the character of [the] sister began to emerge." Whereas readers are justifiably impressed by the technical brilliance of Faulkner's novel, they are apt to forget how simple and moving is the basic story that grew from temporal experience charged with the power of imagination.[3]

The shrine of place is where you have your roots, where you stand, your base of reference that provides validity in the raw material of writing. Fiction especially is bound up in the local, the "real" environment, the present, ordinary day-to-day of human experience. As Eudora Welty says, "The moment the place in which the novel happens is accepted as true, through it will begin to glow, in a kind of recognizable glory, the feeling and thought that inhabited the novel in the author's head and animated the whole of his work." Place, she contends, helps to make characters real and believable. "[T]he likeliest character has first to be enclosed inside the bounds of even greater likelihood," because so confined is "set to scale in his proper world to know his size."[4] If the gods that abide in and speak from the shrine of time withhold their secrets, the shrine of place will help to focus the feeling and meaning that permeate your personal life. A world steadily visible from its outside meets our requirements for belief, *then* liberates the imagination to create an environment of freedom for such otherwise incredible characters as Don Quixote, Huckleberry Finn, and Lolita.

Nowadays some theorists of language deny the importance, even the existence, of imagination. They maintain we are more the slaves than the masters of our language, that the creative spirit is not the source of literary events, but a sort of bureaucratic set that discloses predetermined social and political codes. Claiming to apply a scientific model to our mental transactions, these theorists would deny to imaginative writing the possibility of creation, freedom, play, and pleasure. Or they would denigrate the worth of these by making imagination a self-indulgence of the private life. To them, "mind" means rational consciousness, so they complain that imagination, unlike "mind," is irresponsible and impractical, doesn't improve access to technological information, doesn't increase our control over a world made dangerous by technology. Because imaginative writing fares badly in the marketplace, they argue that it is undemocratic! But there is no inevitable quarrel between mind and imagination. Mind is not limited to purely conscious events, but includes the intuitive, the nonrational, the unconscious. Indeed, imagination is superior to "mind" that is only rational consciousness. The imagination regards rational consciousness as a totalitarian civil servant that imposes categories upon experience with little thought for the nature of the experience. Thus, for example, imagination might conceive of a woman's beauty as a drop of pure mountain water, but a Chinese poet who made exactly that comparison was sentenced to prison because he was supposed, when thinking of water, to think of hydroelectric plants. Luckily, imagination is not committed to categories. With freedom its cardinal virtue, imagination is the *only* force able to accommodate and to cope with the vast chaos of events constituting the occasions of our experience. When a writer brings feeling to the condition of form, imagination makes experience truly known. Imagination discerns the hidden connections of things and promises an incorporating fiction, where true, universal democracy lies, immune to time and, particularly, to the ideologies that are myths manufactured to control the world.[5]

In America, the imagination is engaged with forces it cannot hope to defeat, forces such as technology, big business, the military-industrial complex, advertising, public education, professional football, politicized evangelism, teachers, parents, and other organized crimes. These forces are inhospitable to imagination, which at its happiest would find real substance in the world of history and society.

This is where revolt comes in.

The imagination at work in many major books of American literature seeks to expand human consciousness by revolting against the social forces that otherwise dominate American realities. Emerson, Thoreau, Hawthorne, Melville, Whitman, Mark Twain, Henry Adams, Henry James, Scott Fitzgerald, T.S. Eliot, Faulkner, Frank Waters and many other writers try through style and structure to free themselves and their heroes from historical systems. Works like *Moby Dick*, *Huckleberry Finn*, and *The Ambassadors* are "designed to make the reader feel that his ordinary world has been acknowledged, even exhaustively, only to be dispensed with as a source of moral or psychological standards."[6] Now, earlier, I admitted a degree of validity to stories set in outer space. One is letting go of ordinary realities—family, society, the past, even our planet—and one is letting one's characters exist in some seemingly free, natural state of the true inner self. But revolt against the difficulties of reality requires, not evasion, but confrontation of them. The hostile forces that would destroy what you love must be accorded full room in your fictions in order for the hostility to be felt as a demonic power which forbids individual fulfillment. It is only *within* the massed phenomena of social and economic structures that one can *see* the hero at all. So, sponsored by the revolt of the imagination, part of our task as writers is to provoke the hostile forces into yielding their shabbiness and inhumanity. The provocation may then have some effect upon society, redirecting the confined consciousness of the reader toward ideals of a valid culture. Let us nevertheless remain aware of the price of revolt. Reality ultimately defeats the hero, whose success is inward and invisible. Huck Finn and Jim must abandon the idyl of the raft and return to a society based upon the conventions of slavery. Isaac McCaslin, the hero of Faulkner's *The Bear*, rejects his historical and economic inheritance, his corrupt family, and the plantation he is to inherit. This relinquishment of his inheritance allows Isaac to achieve an original, freed relationship to humanity and to the land. But his choice necessitates a lonely, sexless, childless life. In Isaac McCaslin's revolt against possessions of any kind and in his consequent self-dispossession of personal happiness, we recognize the characteristic career of American heroes and heroines.

Writing is an act not of self-expression but of self-discovery. When you pay close attention to your experience of time and place, the mind's essential power—the imagination—surpasses experience and expands into a created world, the poem or story, wherein we see our real world as if for the first time. And in America, that real world is apt to be felt as preexisting organizations of power, against which the imagination revolts, producing works that demonstrate a turbulent, agitated desire to make a place for the imagination's freedom and to stabilize certain feelings and values of the individual self that have been and continue to be diminished by a technological, urbanized, materialistic civilization. Imagination succeeds on its own terms in the face of apparent defeat.

THE LONG HABIT OF LIVING

Blackburn, William Maxwell (*20 April 1899 — 9 December 1972*), educator, son of Charles Stanley and Amy Malvina Waring Blackburn, Presbyterian missionaries, was born in Urumiah, Iran, and died in Durham, North Carolina. His paternal grandfather was a church historian and college president in South Dakota. His mother's family in Columbia, South Carolina, could claim descent through Hinmans to John Howland of the Mayflower. When five years old, Blackburn came with his parents, a younger sister, Malvina, and brother, George, to live in the Upcountry of South Carolina. The family, eventually including another brother, Clark, moved from small town to small town, living off the meager rewards of Charles Blackburn's ministerial vocation. The memory of those hard times was to haunt Blackburn all his life, yet in a short, posthumously published memoir, he wrote with lively warmth of his boyhood in Seneca, South Carolina, and of the shaping influence on a poor preacher's son of his grandmother, Malvina Gist Waring, a novelist and "old reb" who had served the Confederacy. It was she who encouraged his intellectual growth and independence and in 1917 sent him to Furman College, where he was graduated in 1921 with an A.B. in English. There followed a scholarship to the graduate school at Yale and a year of teaching at Carnegie Institute of Technology. Then came recognition of his learning and strength of character: he was awarded a Rhodes Scholarship. The years at Hertford College, Oxford University, 1923-26, were among the happiest of his life, leading to B.A. and M.A. degrees in English literature and, perhaps of greater importance, confirming his sense of mission as a humanist educator. At Oxford, the passionate ethical idealism, the "sweet reasonableness" of Matthew Arnold, left its strong impression and further liberated Blackburn from the constraints of an upbringing in Christian fundamentalism. The immense learning that produced pioneering studies of *Literature and Dogma* (subject of his Yale Ph.D. dissertation in 1943) was partly a debt paid to Arnold. Still, the Elizabethan and seventeenth-century English writers such as John Donne, George Herbert, and Thomas Browne appealed more than the Victorians to his sense of self-doubt and of language with an accent of greatness.

In 1926, Blackburn was drawn to Duke University in that institution's effort to assemble a strong faculty for an "Oxford of the South." Here he was to teach English for forty-five years, with the exception of a period with University Training Command, Florence, Italy, in 1945. Throughout the Duke years, he remained professionally active in associations of college English teachers and of Rhodes Scholars. He became full professor in 1953. In May 1966 he first served as an advisor to the National Endowment for the Arts.

Blackburn placed his own considerable literary talents, known to his friends and family through the terse, diffident, avuncular letters he wrote them, at the service of other writers. After publishing his book, *The Architecture of Duke University*, in 1938, he edited three successive volumes of narrative and verse by Duke students. Some of them, thus initially encouraged, made their way to literary fame. In 1969 there appeared *Love, Boy*, poignant letters from one of those former students, Mac Hyman, revealing how tormented had been the humorist who wrote the best-selling novel, *No Time for Sergeants*. Earlier, in 1958, Blackburn's ingenious discovery and penetration of the materials published as *Joseph Conrad: Letters to William Blackwood and David S. Meldrum* earned international critical acclaim, not least because, from their editing, the letters show the heroism of Conrad's early struggles to achieve success and recognition.

With imaginative power and a gift for sympathetic insight, Blackburn was able to grasp the essential design of a literary work as it begins to surface from the creative process. This almost uncanny comprehension of design was crucial to his success as a teacher of writers at Duke and, from 1969 until his death, at the University of North Carolina at Chapel Hill. When the *London Times Literary Supplement* editorialized in 1965 about the teaching of creative writing, Blackburn was hailed as a rare teacher possessing "the combination of critical acumen and charisma"[1] feasible for the job. He himself, however, persistently refused to take credit for the successes of former students. Even when featured on national television, Blackburn characteristically turned attention away from himself and onto his famous students. His modest claim was that he helped writers to become good readers, though it was clear to the writers themselves that Blackburn's discovery of their talents was really the decisive event. No history of forces shaping modern American letters will be complete without notice of the influence of this eloquent, plainly devoted teacher—a large man of noble bearing and mien, one whose unifying qualities of courage, humor, and moral integrity helped to guide and inspire makers of literature.[2]

The memorial service is held in the late afternoon of 17 December 1972 in the Duke University Chapel. The sun outside is bright. The stained-glass windows shimmer and dance against its blaze. Soaring through the vaulted arches are the tones of the great organ. More than a thousand people are gathered in this Gothic cathedral, once described by Blackburn as "a study, in terms of stone, of how the spirit of man may escape the fetters of the earth."[3]

Dad, as you lay dying, your sight gone, your rapturous voice gone, some of us were reminded of your recitation of a passage in *King Lear*:

O, let him pass! He hates him
That would upon the rack of this tough world
Stretch him out longer.

Like the character of whom those words are spoken, you

showed us how to take the measure of that toughness and that torture, and transcended both.

The eulogy is brief. James Applewhite reads Donne's "Hymn to God My God, In My Sicknesse." Fred Chappell, in a resonant voice that reminds us of his origins in the mountains of North Carolina, reads Henry Vaughan's "They are all gone into the world of light," and Reynolds Price follows with readings from Milton. Then, in a sibilant hush, William Styron mounts to the pulpit and begins to read from Sir Thomas Browne's *Hydriotaphia, Urne-Buriall, or, A Discourse of the Sepulchrall Urnes Lately Found in Norfolk*—a selection that includes the title of Styron's brilliant first novel, *Lie Down in Darkness*.

"'The long habit of living indisposeth us for dying'," Styron quotes. After a pause, he points out that Blackburn considered this sentence as one of the greatest understatements in the English language.

William Blackburn. "Sketches for a Memoir" (excerpts).[4]

I spent my boyhood in Seneca, a small town on the main line of the Southern Railway, between Greenville and Atlanta. Seneca is in the foothills of the Blue Ridge. I went back there about ten years ago [1938?]. When I saw the contour of the hills, I realized I had returned home. On that visit I was astonished at how things and events and people, long since, apparently, forgotten, flooded my memory:

—The family of Charlestonians up the street who taught me that all South Carolina is divided into two parts: (1) Charleston and (2) the unfortunate remainder of it.

—The first automobile I ever saw, a Maxwell ("Get Out and Get Under"), owned and operated, much to the astonishment of the population, by the enterprising dentist, who lived just down the street from us.

—My first fight in the woods behind the schoolhouse and making up afterwards with my erstwhile enemy by giving him a pocketknife—just to make everything square.

—My visit with other boys to the town calaboose, where the local prisoner, furious at our intruding on his privacy, dashed water at us through the iron bars above the door.

—The Sunday afternoon reader sessions in the family, when Mother read the Bible to us and the *Youth's Companion*, or, sometimes, Bunyan's *Pilgrim's Progress*. This last book, a sure means of conjuring up visions of Old Nick himself, as soon as it got dark.

—Feeling noble the night when John Cary and I brought Julian Holloway, who had been bitten by a snake while we were on a camping trip, to a doctor in John's donkey cart.

—Hearing my father taking the tenor part in "Lead, Kindly Light" at Gus Tribble's funeral and wondering about death and of how Gus met it, driving his taxi on a lonely road.

—Fabulous tales of Train No. 97, the crack mail train, Atlanta to New York, and sometimes hearing it at midnight blow for the crossing. "She was going down grade, making ninety miles an hour."

—The summer visits of Grandmother Malvina Waring, from Columbia. The climax of the visit, an annual pilgrimage in a hack, to Clemson College, nine miles away. Our admiration for Fort Hill, the old home of John C. Calhoun, and Mother's constant reminder: "Now, Billy, you must always remember that your great-great grandmother was the sister of John C. Calhoun's mother." I never got the family connection, but I think I know what she meant. [John C. Calhoun (1782-1850) was senator from South Carolina, secretary of war, secretary of state, and vice-president in the administrations of John

Quincy Adams and Andrew Jackson. His mother, Martha Caldwell, was like his father of Scotch-Irish descent.]

The grand event of the year was the family trek at Christmas to Columbia—a distance of 120 miles, covered in about seven hours in a train as picturesque as it was slow. There in the big house on Laurel Street the clan would foregather: Grandfather Waring, a great hulking figure of a man, with a white beard and a twinkle in his blue eyes and a genius for guessing when exactly children wanted stick candy; Aunt Bessie, who ran the house with quiet efficiency and great good humor; her husband, Uncle Fitz [Fitzhugh McMaster, Lt. Governor of South Carolina], with his laughter and sarcastic wit; Uncle George Waring, boisterous and great-hearted, who used to take us four children to the shoe store and have us shod for the year—as a gesture of good will towards a poorly paid profession; and, of course, there was Grandmother, who, though going blind, had an infectious cheerfulness and an amazing knowledge of the heart, particularly of the young heart. Up to the time when she went completely blind from cataracts, she would play on the piano daily and sing the old songs. She wrote poems and novels. Her last novel, a story of Reconstruction, was published when she was well over eighty. To me, she was the personification of courage, and I owe to her precept and example more than I can say.

She would tell us stories of the Civil War: of Sherman's march to the sea and of the burning of Columbia; of her marriage to Major William Gist, son of the "States-Rights" Governor of South Carolina; and of how, one day while she was taking a walk on the Gist plantation, a little Negro girl ran up to tell her that her husband had fallen at Chicamauga: "Miss Mallie, Mistuh William—he done dead, done dead."

Then she would tell how, after the loss of the major, she

went to Richmond and there signed bank-notes in the Confederate Treasury. Among my most priceless sentimental possessions are some notes signed in a clear, bold hand, "M. Gist."

Grandmother had a way of encouraging her grandchildren to try their mettle, and my brother George and I began early the game of making a shining penny when we could. We used to meet Train No. 38, the Crescent Limited, at Seneca, and sell baskets of figs to the, presumably, rich Yankees on their way south. We sold newspapers. And one summer we went to Akron, Ohio, to work in the Goodyear Tire factory. I never quite learned the art of making cord tires, and I have often wondered how many blow-outs I have been the unwitting cause of. I came along before the Fuller Brush Man entered into his present fame, but in my time I have sold brooms in a house-to-house canvas. And once, the year before I went to college, I dispensed "The Knowledge Book" wherever I could find innocent takers in Orange County, Virginia. There's nothing quite like a house-to-house canvas to learn both the hardheartedness—and the kindness—of the world. Or to learn that one is not cut out to be a salesman.

It was Grandmother who sent me to college....

My teachers at Furman I remember with affection, even those who despaired of my abilities in chemistry and mathematics. I have space, however, to mention but one of them—Robert Norman Daniel. It was he who awakened my interest in English literature. He awakened it by reading poetry as if it has life in it.

My parents had hoped that I should follow the family tradition and become a minister. My father was one; my paternal grandfather had been in his day a distinguished church historian and college president. I had been brought up on the Bible. The ignorance of this wonderful book among present-day undergraduates is appalling—a few years ago I was shocked to read in a sophomore quiz a reference to the best-known fact in Christianity as "the religious angle."

But English poetry and, perhaps the more worldly wisdom of my grandmother—together with my distaste for the role of being a preacher's son—turned me toward a more secular career....

Dr. Samuel Johnson complained of his experience as a teacher that it was dull and unvaried—"One day contains the whole of my life." I must confess I haven't found it so. English literature is so rich in connotation that, even in handling the old assignments, I see something new and, to me, wonderful every year. Nor are the students all alike but, on the contrary, as varied as human nature itself. The ones I admire most are those who come up to college badly prepared but are willing to put up a fight to get an education. This is not, of course, a plea for poor preparation.

Dad, I know you won't mind my putting in a word for Tris, my mother. She was raised in New Orleans, New York, and rural Connecticut to lead a life that might have been suitable for Czarist Russia. By taking up nurses' training, she shocked her family the first time; by teaching herself to become a critical reader of literature and to write witty verses, she reeled them again; by marrying a penniless Rhodes Scholar on his way from Oxford to a tobacco-manufacturing town in the defeated South, she doubtless mortified them permanently. Unknown to your students, she was often their first reader, and you incorporated her lengthy notes into your own.

Although you were too complex a man to be found described in a psychologist's textbook, Tris marked passages in *The Abnormal Personality*[5] that offer us some speculative insight into a type of perfectionist—a man who is at odds with himself,

unable to use his capacities fully; a man who develops self-suf-
ficiency and "paternal" responsibility in order to satisfy the iron
rule of his mother and to avoid becoming as contemptible as his
father; a man who feels guilt-ridden after an acute fright of disillusionment and loss of belief. You never guessed, I'm sure,
how your occasional looks of gloomy desperation filled our
hearts with anxiety. We all laughed together, though, when,
snapping out of your mood, sighing deeply, and clowning with
a self-minimizing shrug, you declared, "Never take the gloomy
view." As for your idiosyncrasies, I still don't understand why
you tied a red bandanna over your eyes every night before you
went to bed. Were you shutting out the sight of those wild
Kurdish tribesmen who used to yell outside Grandpa Charlie's
missionary compound, or did you really believe that Old Nick
himself was out in the dark? You seldom left the house without
a hat on, and you always wore rubber overshoes when it rained.
Grandma Amy trained you well.

The house on Laurel Street in Columbia is gone now. It survived torching by Sherman's troops, but fell to urban renewal
and is now a parking lot.

One afternoon Aunt Bessie was showing me around the
house when I asked her about a particularly wicked-looking
Confederate officer's saber that hung, gleaming, over her man-
telpiece. It had a dark splotch on the blade.

"What is that black spot, Aunt Bessie?" I asked.

She drew herself up stiffly inside her tiny frame. Her eyes
blazed. "Yankee blood!" she declared with fury and pride.

I read something of you, Dad, between the lines of your collection of Conrad letters. Like Conrad, you often felt powerless
but fought through to fulfillment with no surrender of purpose
or principle.

While writing *Lord Jim* and *Heart of Darkness*, Conrad often
had days when he couldn't pen a line. He enlarged on this
theme to David Meldrum, the London agent of the Edinburgh
publishing house of Blackwood:

The worst is that while I am thus powerless to produce my imagination is extremely active: whole
paragraphs, whole pages, whole chapters pass
through my mind. Everything is there: descriptions,
dialogue, reflexion ...everything but the belief, the
conviction, the only thing needed to make me put
pen to paper. I've thought out a volume in a day till I
felt sick in mind and heart and gone to bed, completely done up, without having written a line.

During the "long blank hours," Conrad was tortured by
self-doubt. "I ask myself whether I am fitted for that work."

Conrad was also driven to despair over his debts. "I must
drive on," he told Meldrum in 1900. "One decent success with
a book would give me a chance to breathe freely."[6]

Dad, I'll never forget your agonizing over money. Once, you
settled into a blue funk for a week because you misplaced a
twenty-dollar bill. But you helped to support your parents and
sister all their lives. I am writing this piece while seated at the
huge pine desk you bequeathed to me.

Excerpts from letters, **William Blackburn** to **Elizabeth
Blackburn**, 2-7 October 1927.[7]

Papa rolled in last night at 11:30 p.m. He hasn't aged at
all, so far as I can tell, and I'm astounded at his seeming
good health and spirits. I spent the afternoon yesterday
getting up pictures and tapestries, cleaning the
bath-room—and other domesticities: I hope in this way
to instil subtly into my father a certain amount of self-
respect. If, as Mother says she hopes I will be clever
enough to do, I can keep him from pondering man's
capacity for sin and wrong-doing, the visit may easily
turn out to be a happy one....

Yesterday, Sunday, went better than I had expected. We went to church at Trinity Methodist, and Parson Peel preached a sermon quite in keeping with Fundamentalism. I was a little embarrassed when Dad asked me to join him in partaking of the sacraments; but he's said nothing about my refusal later. He's perhaps worried about me, but his tolerance is far more remarkable than your mother's, for example, and his spirit is sweeter, too. He was shocked at the merry conversation we heard at Lewis' [Lewis Patton, Greenville chum and Duke colleague] yesterday afternoon; in his heart he liked it. I'm actually flippant with him—have suggested the circus for this afternoon, but he passed over that suggestion with, "Well, we shall see"—which means, "I don't approve."

After supper last night Pa and I took a long walk. He introduced the subject of debts by saying that he had just heard from one of the banks which lent him $700 years ago. The bank made him a proposition, namely, that they will reduce the rate of interest from 8% to 6% provided that Dad will attempt to reduce the capital by $10.00 a month. I seized on this idea immediately, as it struck me as very practical indeed. C[harles]. S[tanley]. B[lackburn]. said he was tempted to try it. If he will do this, it will certainly ease Mother's mind a great deal, for the thing about Dad's behavior which worries her most is his oblivious forgetfulness of all his debts. "Mother doesn't understand," he says. "She feels I should put what profits I do make on books into paying debts, whereas I feel I should invest in more books." Without capital, of course, he is quite helpless; and the dilemma is bewildering. But Mother is right, of course, and if I can very subtly let him know that I agree with her, I shall do so before he leaves Durham. The bank's offer makes him think of his responsibilities—an odd thought in his fantastic mind! He fools himself time and again by saying, "Well, I made 100% (or 150%) on that book"—but he doesn't make anything like that on his investments as a *whole*. On his investments *as* a whole, so far as I can see, he has in reality made very, very little or nothing. I was awfully embarrassed yesterday afternoon when he offered all sorts of advice to Mr. Miller of the Booklover's Shop. It was too ironic for words, past belief, past my naive understanding.

On the walk last evening, I brought up the personal items one by one. After discovering that the Benjamin debt was really $400 (and not $320 as George reported last August), I was amazed to learn that, although Benjamin waved aside the matter of 6% interest, he, Charles Blackburn, felt that interest should be paid. Fortunately Dad paid interest up to the year 1921; so he is only 6 years behind (about $150) instead of 15 years. After Benjamin was discussed, Dad said, "That is all." "But," said I, "what about the house rent debt of $150"— "Oh, yes," he replied, "there *is* that." "And the debt to Karl Goldsmith of South Dakota?" "Oh—I forgot that!!!" "And the note J.O. Jones signed for you to buy books?"

Well, to be short, that note for $200 is coming due November 17. In order to meet it, Dad has gone to the Planter's Bank in Greer, S. C. (where he owes $860 already, according to George's figures) and proposed that they lend him $200 for six months to carry him over the emergency; he also proposed that *I* sign the note for him. This, he explains, involves nothing but my name, as his property in Pierre, S. Dakota is on the market this fall, and ought to net at least $350 at the very lowest. Even if he does sell this, and pays the bank the $200—he is using his last resources to pay for his *book* venture (in which field he doesn't see he's making a fool of himself, whereas he admits he played the fool in the oil gambles of 1917), whereas I feel that his last resources should, in all decency to his family, go toward his long-standing debts. But this idea hasn't occurred to him, and doubtless

never will—so muddled is his thinking and his life....
The talk made me pessimistic. "I don't see any end,"—to
which the reply was, "Well, we'll just have to do the best
we can."

Dad and I are getting along splendidly. The reason is
this: I've tried very hard to avoid all clashings of opinion.
Before he goes, he's sure to bring up the subject of religion, and I dread the inquisition. I shall also put in a
word for common sense in his business—which word I
know will do no good—but I can't be dishonest and hide
my feelings in the matter....

Dear Tris

I hand you the palm for objective analysis of various
people I have known. Your last portrait of your sheltered
and petulant sister [Helen] is excellent reading. Of
course, I see in it the sister Elizabeth who wrote it, and
who feels at last that she's superior. But I take no exception to that conclusion; it flatters me as well as you. And,
goodness knows, you are superior in character—and
character is everything. I think your hospital training
has fitted you (to say nothing of your natural talents) for
the task of motherhood, and you are intolerant of
women who do not see their responsibility as clearly as
you do. You will have to admit that the temptation of
boredom was pretty insistent last summer; but, on the
whole, I'll say you didn't yield to it. That's the point. The
way you have managed to keep yourself alive this fall
pleases me very much more than I can say. It seems to
me you are more alive mentally than ever: and this
renascence pleases me mightily, as it is the fulfillment of
one of my cherished hopes for you, namely, that you'd
get off your former fatalistic, self-pitying attitude toward
life. Love, ah love, is not only sweet, but is light for the

darkness. Oh, it's wonderful. And within a few weeks there will be a baby to fill in all the vacant places of our lives. And doesn't Love answer all our wants beautifully? And aren't we lucky to have each other? We're pretty clever, too, in being so independently-dependent. It's simply great to live, and that's all.

Pa says I'm a good teacher! He insisted on coming to classes with me this morning—"as a compliment to me." I felt rather throttled at first, but managed to regain my self-possession. I read the passage (which is expurgated in the edition the boys use) concerning the Lilliputian fire-department: Gulliver, awaking one night to the call of FIRE, rushed out to find the palace of the Empress of Lilliput ablaze. The Lilliputians were at a loss, water was distant. So Gulliver, fortunately having drunk much wine and still more fortunately having forgotten to go to the toilet before bed, took out his hose and peed on the place, thus quenching every flame. The Empress was terribly displeased, just as Queen Anne was displeased with Swift's dirty satires. Thus politics justified the read- ing—and the boys whooped, too. Even Dad liked it!

Excerpts from a letter from **Elizabeth Blackburn** to **Amy Blackburn**, 11 September 1935.[8]

The Florida storm was very exciting indeed. We drove through torrents of rain to Myrtle Beach the morning of the 5th, partly to find out what the hurricane was expected to do.... They told us at Myrtle Beach that the Weather Bureau had telegraphed that the Florida storm would pass out to sea between Savannah and Charleston, missing all the beach resorts. So we went right ahead with plans for Alex's [sixth] birthday party that after- noon. It seemed a bit ominous that the tide did not go out at all, staying as near the house at low tide as it had been at high. The Nixons, who had lived at [Cherry Grove] all their lives, said there was nothing to worry about; however, when I went to the little store next door to invite the Nixon children to Alex's party, I found that their mother had taken them inland.

The two little Springs girls arrived for the party at four. The wind had risen to a howl, rain was coming through the roof and under the walls of two bedrooms, and the shack was shaking. We set the lighted birthday cake on a table in the only dry room. The children dressed up in masks and paper hats, and we played Black Spider, Miss Ginia Jones, and All the Great Men. When the children's father came for them, the wind was blowing so hard the children could not stand up in it and had to be carried by Bill to the car. Miner [the cook] served supper weeping and moaning and wringing her hands. As she threatened to run off into the woods to get away from the beach, Bill decided to take her home in the car—if only to stop her from making such scenes and showing such terror in front of the children. The Nixons still said, "Don't go; Cherry Grove never has bad storms." While Bill was away with Miner, the wind increased even more. It was beginning to get my goat, and I felt like the band playing while a ship sinks, as I read aloud to the children to make them forget the danger, obvious to them, for ours was the only cottage on the beach itself, unprotected by sand dunes, ours and the little store. There were no more reports of the storm missing Charleston. Now it was due to strike *us* at 9:30. I didn't see how it could strike any harder than it was striking already.

At 8:30 Bill rushed into the room, all greeny color with terror. While taking Miner through the forest, [he had observed] great trees crashing around him, some across the road.

"We're getting out damn quick," he said.

There were two dangers: that the only path from the beach was blocked by fallen trees, and that Cherry Grove had become an island, the tide backing into the swamp. I threw some things into a bag, so we would have something dry to put on, gathered Andy [the cocker spaniel] in my arms, and ran out the back door into a whirlwind of rain and sand. The car was parked behind a dune. The children got themselves into it. We started without getting stuck in the sand and plunged through deep pools as if the car were a boat.... Trees were down in the forest road, but we managed to get around them.

We decided to make for Conway, inland from Myrtle Beach, about forty miles away. Every time we passed a forest giant knocked over by the wind, our hearts seemed to rise up in our mouths—would the next tree hit us? The longer we drove, the nearer the time came for the storm to really hit, at 9:30. Alex was big-eyed and tense; Mary April, as always, the perfectly expressionless little stoic.

Suddenly we saw the lights of a car, on the highway ahead of us, flashing on & off, on & off. We took it as a signal to slow down, which, luckily, we did; we could not see the huge tree blocking the highway until we were almost touching its branches. Bill jumped out in the rain & he & the man in the other car—who was fleeing *from* Myrtle Beach where we were trying to go—surveyed the ground with flashlights. The tree was too big to move & there was a deep ditch on either side of the road. It took us some time to get our car turned around; there were other big trees near us & we were afraid to look at them.

You know how your heart & stomach feel just after a near-accident, after the car skids or you nearly run over a child? Well, that is the way Bill & I felt *all* the time, for about two hours. We had a choice left now of two highways, one inland on a dirt road lined with trees, the other on the seacoast 80 miles to Wilmington. We chose the inland road. For one thing, our gasoline gauge was broken & we were pretty sure we didn't have gas enough for 80 miles. We had only gone about five miles, noting as we went the trees that had blown down since we passed that way before, when we came to another monster tree blocking the highway. Other refugees' cars were stopped by it on either side, people wringing their hands & behaving the way we *felt* but didn't behave. Without a word, even to one another, we got the car faced around again & sped towards the last road left open....

We got safely to Little River, where it seemed comparatively sheltered, though only a mile or two from the sea. We found a tourist home & dashed through wind & rain to the door. Here Andy, held high in my arms, was attacked by two little white dogs. We rushed, dripping, into the parlor, where several other refugees from Cherry Grove were sitting. Besides the refugees, all of whom I knew, there was only one grim-visaged dame, writing a letter on a pad on her knee. As she did not look up or change expression, except to hiss out of the side of her mouth, "Can't you leave the dog outside?," I jumped up again & said, "Oh, I hope I haven't barged into someone's private home!" The grim one didn't move or answer; she continued to write her letter. I turned to Mrs. Saunders (from the beach) & said, "*Can't* they give us a room here? I can't take these children out in the storm again!" She assured me it *was* a tourist home & that the grim one was my hostess.

The grim one looked up & I noted (1st) that the effort of keeping her false teeth from falling out was about all the poor creature could cope with at any given moment & that (2) she saw a ghost.

The ghost was Bill. He really looked unbelievable. If all his acquaintances at Cherry Grove had not burst into laughter at sight of him, I believe our hostess would have sicced the dogs on him. In the excitement of the hurricane I just hadn't noticed that he was driving the car barefoot. On his head was *my* red bathing cap. His face was ashy pale & rain dripped off his nose & ears. He had on a soggy yellow leather coat, which crochetted on his shirt & arms in yellow streaks; he had dark blue cotton shorts, & yards of wet hairy legs, ending in muddy toes.

He bowed & we all roared with laughter until a gust of wind sent branches tumbling on the porch & shook the house like a terrier with a rat....

When I, Alex, was twelve years old, Dad took me back to Little River. I described "My Deep Sea Adventure" for my seventh-grade English teacher.

What a day it was for fishing!
My father and I climbed aboard a deep sea fishing boat at Little River, South Carolina. When everyone was aboard, the boat rumbled up the river, across the breakers and out to sea. I was anxious to drop my line and soon, when we were some way from shore, my chance came. Scarcely had I dropped it before I felt a tug, and pulled up fish number one for the day.
After an hour of luck the boat had an odor of dead fish, but the swift, cool, salty air soon blew it away.
Suddenly my line jerked out of my hands! I recovered it and started tugging and pulling. The weight was so great that I called some men to help.
The men hauled up my prize, a shark, still wriggling and scarred. His life was beaten out with Coca-Cola

bottles and the demon no longer molested the deep.
I was certainly the proudest of everyone, even when
we docked and started for home.
I think fishing is a great sport and it isn't everyday
that someone has such an exciting adventure as I
had.

Half a century later, I recall that it took three men to haul up
the shark and six men to beat it to death with pikes, shovels, and,
yes, Coca-Cola bottles. The shark was as big as I was and at the
dock it would be found to weigh about twice as much as I did.

I recall that Dad told me he was proud of me and asked if I
would like to have the shark mounted and taken home.

I looked at the "demon," all battered and bloodied after an
unfair fight. I don't recall exactly what I said, but it would have
been something like this, in the Carolina lingo I had at that
time. "No, sir, it ain't the same."

From **Fred Chappell**:

He wasn't always right, but he was more valuable
than if he had been. It takes a long time for a teacher
to realize that his task is only partly that of the critic.
He must uphold substantive critical values, right
enough, but he is never to rank or grade literary production. Some teachers never learn this fact, but Dr.
Blackburn probably knew it by temperament.
This is to say, he erred on the side of the angels. His
mistakes were those of precipitate enthusiasm and generous sympathy—not forced or dishonest. When he
liked something you had written you felt momentarily
equal to Sidney or Drayton.... Well, to Arthur Hugh
Clough, anyway. And though you knew at the time that
the exhilaration was fleeting and would have to be tem-
pered by knowledge of his generosity, the excitement

was no less heady.

He never taught writing as merely writing. He taught writing as literature, as part of a civilized discourse that always had been and always would be going on. When you wrote a story, no matter how naive or clumsy, he made you feel that you had contributed to the great conversation.

He impressed you with the idea of writing as a moral act. When a story was phoney or cute or pretentious or callow, you felt that you had done a wrong thing, like telling an inadvertent lie. Not something to ponder remorsefully, but something to correct; an error curable by earnest labor.

That's how it was: he taught pride and humility. I know of no other teacher who can do it.[9]

———◦◦◦———

From **Reynolds Price**:

William Blackburn taught by what at first seemed a kind of easy magic—a powerful body, a noble head, a 17th-Century bishop's voice, all ignited by an instinctive wit and eloquence.... It was only after a few of us came to know him closely that we learned how far the magic consisted of rich intelligence subjected to enormous labor. I have never known a teacher who worked harder—both at the homely grind of daily preparation and, more crucially, at the endless, frightening and exhausting task of repairing and enriching the self, at being a better man.[10]

———◦◦◦———

From **William Styron**:

A large, bulky, rather rumpled man (at least in dress), he

tended to slump at his desk and to sag while walking; all this gave the impression of a man harboring great unhappiness, if not despair.... I began to know Blackburn, the great-hearted, humane, tragicomical sufferer who dwelt behind the hulking and lugubrious façade.... He must have known that he possessed that subtle, ineffable, magnetically appealing quality—a kind of invisible rapture—which caused students to respond with like rapture to the fresh and wondrous new world he was trying to reveal to them.... Whatever—from what mysterious wellspring there derived Blackburn's powerful and uncanny gift to mediate between a work of art and the young people who stood ready to receive it—he was unquestionably a glorious teacher.[11]

A few months before he died Dad visited with me and his grandsons then living in Oxford. I took him to "The Perch," a thatched-roof pub reputed to have been the site for Chaucer's *Miller's Tale*. Although we were not discussing literature or philology, he suddenly clenched his fist and brought it down with a kind of chopping gesture. "Alex," he declared, "I believe I'm finally beginning to understand the English sentence!"

As understatements go, I think that one deserves a place with "The long habit of living indisposeth us for dying."

The familiar question of whether anyone can *teach* creative writing hardly seems valid. No serious student of literature can overlook the fact that young writers have often learnt from other writers and critics of their own time, as well as from the past. If the real question is whether or not this process can be regularized within the academy, or whether inspiration and individuality are at risk, then William Blackburn's guidance of a generation of southern writers is a partial but affirmative answer.

He had a cartoon tacked up on his office wall to cheer us on—himself as well—as we went forth to encounter inevitable failures and rejections.

"Up Rodney!" the caption read. "Up like a sport!"

the wedding day which is not long—
Sweet Thames & sing gently etc..

He revived what I imagine must have
been the poet's original impulse &
feeling + his genius in getting it
right.

I'd be in touch as
with great sorrow that
w. the great book has
finally changed — soon
repeated upon nature —
poetry changed forever.

His kindness was hot
pursuing — his criticism
never withering —

Some of the best writers have
been afflicted w. self
doubt — you're in good
company —
when the doubt & becomes
pathological — when it
begins to stifle the
creative mind, we
must treat —
potential talent —
I feel there is representative
& state here, part of
his destiny

ON TEACHING CREATIVE WRITING

Teachers of writers often think of themselves as alienated outsiders whose presence in college and university departments of English is regarded by traditionalist colleagues as a source of embarrassment to "serious" education. The truth, however, is that teachers of writers are among the most hide-bound traditionalists in the academy. They teach what used to be called rhetoric, the design and effectiveness of compositions, and they involve students in a conversation, one about literary forms, carried on at least since Aristotle. If "traditionalist" refers, satirically considered, only to those learned doctors so accursed by narrow specialization that they have lost touch with the creative spirit and with the love of literature itself, then the genuinely traditional teacher of writers may be among the academy's most inspired and inspiring resources. At his or her best, the teacher of writers not only is not confined to swatting up the trivia about Chaucer or Pope or Wordsworth but also is educated in classics, ancient and new, and in the literatures of the world—the living tradition.

In America the long conversation about writing occurs in a culture where a writer's calling is misunderstood, even resented. As Richard Hofstadter declares in *Anti-intellectualism in American Life*, there is a "national disrespect for the mind."[1] A writer, intellectual by definition, cultivates distinctive qualities of mind in order to transmute the base metal of experience into words of gold. Usually apprenticed to a master alchemist, the printed book, a writer may need no companions other than the living voices of the past. But left in the cold too long, regarded as a useless dreamer, a writer may suffer the failure of silences or the suicidal success of a Ross Lockridge or Tom Heggen.[2] The anti-intellectualism fostered by evangelical religion, by "primitive" preference for intuition over reason, by contempt for the past, and by a national devotion to practicality and commerce stereotypes the writer as vain, frivolous, erratic, introverted and somehow immoral. If a writer succeeds—makes money, I mean—he or she is apt to be socially acceptable for wrong reasons, as an example of the virtues of assiduous application. Hofstadter sums up our national attitude: "It seemed to be the goal of the common man in America to build a society that would show how much could be done without literature and learning—or rather, a society whose literature and learning would be largely limited to such elementary things as the common man could grasp and use."[3]

Although most students of creative writing share a common interest in coming in from the cold, they still live in a society that, though passionately intent upon education, expects it to pay dividends and values personality, conformity, and manipulative skill over individuality and talent. For the student seeking to learn the craft of writing, such a tendency of culture may create confusion of means and ends. Perhaps conditioned to think of writing not as an intrinsically valuable activity but as a commodity in which success is measured by volume of sales, a student may seek instruction in techniques that can be rigged for production. When it becomes apparent that there are no fixed rules and formulae for genuinely effective writing, though there may be for popular or "generic" writing, this student may feel that the academy is impractical, divorced from the cash-register mentality of the literary marketplace.

Another kind of confusion, one also induced by the world of consumption and hobbies, is that creative writing means self-expression, only that. According to Ronald Sukenick, a novelist who teaches writers at the University of Colorado at Boulder, "There has been a huge increase in registration in writing courses around the country, but at the same time it's harder to get students to read. Everyone seems to want to 'express themselves'."[4] There is little educational purpose to expression without discipline, without style, without tradition. Jack Kerouac's "free writing"—the removal of literary, grammatical, and syntactical inhibition—is, I think, precisely the kind of disengagement from art that leads not to but away from real self-expression, a form of self-discovery. And rejection of literary tradition dooms a writer to "the tradition of the new," a more or less institutionalized formlessness.

A creative writing course may not make anyone rich or wise, but its place in education now seems established. Among the first of such courses to be celebrated was George Pierce Baker's 47 Workshop at Harvard in the 1910s and 1920s: Eugene O'Neill and Thomas Wolfe attended it. In 1931, Paul Engle, just back from Oxford where he was a Rhodes Scholar, gave direction to the Iowa Writers' Workshop. The same year, another Rhodes Scholar, William Blackburn, began teaching at Duke what he insisted on calling "composition." By the 1940s, there existed a few dozen writing courses in the country, and at the end of that decade one could study with Hiram Haydn at the New School for Social Research, Martha Foley at Columbia, Jessie Rehder at the University of North Carolina, or with Wallace Stegner at Stanford, to name a few of the teachers of writers. The academic climate for these pioneers was frequently hostile. They would often be told that teaching doesn't "count," that is, the professional gaze ought to be lifted toward such lofty pursuits as research, graduate programs, and anything called "national." The teacher's novel or book of poems "counted" but not on a par with research. So it has taken a long time for the academy to recognize an asset in the creative writing courses and in the teachers of them. During the past forty years, though, this situation has changed dramatically: there are in the 1990s more than 200 graduate and undergraduate programs in creative writing in the United States and in Canada. As M.F.A. and Ph.D. programs in writing proliferate, we have clearly come a long way from that "traditionalist" orientation of English studies to which I have referred.

We have come so far, in fact, that now a legitimate concern of educators is what to do with the wealth of talent. Welcome as is the acceptance of creative work on a par with research, the question, "What are we training writers *for?*," involves a serious moral dilemma. The fact that government financing for libraries, which bought books from hardcover houses in the 1950s and 1960s, no longer exists, has, along with other problems, made the publishing of literary work tenuous and problematic in our time. With few exceptions, quality publishers nowadays are wary of taking the financial risk of publishing serious imaginative literature. Novelist George Garrett maintains that the publishing system is running out of control and cannot, therefore, be "beaten." There is, he warns, no real money to be made in the business; writers in fact are engaged, by secular standards, in a highly irrational activity. Therefore the teacher of writers should feel morally bound to advise students that literary culture as we have known it in the past may be disappearing. In Garrett's view, we need to produce a large audience among writers themselves. Students in creative writing programs should be educated to become better readers, hence better book-buyers.[5]

Now that the academy has liberalized its understanding of the variety of styles in intellectual life, including the passionate and rebellious, it may well be the best home for writers. An American Bohemia of writers and artists struggling with the world can no longer seriously be said to exist. Although some of the Beatniks lived close to poverty, they repudiated the life of the mind and remained at the level of adolescent inspiration, their alienation becoming an orthodoxy akin to the Organization Man's.[6] A lack of historical perspective, a life-style as conformist as that of hated "squares," and a humorless solemnity about the relaxation of literary forms: these have manifested themselves more frequently in Bohemia than in Academia. Since, too, a writer needs to develop resources for facing the world alone, his or her fears of the academy, that it inhibits creativity and independence and stifles dissent, must be measured against fears of poverty encountered outside of it. As long as the academy practises its major virtues of being open and generous in its understanding, encouraging writers in self-fulfillment, there is probably more freedom for a writer in the academy than in Haight-Asbury. This is not to say that life outside the academy cannot be productive and noble.

"Reading maketh the full man, writing the exact man." Sir Francis Bacon's words almost four hundred years ago help to clarify why, today, the aims of the study of creative writing can be consistent with those of the academy. The academic ideal since ancient Athens and Renaissance Europe stresses the liberation of man from the idols, shibboleths, and dogmas of cumulative historical existence. The pursuit of knowledge is worthwhile in itself. The cultivation of excellence is not a form of special privilege but the noblest activity of man. Ideally, the study of literature is a way to truth, an act of knowing, an adventure in being human. Therefore, a writer and a scholar represent two sides of the same coin. Although, so to say, a scholar works *on* a subject and a writer is submerged *within* it, these differing mental processes are joined together in the general effort of extending awareness of life. Keeping academic orientation in mind, then, I discern at least a five-fold purpose to a writing program: (1) to bring intimately together a group of students and teacher-writers who share a common intellectual interest; (2) to give students an opportunity to discover literature via the creative process, itself; (3) to make students better readers; (4) to guide students toward more exact and vigorous use of language, broadening their sense of writing as a moral act; and (5) to provide a means for the discovery and guidance of talent. The key to realization of these aims is growth—growth in knowledge, growth in character, growth in understanding the difficulty as well as the pleasure of becoming, in Bacon's words, "full" and "exact."

A general academic purpose protects students from certain dangers in the teaching of creative writing. One kind of teacher will see the writing class principally as a means to discover and to develop talent. The danger here, aside from uncertainty as to the nature of talent, is that the teacher may feel tempted to send a gifted student forth to a life of toil, with hopes inflated for fame and fortune. Another kind of teacher likes to dispense indiscriminate praise instead of honest, balanced criticism. Fortunately, the serious student writers who are risking their innermost selves in their writing are not likely to tolerate syrupy intellectual permissiveness. This is not to say that a teacher shouldn't encourage writers. On the contrary, the teacher of writers should show that everything written by a student is in some way acceptable, and from this basis of acceptance proceed to comment upon what might be improved, and why. The worst teacher of all, because a relationship of mutual respect and trust is indispensable, uses student compositions as a means of "encounter," as if to prove writing interesting only when indulged in by maladjusted children whose work displays signs of psychic upheaval. Of course, I overstate the case. But if a young woman chooses a horse as subject for a poem or a young man writes about underwater caves, are we to take them as significant sexual symbols? In a composition, a writer is often working out a private problem, with the act of writing a means of finding a solution to it or of releasing tension. If writing is therapeutic for a writer, so much the better. To expect or to demand highly personal writing, as a kind of distasteful prying into what makes authors tick, will sooner or later destroy the learning experience. All writing is, in a sense, autobiographical, but if a poem or story *works*, it will do so because subjective emotion has been "outered" into imagery, and artistic form has been given to a pattern of events in itself chaotic.

Two of the best creative writing teachers whom I have ever encountered were themselves not published creative writers.[7] But they were scrupulous and imaginative critics. They had compassion. They understood writers, their compulsions, their needs for understanding. They tolerated experiments in language. Painstakingly, they annotated and discussed student writings as if these were always potentially Chaucer's. Such was their honesty and integrity, they were trusted by the students whom, after all, they were leading toward a necessary and sometimes dark voyage into the interior of selfhood. Recognizing that most of us do not examine the experiences we've had or don't know what to look for in the elusive depths of the past, they taught us to perceive what is *really* involved, what love, what death, and they taught us to probe feeling until true images emerge. Above all, they communicated this glory of the creative spirit: upon words, writers confer reality in order to preserve it from passing.

There is such an intimacy in the teaching of creative writing that it is not far-fetched to say that *souls* are at stake. A writing group without the presence of the teacher's authority may degenerate either into spiritual warfare—in which conditional emotions are nakedly expressed rather than gathered in the literary work—or into Prufrockian toast and tea. With the teacher's authority present, the group is protected in its give-and-take. Properly prepared for, the collective experience of a creative writing group may exceed usual educational goals and become a sharing of the bread of life.

Revision is essential to the writing process. If the student has not yet engaged his or her material, the teacher may want to explain pre-writing, false starts, the surface brainwork that precedes submergence in the work. Once the student's material has been engaged, the teacher's imaginative and critical faculties can be brought into play, and the energies of a manuscript may be recognized. This may be the first and most important moment of recognition in an author's life. When an entire group contributes to an author's recognition, the mutual—and, astonishingly, seldom envious—sense of breakthrough to achievement is truly one of awe. Sometimes the way to a revision will be obvious. Usually either teacher, author, or fellow writer will quite suddenly "see again" what the poem or story wants to do to achieve form. If nothing "happens" in class, a good procedure is for the teacher to confer with the student writer, often for many hours, in a session wherein every word of a composition is tested, justified, omitted or replaced. Such caring by the teacher, such passion for words, is often accompanied by a writer's swift growth, a palpable event indeed.

Reading aloud is one of the essential methods of a creative

writing class. It is axiomatic that a writer's voice is his or her unique way of telling the story, of singing the poem, and when a work is read aloud, the reading quickens the process of *seeing* the words as they surface from the creative act. Flat, prolix, or commonplace passages show up as disturbances to a voice's "flow." Narrative scenes that are undramatized, or lack appeal to the senses, or that shift points of view awkwardly will imperil an audience's powers of attention. A writer needs to cut the cackle and get to the horses (as an Irish writer, perhaps Sean O'Casey, once said). The hoofbeats of Pegasus need to be heard.

Increasingly nowadays writing classes are opened to students who have seldom written anything but who are attracted by a tiger-in-the-tank word like "creative." For these students, criticism appears as a personal affront or the kiss of death, and the teacher is faced with the elementary problem of getting them to put words on paper. These students aren't blocked in the usual senses (emotional, aesthetic); they are flummoxed because of a sudden, cold realization that they have nothing to say. And, of course, they are wrong. They *do* have latent creative powers. So now the teacher's basic approach is to stress creativity over criticism.

That is the approach recommended by Dr. John Schultz in his Story Workshop at Columbia College, Chicago. The teacher actively stimulates students to write imaginatively. First, there are oral word exercises, initiated by the teacher's directing of students to give the "felt word" or "the word that surprises you." With practice, students experience word progressions as multiple leaps of imagination. Second, there is image-telling:

> The director can isolate a 'felt' or 'aware' word that was given: 'Everybody see his rope,' pointing to the person who originally gave *rope*, 'and *use* it, do something with it...Now what's happening? What do you see? *Who* do you see? What is that person *doing* with the rope?'

These directions enable students to go from the moment of the word to its *movement* in time, place, and dramatic situation. For example, one of the verbal responses in Story Workshop was *tail-light* plus *moan*. These words

> may conjure the presence of a man in a white shirt with his sleeves rolled up driving a country road at night in an old station wagon. There is a smell of creek water and the raw scent of fresh oil blowing in the windows. He is warm, his legs ache, he is sleepy, and he must sing to keep his eyelids from sneaking down. The loose muffler rattles and drags on bumps, and up ahead the red gleam of another tail-light moans around yet another dusty curve that he must follow before he can lock the car and fall on his bed and sleep.[8]

From word exercises and oral "tellings" the students go on to actual writing, to get perceptions onto paper with a minimum of interference. "Tell it to the paper! Write it the way you tell it! See everything you write! Be aware of the place, see objects, see what the people are doing with objects!" These directions force students back upon their own realities, those aspects of their lives which are lively and important to them, aspects just surfacing from the long sleep of dreams.

Perhaps it is a truism, but how often have professional story writers and novelists had to remind themselves to begin with an image rather than with the outline of a plot! Usually by the time that plot is outlined, the story has gone stale and a writer has lost interest in the characters, their fates already known. But when a writer begins with an image, it may quickly move to suggest character, conflict, and place, with plot now the natural development of causes and effects incident to these. Here is an example of this procedure from one of my workshops at the University of Colorado at Colorado Springs. The class was presented with a number of static images, emphasizing sensory experience; each student was asked to select one image, to *see* it, and to start writing at once for thirty minutes.

> You are a naked woman contemplating the sea. It is hot, the air is light, sticky. Your eyes are closed and you are massaging your scalp, especially near the nape of the neck which you stroke with your thumbs.

That was one of the images. One student selected it and wrote as follows:

> Evelyn dropped her robe to the sand and with one foot edged the sandal off the other, then using her bare toe removed the remaining one. She tore her toes in little circles deep into the new-felt ground and at last felt the cool damp of the grains. She straightened her body, tossed her hair, lifted her arms as if in flight and aimed herself toward the surf—and paused at the side of the sea.
>
> It felt good, feeling so free. It seemed she had released herself from the awful fact of the horrid argument and disbelief that she and Court had really decided to quit, to divorce. She felt the almost too-hot bay breeze wrap around her like thin lingerie; then felt herself shiver, whether from actual chill or something within; some fault, some degree of wondering— if she had let go of too much. She ran her hands up the side of her shapely hips to the outer curves of her breasts, embraced her own shoulders and began massaging her scalp, feeling the fine fuzz of her hair at the back of her neck. At the feel of her own touch she began sobbing, quietly, and finally burst out loud in uncontrollable anguish. Madness seemed to come like a storm, and turning her total naked being back toward land she whispered, "No." She cried, she murmured softly into the departing wind one single and last word—"Court!"

Then, slowly, deliberately her tired form toward the sea, walked. The first small wave scraping, almost itching little stones away beneath her searching feet. Her second step took her to a deepening swirl of sand. The water embraced the calves of her brown legs; she felt a pull deeper as the water rushed back into the deep; she stumbled and as she braced herself to regain her stance, the water slapped her in the face. It was salt; it was bitter, choking. She rose—and fell forward and began frantic swimming strokes, pausing only for the waves to pass her up and down before going on—

It was the sea; endless, yet final.[9]

The student who wrote this little narrative was a Vietnam veteran with many gruesome memories he was later to purge through writing about them. The fact may explain why the narrative is so agitated, so melodramatic, so morbid. The point here, however, is that the image *does* move as if by magic, like Galileo's celestial sphere.

Once, back in 1974, another Vietnam veteran came to my class with a thick manuscript of poems, many of which I soon published in *Writers' Forum*. Here is one of those poems in its original, unrevised version.

Why did you stay away
So long? I've buried another
Husband, since I last saw you.
I hear where you now live,
It snows year round.
The pear and apple trees
Missed you; see their dead
Branches scattered about like legs
And arms? Come closer,
Let me see your face—my eyes

Have almost burnt themselves out;
I see only impressions of stars.
The white boxes
Of honey-bees are silent as dirt;
Silent as your unwritten letters
And missent postal cards
With strange faces and places
With unpronounceable names.
Have you noticed how white
The evening sunlight
Has bleached my fading hair?
The old stable has slouched
To the ground, gone to dust
And iridescent worms.
Cyclops—the flaming chestnut pony—
I dug its black hole
Two years ago.
Milkweed and blackberry brambles
Now keeper of the cornfield.
And Anna, that beautiful girl
You once loved enough
To die over and over again for,
Now lives in New Orleans,
Working both sides of Bourbon Street.
She has three children,
Who have never seen
The faces of their fathers.
Now don't go fretting none:
Let bygones be bygones.
That's the way the cards fall.[10]

The author of this poem, a professor now at Princeton University, is Yusef Komunyakaa. In 1994, he won the Pulitzer Prize for Poetry for *Neon Vernacular* to which volume the revised version adds power.

In a society which likes to do things without literature and learning, classes in creative writing may seem strange to students as they try their almost forgotten wings. Nowadays, college and university teachers of writers hardly expect literary language to come "naturally." But we remember that, though a whaling ship was Melville's Yale and Harvard, he was educated at Albany Academy. We remember that Shakespeare, at Stratford Grammar School, studied rhetoric.

CHARACTER AS STYLE

Frank Waters[1] was always able to look on the bright side of life. He was able to communicate with people from all walks of life, whatever the differences of age, class, gender, and race, and he left with those who met him a lasting impression of his aliveness. As a man, he never stopped living.

One star-frantic night in Tucson, Frank, Barbara, Inés and I were driving to a mountainside restaurant. The headlights picked out four coyotes loping across the road just in front of us. Frank leaned forward, alert. Although I didn't know it at the time, he is an honorary member of the Coyote Clan of the Hopi Indians, so these were "his" coyotes, perhaps personally significant. "Frank," Barbara said, "four is a good number for you, you always say that." I remembered Frank's many references in books to this number: the Four Corners, the four directions of Indian myth and ceremony, and the like. If you are the center of four points, you represent a fifth point of emergent consciousness. You are attuned to life. We went on to the restaurant. Frank, as usual, had a wonderful appetite.

A couple of years later, the four of us were headed for a picnic high in the Sangre de Cristos. Frank was driving. As we came down the narrow road from Arroyo Seco in his old Galaxie, the one that pretends to have shock absorbers, he was doing 65 in the 45 mph zone, and he was on the wrong side of the road. Nearly 90 years old, he was slightly blind. "Frank," Barbara asked calmly, "do you see that car coming straight at us?" Frank said something in that low, slow voice of his. I didn't hear what it was because I was suffering a bit of emotional dysentery, waiting for the mother of all automobile collisions. Frank swerved at the penultimate moment. We all sighed and looked at him. He had this big nothing-to-it grin on his face.

The picnic site was in a wooded glade at over 9,000 feet, next to Coronado's trail from the sixteenth century.[2] After a delicious luncheon of sandwiches, devilled eggs, and fruit, together with a bottle of light wine, the women went for a walk, leaving Frank and me to talk—or not. We chose not. Frank leaned against a log and let the sun pour down on his face. Above us a cathedral of giant trees lay spread against a sky bluer than blue. I have seldom known such perfect silence.

Frank has written a lot about silence, silence and humanity. Here's a passage from *Flight from Fiesta*:

> Hand in hand the old Indian and the little White girl walked down the nave of the great forest cathedral on a carpet of pine needles and entered a world that was old when this one was young, a world that would still be young when this one would be old and worn and weary. This was more than a single day they spent together feeling safe from pursuit and lost to the stark reality of their tragic flight. Always for Elsie it would preserve the strange and tenuous dimension of a timeless interlude that nothing could ever touch, as she remembered being shown by an old Indian the secrets of its wild and pristine beauty. For Inocencio, too, the day held all the mystery of a supreme adventure whose intangible components he had no mind to perceive. He had never had a child of his own, and the children of his pueblo had shunned him and his bottle. Now at last he was awakened to the paternal pride of responsibility and the joy of sacrifice. Always he had nursed an unconscious fear and hatred of Whites; a racial barrier through which, with this small White girl, he had finally broken to their common humanness.[3]

One listens to the silence of this idyllic interlude as if its grace comes largely from effects produced without apparent effort, from subtle simplicity. "A butterfly sleeps on the village bell," says an old Chinese poem. Perhaps the reason Frank never stopped living is that he never lost his sense of being within a timeless mystery.

Was he always such a kid?

Evidently. Some of the old ladies from the north end of Colorado Springs remember Frank as an excitable kid who broke front gates from swinging on them and who liked the company of "railroad tramps" along Shooks Run.[4] I get a picture here of a Thomas Bailey Aldrich "bad boy," a fearless and unpretentious fellow, and I think of Frank's driving his car. But Frank can give us his own portrait of the artist as a young dog. This is what he wrote for the dedication on 27 April 1991 of the Frank Waters Park in Colorado Springs:

> Columbia School was a long walk up Bijou, through the underpass of the railroad embankment, to El Paso Street, then north and west to a two-storied red brick building on the edge of the prairie. It was here, in the eighth grade, I first saw her. The new girl who had just entered school. Leslie Shane. She looked up to meet my stare, and in that instant it happened. That single glance revealed for me a strange truth and a mystery never since explained. My soul rushed out to her in a flood, as if I had long awaited her coming . . .
>
> Leslie was a small girl with apricot-colored hair, a pale face covered with freckles, large brown eyes and stub nose. She seemed the most beautiful girl I had ever seen. Bashful as I was, I began to walk home with her. She lived with her parents and younger sister on top of Bijou Hill, a block west. That October she assented to go with me to our class Halloween party.
>
> "Why don't you just drop by on your way?" I suggested. "There's no need of me climbin' the hill just to come back down."
>
> "I guess that'll be all right," said Leslie.

I didn't tell anyone at home I was taking Leslie to the party, but the night of the party I waited anxiously till I heard a loud knocking on the front door and rushed to open it. Standing before me was Mr. Shane, grinning good-naturedly. "Well, young man!" he roared. "I've brought your girl here for you to take to the party. But you make sure that you bring her home. Understand?" He pushed Leslie over the threshold and walked away.

Leslie came in to meet the family at the supper table. Mother was dutifully shocked at my lack of gallantry in not calling for Leslie, but Leslie was not embarrassed. And I did walk her home in the dark in the middle of Bijou Street.

Our class graduated from Columbia that year, and entered high school just three blocks from home. This ended my daily walks with Leslie, and I saw her seldom. A short time later Mr. Shane moved his family away—where, I didn't know—and I never saw Leslie again.[5]

After supper at the Waters's adobe in Seco, it was Frank's custom to wash the dishes. There may be some improvement in gallantry, there. I think, if he hadn't injured a hip when he fell from a horse in the Mexican backlands in 1931, he would have remained a passably mean swinger of gates.

The character of a writer is not always or even usually regarded as the foundation of his style. Yet when we inquire about the qualities that endow language with persuasiveness or power, a moral and psychological approach seems indispensable. "*Le style est l'homme même,*"[6] said Buffon—that is, style is personality clothed in words. Deeper than "correctness," more fundamental than technique, style is thus something more than a special manner deliberately cultivated and peculiar to one's individual self. It is, in a word, soul. If your soul is mean or peevish or vain or false, no cleverness and no technique are likely in the end to save you. The readers worth winning—the ones who read between the lines—will find you out. Sooner or later, they will feel repelled if your writing is muddled, dull, pompous, prolix, pretentious, self-assertive or exaggerated; but if you are warm, honest, courteous, good-humored, vibrant, urbane and wise, and these qualities manifest themselves in your writing, readers will feel charmed and delighted. They may even love you.

Frank Waters, like Stendhal before him, has had to wait to be appreciated, but a steadily growing number of readers attests to a love for his work, the acceptance of a greatness that stands above narrower perfections. Waters the writer is loved because he has shown his unknown audience the courtesy due to any audience, of communicating as clearly as he can what he thinks and feels, of refusing to defer to popular taste, and of considering the feelings of others, not imposing his ego on others. Writing to serve people rather than to impress them, he has acquired both clarity and brevity. He never overstates a case; hence his style gives a strong impression of sincerity and authenticity. Above all—and this may surprise people who think of western writers as hayseeds—Waters's style has the courtesy of urbanity.

"Urbanity," says F.L. Lucas, a Cambridge don whose book, *Style*, is full of surprises, all justified, "is that form of true politeness which sets men at ease ...and it is largely based on simple sympathy and unpretentiousness."[7] It is not a sort of effeminate elegance. It doesn't play oracle and lay down the law (in the manner, say, of D.H. Lawrence). Urbanity, Lucas suggests, is the "smiling headshake of Montaigne, tranquil on his pillow of doubt."[8] Urbanity is a main means of strengthening sympathy between writer and reader.

A great deal about Waters and his style is revealed in one sentence from *The Man Who Killed the Deer*: "So little by little the richness and the wonder and the mystery of life stole in upon him."[9] Thomas J. Lyon, the first critic to note what a remarkable sentence this is, sets in opposition to it the first sentence of Jack Schaefer's *Shane*: "He rode into our valley in the summer of '89."[10] Schaefer's character is solid, separate, and alone; *he* acts upon his world, a kind of cowboy Messiah whose word is a gun. But Frank's character, the *him*, receives the action of the world; Martiniano has come to realize that everything in life is connected, that he is part of the tribe, society, nation, planet, and cosmos. Here in a simple sentence from *Deer*—its only irony the dramatic one of a belated discovery—is the essence of a profound world-view. The Shanes of literature impose themselves on others, assert their individuality violently, and represent a spurious male myth of intervention in the scheme of things. The Martinianos, by contrast, have to lose their ego-identity in order truly to be alive. The ethic of their self-fulfillment is atonement with a living universe.

So when I refer to Frank as a man who never stopped living, I mean that he never stopped living within the richness and the wonder and the mystery of life. Whatever faults or foibles he may have displayed in a long and active life—his biographer can cope with these as and when they are found—he had a character fine enough to imagine types of human nature at its most lovable and enduring. Martiniano, Maria del Valle, Tai Ling, Helen Chalmers and the tragic Rogier are portrayed with a vibrant quality that seals itself on the reader's mind.

Let us look at some specimen passages.

(1)

> As this solitary and silent girl stood there in the moonlight, a straight slim figure, clothed in a plaitless gown, the contours of womanhood so undeveloped as to be scarcely perceptible, the marks of poverty and toil effaced by the misty hour, she touched sublimity at points, and looked almost like a being who had rejected with indifference the attribute of sex for the

loftier quality of abstract humanism. She stooped down and cleared away the withered flowers that Grace and herself had laid there the previous week, and put her fresh ones in their place.

"Now, my own, own love," she whispered, "you are mine, and on'y mine, for she has forgot 'ee at last, although for her you died! But I—whenever I get up I'll think of 'ee, and whenever I lie down I'll think of 'ee. Whenever I plant the young larches I'll think that none can plant as you planted; and whenever I split a gad, and whenever I turn the cider wring, I'll say none could do it like you. If ever I forget your name let me forget home and heaven! ...But no, no, my love, I never can forget 'ee; for you was a good man, and did good things!"

(2)

On the doorstep lay an empty pair of shoes. She closed the door and carried them into the candlelight. The shoes were old and shapeless, caked with mud and spotted with dried blood. They were Onesimo's.

The sudden meaning of their appalling emptiness stabbed her like a knife. It carved out her heart and bowels and mind. She stood more empty than the shoes, one hand clawing at her face, holding her breast, then pressing against her belly.

Teodosio and Niña were gulping goat's milk from wooden spoons. Maria bent down to her own bowl, and lifted a hair from the milk with her forefinger. Suddenly she straightened. With a fearful howl she flung open the door and rushed out into the night.[11]

The first passage, from the close of Thomas Hardy's *The*

Woodlanders, shows the grief of Marty South; the second passage, from Waters's *People of the Valley*, shows the grief of Maria at the moment when she realizes that Onesimo has died during the Penitentes' reenactment of the Crucifixion. There is a bleak, yet compassionate honesty in both scenes, and a tense reticence in the portrayal of people who feel much, say little. Some readers nowadays may wish that Hardy had been even more restrained than he is, had cut the business about "sublimity" and "abstract humanism," and had not surrendered to the Victorian taste for graveyard sentiments and soliloquies. I confess, however, that I find his scene true and convincing. It has a quiet dignity.

But the controlled brevity of Waters's scene has a power of implication greater than Hardy's. Not a word is spoken, yet we know that the hair in the goat's milk is Onesimo's, without being told, as we are about his shoes; and it is this thread of human connection which, more than the detail of the empty shoes, conveys just how unbearable is Maria's loss. In fact, the scene proves the vitality of concrete, vivid details. Whereas Hardy gives us some homely touches—for example, how Marty's lost love could turn a cider wring—Waters lets details reveal a world of loss. The dried blood on the shoes has been shed by a man who died on a cross. Now, Flaubert was a master of this kind of concreteness. We recall his Emma Bovary gazing nostalgically at the stain of yellow wax on her dancing-shoes, which recalls her momentary glimpse of her false paradise in the ball at the château. The yellow wax and Onesimo's bloody shoes: we see, we remember.

Ernest Hemingway has taken a drubbing lately from readers who deplore his projection of excessive masculinity or his insistent nihilism. Yet a problem with Hemingway, I think, is a matter of style—the very thing upon which he most prided himself. To be sure, this criticism rests upon a distinction made earlier, that style is more than a cultivated manner. I shall gladly be first to grant Hemingway his large achievement in the disciplining of language. Nevertheless, let's look at *A Farewell to*

Arms, the Caporetto section usually singled out for representing Hemingway at his best:

> Two carabinieri took the lieutenant-colonel to the river bank. He walked in the rain, an old man with his hat off, a carabiniere on either side. I did not watch them shoot him but I heard the shots. They were questioning someone else. This officer too was separated from his troops. He was not allowed to make an explanation. He cried when they read the sentence from the pad of paper, and they were questioning another when they shot him. They made a point of being intent on questioning the next man while the man who had been questioned before was being shot. In this way there was obviously nothing they could do about it.[12]

The point of view here is that of Lieutenant Henry, and he is about to make his escape to the river. Certainly in the circumstances he is entitled to believe that he is up against an impersonal war-machine and cannot possibly expect a reprieve. That's fine. I suspect, however, that Hemingway, in complete agreement with the protagonist, has allowed himself to force the issue about the Italian soldiers. Did they all, without exception, make a point of being intent on the questioning, so that "there was obviously nothing" to link them responsibly and humanly to the executions? Was there not present a single soldier who betrayed a lurch of disgust or pity, not a single officer who hesitated before reading from that pad of paper? Hemingway could have avoided our suspicion of falsity by adding a single qualifier, "perhaps": "Perhaps they made a point of being intent," etc. Hemingway need not be suspected of insincerity, but in trying to set up the reader's response to a seemingly monstrous situation, he has taken for granted that his conception of warfare must be shared by others. This is a kind of obscurity due to egotism; this is a kind of spleen-venting that seeks to make other people feel sick to death of war. I believe most of what Hemingway wants me to believe, but not all.

Artificiality in the service of literary tact has much to be said for it, especially in these days of the aggressively unbuttoned bodice. However, readers quickly detect the difference between decorous cleverness and earthy simplicity, when it comes to understating the obvious. Here are two examples of pastoral love-making, the first from Hervey Allen's best-seller, *Anthony Adverse*, the second, again, from *People of the Valley*.

(1)

Brushing aside the long, trailing tendrils like a veil, Denis laid Maria softly in the nest of dry ferns ...To the curious sheep cropping nearby it seemed as if the man and his burden had vanished into the old wall. Soon their bells continued to sound again gentle.

Only once more during the noontide were they disturbed; this time by a soft, tremulous cry.

Attracted by so lonely and virginal a store of honey, a bumble-bee lit upon this blossom and after stroking its petals for sometime as if he were in love, began to tear away the small green membrane that still defended it from his assault. The petals opened slightly and began to curl. Settling back as it were upon his haunches, and raking his body back and forth over this small opening the bee finally succeeded in inserting himself into the flower. Here, as if in ecstasy, he dashed himself about.[13]

Unfairly neglected now, Allen (who died in 1949) was a good poet, a large-minded and zestful writer of historical fiction, and author of one of the most compelling eyewitness accounts of soldiering in the first World War. But his stylistic transgression in this passage is against good sense. How did he know what those "curious sheep" were thinking? Why did he indulge in soft pornography about bees and flowers?

(2)
> So through the afternoon neither moved. The goats stirred like phantoms through the brush. Major crunched grass with the bit still between his teeth. A magpie chattered in the pine, a hawk hung suspended overhead. The stream rippled noisily in the silence. It was all one song, a song heard by none but sung by all. And in the yellowing sunlight the wild August plums hung darker, softer—green no longer, but yet not wholly ripe.
>
> They sat up suddenly, as if conscious of the shouts of mule skinners passing on the road as they had all afternoon.
>
> "I ought to be goin' back to the fort," the soldier said, staring at a tuft of dust shot through by the fire of the setting sun. But instead he tethered Major out of sight in the brush. Maria called softly to her goats, as if merely to hear their crackling in the thicket.
>
> The shadow of the pine grew longer, blacker. A breeze was coming up. And yet neither man nor woman spoke.
>
> When the sun went down they moved back into the wild plum thicket. Here it was warmer, darker, and then there was nothing to be seen or heard, not even the first ecstatic trembling of the plums overhead ...[14]

The first thing one notices here is that Waters, unlike Allen, is creating a genuinely pastoral setting. The goats belong to Maria, not to the conventions of Theocritus and Virgil. Second, sexual attraction ("all one song") is shared by all of nature and not conventionally delegated to bees and flowers. Third, society, such as it is, has to be reckoned with: mule skinners pass on the road, the soldier has duties at the fort. Fourth, the wild plums are not extraneous props but a symbol of Maria herself as she moves from ripeness to fulfillment.

Just how much brevity serves the cause of sincerity remains debatable. In one of his poems, W.H. Auden wrote, "Love was made," and that was it, passive voice and all. According to Lucas, the late Sir Edward Marsh, composing his memoir of Rupert Brooke, wrote, "Rupert left Rugby in a blaze of glory," and the poet's mother changed "a blaze of glory" to "July."[15] I think we are much more likely to accept Waters's trembling plums as sincere feeling than we are Allen's dashing bumble-bee.

Here is a final set of specimen passages, the first two considered glories of American literature.

(1)

> The Supreme Critic on the errors of the past and present, and the only prophet of that which must be, is that great nature in which we rest as the earth lies in the soft arms of the atmosphere; that Unity, that Over-Soul, within which every man's particular being is contained and made one with all other; that common heart of which all sincere conversation is the worship, to which all right action is submission; that over-powering reality, which confutes our tricks and talents, and constrains every one to pass for what he is, and to speak from his character and not from his tongue, and which evermore tends to pass into our thought and hand and become wisdom and virtue and power and beauty. We live in succession, in division, in parts, in particles. Meantime within man is the soul of the whole, the wise silence; the universal beauty, to which every part and particle is equally related; the eternal One.[16]

(2)

> ...and he did what Sam had coached and drilled him
> as the next and the last, seeing as he sat down on the
> log the crooked print, the warped indentation in the
> wet ground which while he looked at it continued to
> fill with water until it was level full and the water
> began to overflow and the sides of the print began to
> dissolve away. Even as he looked up he saw the next
> one, and, moving, the one beyond it; moving, not
> hurrying, running, but merely keeping pace with
> them as they appeared before him as though they
> were being shaped out of thin air just one constant
> pace short of where he would lose them forever and
> be lost forever himself, tireless, eager, without doubt
> or dread, panting a little above the strong rapid little
> hammer of his heart, emerging suddenly into a little
> glade and the wilderness coalesced. It rushed, sound-
> less, and solidified—the tree, the bush, the compass
> and the watch glinting where a ray of sunlight
> touched them. Then he saw the bear. It did not
> emerge, appear: it was just there, immobile, fixed in
> the green and windless noon's hot dappling, not as
> big as he had expected, bigger, dimensionless against
> the dappled obscurity, looking at him.[17]

Emerson in "The Over-Soul" and Faulkner in "The Bear" are
both concerned to arouse in us the sense of awe and wonder
and mystery. Both want to overwhelm us, Emerson by means
of a hectoring, trumpeting, sermonizing style which, though
generous, is exaggerated and pompous and hifalutin. It seeks to
glorify the self rather than the theme. Faulkner is far more con-
siderate of his readers than Emerson and leads us to share in a
boy's initiation into a magical wilderness. And yet Faulkner, it
seems to me, is spouting a Niagara of words as if turning up the
rhetorical volume will deliver salvation. Look, for example, at

the pile-up of negative universals: *tireless, soundless, immobile, windless, dimensionless.* These words have the aim of convincing us that an abstract and absolute reality exists; and, of course, you may embody a whole vision by using epithets that strengthen effect. I needn't argue against the power of these passages (especially that from "The Bear"), but they bruise my feelings in ways that plain prose does not.

It is quite possible to take the gates to the sacred not by storm but by gentle surrender. Frank Waters knew this aspect of style better, I think, than most writers. When he writes of his own spiritual experiences, he creates a mood that is at once dramatic and plain-spoken. Here is one such story from *Mountain Dialogues.*

(3)

It was late afternoon. My brother-in-law Carl had gone fishing and had not yet returned. While waiting for him, Naomi and I went for a walk up the road toward the base of the mountains. When the road ended, we cut south toward the mouth of the Lucero across an open, high meadow. It was a lovely spot whose peace and silence were enhanced by the wild flowers underfoot, the mellow glow of the sinking sun. Ahead of us lay the thick growth of scrub oak I have mentioned.

Suddenly Naomi, with her acute perceptions and fey intuition, stopped short, and I noticed on her face a look of trepidation. At almost the same time, I was halted by what seemed an invisible and intangible barrier. For a moment, I believed that she had instinctively sensed the presence of a bear, which had come down to feed on the acorns. Previously, I had been warned not to ride in this vicinity, as Cry Baby would be spooked by the smell of bear. Yet as I tried to step forward anyway, I was held in check by that mounting, intangible wave that had no sound nor smell, but was more impassable than any physical barrier.

At this instant, the cloying silence was broken by a shrill cry that seemed to come from the cliff walls at the mouth of the Lucero. It was so loud and clear that it filled the meadow. Wild and frightening, it came from a human voice imploring help, but in words I could not understand. Surely someone over there, perhaps an Indian, had been attacked, fallen from a cliff, or met with another serious accident. Unable to ignore its wild plea, I gave a loud shout, although that intangible barrier prevented me from moving forward.

As we stood there rooted to the spot, another shrill cry sounded. Now years later, I cannot describe it though it is etched indelibly in my memory. It was as if it were uttered by someone who had been pushed or jumped to his death from the cliffs; and now, too late, gave one last despairing, agonizing death-cry. An earthly cry, but unearthly, too, as if it had been filtered through an abnormal or supernormal medium. It filled our small world with a horror that destroyed completely all serenity, and broke against the benevolent Sacred Mountain its soul-torturing anguish.

The story continues as Frank and Naomi get in a car and drive down to the pueblo to find out if someone had met with an accident. They learn that no Indians had gone up the Lucero that day, no trouble had been reported, nor were any Indians reported missing. They are asked to come back next day, to see their friend Albert.

> Early next morning, we drove back to see him, still disturbed ourselves. Albert gave us coffee at his kitchen table. He affirmed that further inquiry had revealed no accidents at the mouth of the Lucero, no Indians missing from the pueblo. The door was open. The morning sun shone in, bright and clear. Out in the plaza, people were serenely going about their daily chores. Yet all this only accentuated the frightening cries we had heard the previous evening, the intangible barrier we had encountered.
>
> Albert was a man of few words. He finally said simply, "Long time ago that happen. You just hear it now."

"Nothing," Waters concludes, "puts into such few words the belief—not only Indian—that time is not a linear flow, as we think it is, into past, present, and future. Time is an indivisible whole, a great pool in which all events are eternally embodied and still have their meaningful being. Into it we may dip by chance, or by a meaningful flash of supernormal or extra-sensory perception, and glimpse something that happened long ago in our linear time."[18]

Waters's story flows naturally from the person and the situation. The surface of the style remains open, simple, clear, a kind of anticipation of the stainless pool of the timeless, his theme, his depth, his aliveness.

The man who never stopped living in his quest for meaning has, once again, courteously and rapturously stopped for us—to light us on our way. Character and style, the man and the writer, Frank and Frank Waters. Happily for friends and readers alike, the pairs coincide.

II. Pícaro

MYTH AND THE PICARESQUE NOVEL

There is at present neither a science of mythology nor a psychology of literature. But we should overlook no approach that casts a cold eye upon the tragic predicament of the Atomic Age and illuminates the grave and constant in human affairs. I, for one, believe the study of myth opens such a possibility, permitting us a glimpse of the creative spirit necessary to human survival. Consequently, the study of myth seems a proper study of mankind not only in the anthropological sense of so-called primitive mentation but also in the psychological sense of the here-and-now in the civilization of the recent West. Our recent mind, that of modern man, is discernible in various phenomena including, as I shall argue, the literature of the past eight centuries, particularly in the novel because, since its appearance as the picaresque novel in the sixteenth century, it has been the dominant literary mode. If indeed myth and the picaresque novel are fused, we should be able to trace a picaresque myth expressive, at a certain depth of import, of man in the modern world.

The proposition that a myth expresses us is not, I trust, to impose a religious idea upon a literary one. I share the skepticism of the young woman who, after reading D.H. Lawrence's *Sons and Lovers*, protested, "But I don't *believe* in the Oedipus Complex!" Nor do I, where faith is concerned. The psychoanalysis of imaginary characters such as Oedipus and Hamlet violates the integrity of art. Similarly, the devotee of archetypes who reduces art to an undifferentiated continuum drives all human experience into a corner in order to make it yield eternity. Nevertheless, we all so to speak are Freudians and Jungians now, with qualifications. Here are some of mine. If myth is discernible in a literary work, the message conveyed may be limited to the work and remain the creative mythology of a particular individual. Then again, the myth may be continued in other works, but the message may be transformed by

them; anyone with empirical knowledge of the habits of story-
tellers must admit that transformations occur to some degree.
Further, the meaning of a myth may not be limited to the archetypal but may be both a product of its overt contents and an
underlying structure of particular materials. This qualification,
namely that the design of a literary work may by itself precipitate the essential story or myth, permits the critic of fiction to
wrestle with the angel, Art, without fully committing himself to
divinity. Myths may express local and ethnic ideas as well as
elementary and recurrent ones. At all events, I think we would
agree that myth takes its source in the imagination and address-
es itself to the psyche, not to historical circumstances, and that
literature often follows the same path, rising to consciousness
out of the unconscious mind.

 That myth and literature are complementary or even identical aspects of the act of creation is a view nowadays widely
accepted. Many of us, nevertheless, have been conditioned in
the attitude that a myth means something Greek at best and at
worst something false. Until relatively recent times such has
been myth's disrepute that it was relegated to the nursery
where it joined such supposedly harmless works as *Gulliver's
Travels* in a junkyard of shadows. Bulfinch's *Age of Fable*, first
published in 1855, continues to be assigned to college students
as a reference work. They remain frostily silent about
Bulfinch's preface wherein he declares that the stories of
mythology are merely a source of amusement and that he has
omitted "stories and parts of stories as are offensive to pure
taste and good morals."[1] But hostility to myth arises, not from
the prurience and superficiality of Bulfinch, but out of misconceptions about the process of thinking and the methods of science. Ever since what Arthur Koestler calls "the Cartesian
Catastrophe" in the first half of the seventeenth century, we've
been conditioned to regard the unconscious mind as a separate
realm divided from full consciousness. This assumption, hard-
ened into dogma in the nineteenth century, elevates science
above organic processes with which the mythic mind is associ-

ated. Paradoxically, Koestler observes, science "operates predominantly with abstract symbols, whose entire rationale and credo are objectivity, verifiability, and logicality," but "depends on mental processes which are subjective, irrational, and verifiable only after the event."Archimedes, one hopes, bathed regularly, but not until his mind was preoccupied with the problem of volume did the rings on his bathtub lead him to cry Eureka. "Conscious and unconscious experiences," Koestler affirms, "form a continuous scale of gradations, of degrees of awareness."[2] Science, like myth, is a spontaneous child of the unconscious mind.

For those still skeptical of myth's relevance to modern man, I shall need to ask what is meant by *modern*. But first let me give a modern instance of what happens when genuine spontaneity becomes inconceivable.

The Hungarian Revolution of 1956 was in every sense spontaneous. For about two weeks a subjugated nation of ten million people, without planning or leadership and originally with no more aggressive intention than to list grievances over state-controlled radio, found itself freed from government, the secret police, and the armed might of the Soviet Union. Leaders appeared among the masses, not simply from the ranks of the intelligentsia, yet everyone had been thoroughly indoctrinated in Marxist-Leninist ideology. Since, as Albert Camus remarked, the gallows don't liberalize, one would have thought the Communist Party had nothing to fear from the cowed and compliant survivors of a long reign of terror. Yet suddenly the people exploded into revolution. It was the kind of reflex that constitutes a creative act: two mutually incompatible codes or associative contexts came to the clash, and habit was defeated by originality. The Hungarians could even invoke the spirit of Lenin in support of their liberation, for they were activating the classical Leninist postulate of revolutionary situations in general: namely, the historical moment when the ruling classes are unable to govern and the oppressed classes are unwilling to live in the old way.

After Soviet weapons had silenced the voices of freedom, and after Janos Kadar had been installed in power determined to imitate his predecessors in ideological autocracy, the party tore off a thousand metaphorical hairshirts in order to explain that shadowy explosion of "unhistorical" and therefore unintelligible forces. Instead of invoking Lenin, the party itself turned to the powers of darkness. According to the so-called objective laws of society—Cartesian logic raped and then married to dialectical thought—the masses, so often erroneous *because* spontaneous, had to be critically supervised, with scientific exactitude, by the party. Since by definition the party is solipsistic, the only knowable or existent thing, it must have been that the Hungarians had been possessed by demons in spite of years of uninhibited terror! As Tamas Aczel, winner of both the Stalin and Kossuth literary prizes, writes, an almost comic situation arose. "The party interpreted the spontaneous eruption of the revolution as a conscious preparation of the class enemy, whereas it attributed its own spontaneous reactions to the conscious efforts of the working class."[3] By means of doublethink, the Party made all the intricate and creative forces of human nature equivalent to an underworld teeming with the demons of the unconscious mind—and unwittingly prompted poets and writers to abandon the alpine air of full scientific consciousness in which hitherto they had been contentedly strangling. Reaching down to the unconscious mind to such literary forms of spontaneity as existentialism, surrealism, pessimism, and biological realism, writers experienced the electrifying shock of being in touch with universality. Living consciously in a world where value-judgements are mass-produced, they discovered or rediscovered the elements of individual morality and truth.

One lesson of the Hungarian Revolution and its aftermath is its approximate repetition of historical conditions in sixteenth-century Spain when the first picaresque novel appears. Extraordinary terror such as that used by the Inquisition in support of an ideology in which man of the Middle Ages no longer believed with a living faith also drove writers inside themselves, to the unconscious mind from which morality and truth could be reborn. There should be nothing surprising in this. When a problem cannot be solved by the same rules of the game which were applied in past situations, the attention is displaced to something not previously noted, dream-like states where codes of rational orthodoxy are suspended. This process of escape—from emotional frustration, intellectual stagnation, boredom, terror—becomes a search for new sources of living a life otherwise consciously automatized. Furthermore, the reality revealed by personal experience is not solipsistic. It was the Communist Party which drove itself into the cul de sac of emotional solipsism, whereas the writers and by implication the spontaneously liberated masses were relearning to experience selfhood as part of a larger whole, a higher unity. Camus's famous repudiation of Cartesian, Rousseauistic, Marxist, and other nihilistic logic is relevant here: "I *rebel*—therefore we *exist*."[4] The fruits of a quest in the depths of the unconscious mind, and bitter fruits they may be, can nourish those starving for authentic reintegration with God, society, and our fellow man.

But let us turn now to the question of what is modern about modern man. Those who believe modernity is here-and-now separated from history have no idea how far back our here-and-now extends its roots. Emulating Henry Adams and Joseph Campbell, I'm going to propose that we identify modern man as a component of western history since the twelfth century A.D.

To begin with, we need a view of myth as an essential process in history in order to describe stages of culture according to their dominant symbolic modes. To the objection of historicism, which is the attempt to get from historical premises conclusions more than historical, I would argue that we cannot remove from human action what makes it truly human. In other words, myths have the merit of showing the way that historicism is justified in taking. Since myths function to awake consciousness to the profound mystery and order of the universe, in the face of which we feel an awed delight or terror at the world of man, we should be comfortable in asserting that part of the narrative of modern man belongs as much to myth as to history. Let me again offer an illustration from contemporary life. Whereas the historian will be seeking social, economic, and political causes for events, the mythographer, like as not, will be considering ways in which we imagine ourselves, internal events, so to speak. For instance, it seems to me one of the most striking facts of our time is our fondness for destruction. What I call the New Millennialism erupts all around us: movies about demons and monstrous sharks, fiction about nuclear and bacteriological holocausts, Y2K hysteria, and so forth. It is as if we can no longer imagine the universal mystery as other than cataclysmic destruction. At the same time, we glory in Future Shock, our own form of evanescence, not really dreading it, of course, but rather attuning our minds to a fortuitous world without daylight or clocks, like a Las Vegas casino. In order to retrieve the creative element from the Dispose-All of Apocalypse Now, we need to separate the idea of progress from that of imminent doom. Both mingle as aspects of contemporary myth; both contribute to the idea of ourselves in time.

Viewing myth as an essential process in history, I approach the picaresque novel of the later Middle Ages as an expression of double consciousness, an artistic event looking two ways at once, in one direction toward medieval man, in the other, toward modern man.

A funny thing may happen to you on your way to the Middle Ages: the closer you think you are, the more they recede like a mirage. Two centuries ago, when Europeans began to study the Middle Ages, the border country seemed clearly visible: the seventeenth century divided civilization from barbarism. Especially in Protestant England, the Catholic Middle Ages represented a cesspool of ignorance, superstition, and vice, and with the rise of capitalism and bourgeois democracy, Gothic Europe became another word for terror. There was, however, a fascination with this abomination. Gloomy cathedrals and damp castles entered literature as backdrop to romances. Ruins, especially, produced instant nostalgia, and if you just happened to lack a Cistercian abbey or Norman battlement in your garden, you installed one called a folly. By the time of Scott and Hugo, the Middle Ages were à la mode, still gloomy and terrifying but now also a time of *Liebestod*, of effeminate knights, lusty wenches, and admirably toiling peasants. The Middle Ages began to recede, leaving behind a sort of wall, the Renaissance. On its bad side, the Renaissance is a slough of all that is uniform, static, and unprogressive. On its good side, all is science, art, democracy, and capitalism. The truth is not so simple. Spreading the barbarism of the Goths and Vandals over the centuries following their invasions does not explain, for example, the achievement of Gothic architecture, and contrasting the ignorance of this age with the enlightenment of the Renaissance disregards, say, the religious fanaticism that flourished throughout the succeeding period. Europe developed unequally in different parts, great economic changes occurred within the epoch of the Middle Ages, and new learning flowed from the East as early as the twelfth century.

Nowadays, many of us would like to abandon the term Renaissance altogether, as conveying false impressions of sudden change and an original and distinct culture, as well as implying that a real rebirth of something past is ever possible. The problem, as I see it, is our conditioning in linear thinking. If we must absolutely have a line, one where medievalism and modernism begin to exhibit a double consciousness, then let us push the border back before Dante to the age of Chartres and the *Tristan* myth of love. But even when we draw the line at the twelfth century and begin to discover our modern selves there, we are hard put to find the Middle Ages. Do they truly distinguish modes of thought and feeling as between Greco-Roman civilization and our own since about 1750? Or are the Middle Ages, however special the gothic imagination of Northern Europe, still essentially a continuation of a stage of history associated with the civilizations and mythologies of the ancient Mediterranean and Near East? If so—and I believe that it is so—then how much deeper and more challenging to the spirit yawns that abyss between us and the receding Middle Ages than we are accustomed to expect! For now the Middle Ages and the Renaissance are largely identical, though differing in degrees of the acceleration of energy or the rapidity with which modern man is born after gestating for some seven thousand years.

This view of history necessitates categories based upon unifying ideas of reality and of authority. Joseph Campbell's great work of comparative mythology, *The Masks of the God*, distinguishes three stages of culture. In the Goddess Mother Stage, man is inseparable from nature as nature is from divinity. In the Monumental Stage, patriarchal mythologies of thunder-hurling warrior gods dominate. The central symbol is a world mountain that has the City of the Lord at its summit and hellish waters beneath. This symbol can be recognized in the ziggurat of Nippur, in the Tower of Babel, in pyramids, in Mount Sinai, in Mount Olympus, in the gothic cathedrals, and in the structure of Dante's universe of Hell rising to the Mountain of Purgatory and to Paradise. In Sumer, Babylonia, Egypt, Jerusalem, Athens, Rome, or Dante's Florence, authority was from aloft, the order of the heavens interpreted and administered by priests, and the lesson that many sought to know and to follow was written "above," for all time and for all people, either in the stars or in the pages of a book presumed to be dictated by God, the words of one come down from on high and miraculously made flesh. But where for thousands of years God has been conceived as "above," around 1200 A.D. the new center and source of awe, truth, virtue, and being becomes for each his own, made known within. Campbell calls this the World Culture Stage and perceives its moving irrevocably into history during the sixteenth and seventeenth centuries. The technical determinants of World Culture become over a period of some eight hundred years the scientific method of research and the power-driven machine; and now the distinguishing feature of the new mankind is that it is one of individuals, self-moved to ends proper to themselves, directed not by the constraint of others but each by his own inner voice. Campbell concludes, "The faith in Scripture of the Middle Ages, faith in reason of the Enlightenment, faith in science of modern Philistia belong equally today to those alone who have as yet no idea how mysterious, really, is the mystery even of themselves."[5]

Modern man, in other words, is created out of the breakup of many millennia of a belief system, the Middle Ages but its last expression. Using the past eight centuries as a target, we may chart a kind of magnetic field of force consisting of concentric circles orbiting around the bullseye of the later twentieth century. Certain moments and individuals are plotted on this target, for *they* are the true "Renaissance," distributed over the entire field, their density of position increasing as we move from the sphere of Abelard and the Troubadors, Gottfried and Dante, to the anonymous author of *Lazarillo de Tormes*, to Cervantes, Shakespeare, the Baroque poets, and on to the inner circle. How else can we explain, on the one hand, the modernism of the *Tristan* myth of the twelfth century and, on the other hand, the medievalism of the Ayatollah Khomeini in 1980? *Time* hailed this Iranian priest as Man of the Year—but his proper year is 2,500 B.C. in the period of the first Semitic kings when the idea of a distinction between God and man first became an important social and psychological force. Significantly, too, as I implied earlier by reference to the Hungarian Revolution, Marxist-Leninist ideology is neither scientific nor modern. Those who continue to believe in it would feel quite at home in the world of the Spanish Inquisition, which, however, had an eschatological as opposed to a nihilistic basis. This analogy was not lost upon Dostoevsky in *The Brothers Karamazov*, and Camus in *L'Homme révolté* exposed it definitively. Pretensions to scientific determinism notwithstanding, Communism is nothing but man's ancient, lunatic desire to convert himself into a god presiding over a never-never kingdom of this earth.

Nevertheless, authentic modern myth such as existentialism with its emphasis upon the free life of choice compels us to
recognize our day of dread. Modern myth, arising, like as not,
from experience of death in the heart of culture, is often
expressed as anguished loss of the older myth. Indeed there is
something to be said for the structural theory of myth pro-
pounded by the French anthropologist Claude Levi-Strauss, in
sum that "the purpose of myth is to provide a logical model
capable of overcoming a contradiction."[6] In functioning to mediate between conflicting cultural elements, a myth may reveal
dramatic tensions without necessarily resolving them. Thus in
The Education (1906) Henry Adams recoils from a central
predicament of modern times: man can no longer reconcile his
mind with the forces of nature it studies. The dynamo and
X-rays symbolize for Adams awesome force that has never
before played a part in man's consciousness, the atom having
previously figured, as in Lucretius, as a fiction of thought. His
education had not prepared him for reality, any more than our
education more than half a century later made it predictable
that Shepherd would take a moon-walk instead of sinking into
fathoms of dust. Now man, Adams recognized, must live in a
universe in which he can "measure nothing except by chance
collisions of movements imperceptible to his senses, perhaps
even imperceptible to his instruments! . . ."[7] How much more
comforting, then, was the mythic energy of the Virgin of
Chartres, the heavenly queen who, far from wrapping herself
in shadows of terror, is harmony and light personified! Her
attribute was humility, her love and pity were infinite; she was
humanly accessible, as the orthodox Trinity was not, and her
emblematic Rose represented for the people of the thirteenth
century light, passion, grace, magnificence, and the promise of
joyous Paradise. If Adams's sense of loss is softened by nostalgia, it is because he is already eased into a modern mythology
whereby the mysterious and infinite can be identified with
nuclear energy. There was little use in crying over spilt religions. But for man in the sixteenth and seventeenth centuries

the sense of loss cut to the marrow: the collapse of his mythology was, for his eternally damned soul, a no-exit situation. Kit Marlowe, the cocksure freethinker of Cambridge, could hardly have been chuckling as his imaginary Doctor Faustus goes shrieking to perdition. Hamlet's discovery of disorder in the cosmos, in the state, and in himself sets him adrift in a world without apparent meaning, inscrutable, unjust, and futile. This disintegration of Hamlet's world view, not coincidentally, is prompted by loss of faith in the Virgin Mother symbol. When we read the literature of four hundred years ago, approximately midway between Dante's Florence and Henry Adams's Chicago, we should anticipate such models of convulsion. Painfully, in spite of the constraint of authority, certain creative spirits feel, think, and do what only they, in the individual sense, must feel, think, and do.

Lazarillo de Tormes, first published in 1554 though possibly composed several decades earlier in the wake of Luther's Reformation, is, I believe, the first modern novel. It had its precursors in Spain, in Italy, even in Iceland and Japan, and especially in the ancient world as we westerners conceive of it; Apuleius's *Golden Ass* is probably a direct influence. But, insofar as I can determine, *Lazarillo* differs from all previous prose narratives to which one assigns, however vaguely, the title of novel. *Lazarillo* offers for the first time a story of character in process—social, temporal process. That technical innovation alone is sufficient to mark a boundary between the way man regarded himself prior to 1554 and the way he has tended to regard himself ever since. Something begins, and in the light of such a distinct beginning we are able to connect myth to the predominant literary form of recent historical times.

The genius of despair and the aggressive, self-defensive reflex of laughter probably drove the *Lazarillo's* anonymous author deeply within the unconscious mind in order to bring forth, doubtless at great danger to his psyche if not to his physical person, the true form and feeling of his age. Here, briefly, is the story. Lázaro, a disreputable town crier of Toledo, has

been ordered by a social superior to give an account of himself
and to explain his marriage to and pimping for the mistress of
the archpriest of San Salvador. In order to evade the issue, this
clever young man devises a narrative strategy that projects his
guilt upon others. He is so adept in the confidence trick of dissolving reality, so convincing in his indictment of a society corrupt from bottom to top, that he almost deceives us into thinking him a pitiable victim who has achieved honor and success
against slim odds. From birth, he would have us believe, fortune conspired both against him and, ironically, for him. His
parents were poor, his father a condemned thief, his mother a
prostitute. But sir, could the Emperor claim better pedigree?
Certainly, sir, no one could ask for a more illuminating education than that provided by a series of masters whom Lázaro
came to serve. First there was a blind man whose brutality
taught him to consider self-interest above everything else.
Starved by a priest and then deserted by a poverty-stricken
squire, Lázaro does indeed have the right to claim that he survived because he learned to do society's work, namely, to
exploit others through deception and compromise. So there you
are, sir. I, Lázaro, am now respectable and prosperous, just as
worthy as the next fellow—no, better than he, for I have not
only climbed the ladder of success but also had the insight to
recognize the conditions of success. Well, that's Lázaro's version
of the story. Authorial irony interjects another version.
Whether Lázaro is a victim or a trickster, he has clearly adopted a dehumanized value system in attempting to cope with the
schizophrenic demands of a society in which so-called "good"
people must act in one way while pretending that they are acting in another. In claiming to have attained the summit of all
good fortune as a consequence of his arrangement with the
archpriest, Lázaro has become like everyone else and wants to
be respected for an accomplishment that, when judged according to a truly human set of values, is no accomplishment at all.
His "success" is inseparable from amorality and spiritual death.
    The mythical aspect of *Lazarillo de Tormes* arises precisely

from the protagonist's or *pícaro*'s interiorization of the prevailing ethos of society. His story illustrates the process by which the dehumanizing values of a corrupt society are imprinted upon the mind of an individual who henceforth creates his own identity. Since the story of the death of a soul cuts far beneath the levels of satire, the author's world view implies not only condemnation of a dehumanizing socialization process but also the tragic predicament of an individual locked into and isolated within society and forced to assume the mask of a confidence man, an outcast without real identity. *Lazarillo de Tormes* gives evidence of a shift from the medieval view of a reality as absolute to the modern view of reality as relative to the individual; an individual, moreover, so unreliable as to be nothingness personified. In the context of religious beliefs of the Spanish sixteenth century, Lázaro is cosmically homeless. His is a strange, inaccessible self held over from the loss of grace, and his journey into self is a confrontation with death and emblematically an experience of it. This novel's systematic procedure, the ironic success-story of character deformation, betrays in its largest configurations a myth of the prying loose and casting out of a free individual and of the spiritual death that results. It is death in life, the archetype of the biblical Lazarus, and this condition of a dead soul annunciates, as it were, the whole history of modern man's quest to become united with the world in the spontaneity of love and productive work—or else to disappear altogether from meaningful humanity.

The presence of a creative myth in *Lazarillo de Tormes* is, I think, confirmed by its continuance in Mateo Alemán's *Guzmán de Alfarache* and in Francisco de Quevedo's *El Buscón,* both Spanish novels of the early seventeenth century. Although these authors interfere with the overt narrative structure of *Lazarillo*, they do not alter the underlying structure wherein a myth of the *pícaro* is felt. Guzmán's alienation from society and Pablos's spiritual invisibility within society state in affective terms the same problem represented by Lázaro's death-in-life and, in the way of myth, offer identical non-rational solutions.

If the problem is that nature and culture, or what I have else-where called spontaneity and full consciousness, have come apart to the extent of dividing the self, then the proffered solution is a return to that very orthodoxy in which the medieval world no longer invests living faith—and that is no solution but, rather, a further turn of the screw. The first picaresque novel-ists perceived the darkness of a spiritual void; the feeling aroused in them, which is the feeling of myth, is one of mystery and terror.[8]

Some Hispanists contend that the picaresque novel is a phe-nomenon exclusively of Spanish culture. "The *pícaro* is not a myth, he is a reality," a Chilean scholar has remarked to me. But fiction and so-called real life part company. The Spanish picaresque novelists—unlike Cervantes, incidentally—portray "real" life as an illusory journey to the end of night. And I doubt if they sat down like propagandists to prefabricate a myth, though they may have attempted consciously to control mean-ings in a myth. The point is, a picaresque myth is, like any other myth, unconfined, crossing historical and cultural fron-tiers at will. Sociological critics alight here, for, having identi-fied the *pícaro* as a lower-class wanderer, they leave themselves no choice but to trace his upward mobility until Smollett makes him an aristocrat. Although this is the usual approach to the question of the picaresque novel outside Spain, it explains nothing, neither the realism of the eighteenth-century novel in Europe nor the symbolism of the novel in Europe and in the United States in the nineteenth and twentieth centuries. Either the *pícaro* reappears in literature outside Spain or he doesn't, and the fact of the matter is that he does reappear, becoming in our own time the very image of the loveless, invisible, disinte-grated soul. Once the *pícaro* is integrated into society, the lone-ly "I" becoming a "we," he has ceased to be a picaresque hero. Where then—in the sense of a masked self within narratives—does the picaresque myth go? He goes underground, that is, the *pícaro* who is at the heart of the myth, and he surfaces in nov-els as the ever-latent threat of meaninglessness and nonidentity. Submerged by the Cartesian Catastrophe, this child of the unconscious mind, like other mythical characters of the late Middle Ages, such as Don Juan and Faust, is transformed into a demon. And it is as a demon that we recognize him in Fielding's *Jonathan Wild*, in Smollett's *Ferdinand Count Fathom*, in Gogol's *Dead Souls*, in Melville's *Confidence-Man*, and in Twain's *Huckleberry Finn*. Although the generalization is sweeping, I submit that elements of the original *pícaro* are quite ubiquitous in twentieth-century literature, not only in novels where he lurks evidently, as in Thomas Mann's *Felix Krull* and Ralph Ellison's *Invisible Man*, but also, disguised, in Franz Kafka's *The Trial*, James Joyce's *Portrait of the Artist as a Young Man* (recall that Stephen Daedalus's is a death-in-life until he experiences the vision of the girl at the seashore), and even in that emaciated picaresque novel masquerading as a symbolist poem, T.S. Eliot's "Waste-Land" (recall that the invisible hero remains in despair, just as Guzmán de Alfarache does). Neither sociology nor genre criticism can explain these connections, but the concept of picaresque myth both explains them and sheds light on the human condition.

The birth of the modern novel, I submit, occurred when the soul of Western man, increasingly aware of death, in itself and in the heart of dominant culture, had been struggling to find its way back to humanity out of the labyrinth of loneliness. The moral passion, the honesty of the authentic picaresque novels, strips from man his social masks until he is "nothing man" or "invisible man" confronting, with ancestral craftiness, the millennia of his solitude. Essentially a con artist, potentially a poetmaker of new social identities and new cultures, the *pícaro* presents a masquerade of episodic adventures that are inevitably "to be continued" as long as experience remains open and mankind sane and human, this side of Orwellian 1984. The informing idea of the myth of the *pícaro* is that it has the power to identify and to reverse modern man's alienation from himself, from humanity, and from the universe. His negatives are necessary to express the light. The autobiographical

"I" dissolving into the communal "we" creates the literature of unity and love. What I have in mind is a bipolarity, a tension between the literature of loneliness and the literature of love out of which the modern novel (and much else besides) has come into being. From *Lazarillo de Tormes* to Joyce's *Ulysses* and William Faulkner's *Absalom, Absalom!* the light of love has been defined by and won from the darkness of not-love. A transfiguring death-to-oneself proceeding from the natural self has been linked to the dialectic of sin and grace, for he who has not love is nothing, in spiritual truth.

He is *Pícaro*.

To the Spanish picaresque novelists, creation of self outside orthodox theological patterns is folly, the way of spiritual death. And though contemporary man, by contrast, sees his salvation in the creative spirit of self-creation, there remains the possibility of frustration and failure, of escape from freedom, and of conditioning into spiritual death. Here, at the psychic root, is a continuity of picaresque myth, for what it comes down to is not just the way of life of vagabonds and juvenile delinquents but any way of life that seems to lead away and down from meaning and full humanity. Such a contingency surely shapes a great deal of twentieth-century fiction and philosophy: modern man struggles to find identity in a less than meaningful world.

The modern artist is akin to the *pícaro*. Not only does the artist recognize that he is both isolated and imprisoned within society, he also understands and accepts the conditions of survival. And he accepts them because in his search for forms, he discerns that everything is created, everything made—selfhood is made, society is made, love is made—and that the good, the true, and the beautiful are forever destroyed, forever reborn. This positive ongoing creation, this view of time as eternal revolution, is latently prefigured in the myth of the *pícaro*, a story of the casting out of the free individual, of his essential aloneness, and of the disintegration of received values and reality. In its original, Spanish form, the myth was profoundly pessimistic because man's nature as free could not be celebrated by the closed systems of prevailing belief. In later, modified form, the myth lingered in a kind of individualism that persists in a "naturally" loveless state outside society. In more recent times, outsidedness has become descriptive of the human condition, the artist has been elevated to the role of representative man, and the myth of the *pícaro* is a universal story, the *pícaro* now neither outcast nor sinner, but the trickster of eternity and master forger, through imagination, of reality. At the same time, the *pícaro* has power to transform outsidedness into insidedness. Insidedness is his freedom, the disaster and the glory of being alive. He is free to choose love and to transcend the destructive element of self through faith in perpetual creation. When every day is a new creation, the old narrative of personal center is preferred to historical chronicle. Something of the intimacy with which *Lazarillo de Tormes* may have been felt is restored. The tragedy of lonely bondage to freedom is returned to consciousness in forms akin to the first modern novel of four hundred years ago. When the artist's quest for a personal mythology fails, identity fails, and it is as if the individual of our times were being deformed and dehumanized by a worldwide confidence game. Then the myth of the *pícaro* dominates and expresses us all. But when the quest succeeds—not an ironic Lazarillo-like social success but a spiritual penetration to essences—the myth of the *pícaro* has lost its four-hundred-year-old hold on human imagination, and a new and hopeful myth, as yet unnamed but powerfully felt, is becoming the shaping force of civilization.

Perhaps the picaresque myth's sustained inquiry into civilization and its discontents has gone all the way to chaos and back. If so, the original story of a dehumanized juvenile delinquent is indeed that dark night of the soul, that path leading us, as myth always does, to the center of being.

THE PÍCARO IN AMERICAN LITERATURE

A *pícaro* is the protagonist of a picaresque novel, a tragicomic narrative form first fully achieved as art in a triad of Spanish works, the anonymous *Lazarillo de Tormes* (1554), Mateo Alemán's *Guzmán de Alfarache* (1599), and Francisco de Quevedo's *La vida del Buscón* (*The Swindler*, 1626). In these novels the *pícaro* is a lonely individual isolated within society, a society which also acts morally and psychologically within him. Loneliness becomes an evolving state, the outgrowth of the *pícaro*'s sense of failed identity, of the instability of an inferior social standing, and of the failure to find human solidarity. (One of the sure clues to the absence of a true *pícaro* in a novel is the representation of a fellowship, e.g., in Cervantes's *Don Quijote* [1605, 1615], Le Sage's *Gil Blas* [1715-1735], and Fielding's *Tom Jones* [1749]). Furthermore, the extent of the *pícaro*'s loneliness may be seen in the compulsive restlessness with which he goes forth in search of life. Increasingly those whom he encounters on the road tend to reflect his own lack of significant reality. His jerky, episodic journey is thus precisely the form this experience takes. The more he seeks, the more disintegrated he becomes. Finally, in order to bring himself into precarious relation to society, the *pícaro* undertakes to create a deceptive identity out of social roles and appearances. Creating a self that his will supports but that he knows for an illusion, the *pícaro* evolves into a symbolic literary being, a confidence man, outwardly one who shares faith in existence, inwardly one reduced to spiritual nothingness.

The hero of a genuine picaresque novel is thus always to a degree archetypal and has potential to be spontaneously reborn in literature outside Spain. Beginning as a kind of novel depicting the adventures of a trickster or delinquent in a chaotic, decadent world, the picaresque has developed, over four centuries, in new modes until, in recent times, the ethos of western civilization can plausibly be described as "picarism." Here the *pícaro* is in the largest sense modern man without a living faith, and the trickster hero of folklore is re-created as the lonely individual cut off from though yearning for community and love.

This recent development is especially evident in American literature from the 1830s to the present. Picaresque and part-picaresque novels have appeared in the United States, usually their *pícaros* symbolically represented as confidence men. And picarism—the way of life historically depicted in the fictional genre—has found ubiquitous expressions (including nonliterary ones) as a cultural outlook of the American people.[1]

The American *pícaro*, viewed against the nineteenth-century literary background, is an expression of disillusionment with Adamic myth. For many writers of the period, appearances became impenetrable masks, the world a stage, and the existence of truth so dubious as to eliminate any difference between it and fiction. There followed a quest for higher or transcendental truth, but, with disillusionment, an artist might see all cultural enterprise as a great confidence trick. Hence the old idea of the *pícaro* reestablished itself in some writers' minds as an image or symbol of disintegration, as a state of being in some way non-human. The symbolic confidence man's character is accordingly unreal or at least opaque and impenetrable because reality has become endlessly contingent; and if ill-will enters into his con game, he is also grotesque. Indeed, as a creature of nihilism, the symbolic confidence man seems to be at times actively engaged in the destruction of whatever reality, goodness, and trust remain in the living world. If, by contrast, the Spanish *pícaro* is the victim of an atomizing process, the American *pícaro*, like as not, may be incarnate atomizer, destructiveness, devil, mankind corrupted, or civilization. In a sense, too, the American *pícaro* is simply "the" American. In various literary contexts one finds the figure of a lonely, rootless innocent, an Adam emancipated from history, from the Europe of the mind, and existing morally prior to the world, yet moving into the world that promises and provides experience. If at first the encounters between this radically self-reliant outsider and the alien world had seemed heroic, in time, two Americans stride forth in Adam's guise, the one creative and Promethean, the other destructive and satanic, both wearing the masks of idealism. The archetypal Adam, protesting innocence and benevolence, might not be a radical new person emancipated from history but might, instead, be history personified—a dead soul, an invisible man with a self consisting of social roles taken on "faith." But the American *pícaro* is not the feudal outcast of Spanish picaresque novels. He is a representative figure who playfully brings to focus the whole paradoxical question of individualism in the American past.[2]

The literary symbol of the American was Adam; the popular symbol was the Yankee, that sharp-witted Brother Jonathan who tricked Old John Bull. The bumptious certitude often scornfully attributed to Americans by foreigners was picked up by the fledgling culture as a nose-thumbing badge of identification. As the Yankee appeared on stage and in the literature and subliterature of the century—and he appears in cartoons to the present day as Uncle Sam—he increasingly reflected the deprecation of everything sophisticated and the exaltation of a shrewd, peasant common sense that was thought to be a native gift. He was a symbol, then, of triumph, of adaptability, of irrepressible life—of many qualities needed to induce confidence and self-possession among a new and unamalgamated people. But he was also paradoxically both innocent and cunning. The primary manifestation of the Yankee was the peddler, whose lonely, wandering lifestyle, true to the promptings of democratic patriotism, romanticism, and free enterprise, was the icon of self-confidence above all. This relatively harmless Yankee peddler emerges into literature as Sam Slick of Slickville, Connecticut, in Thomas Chandler Haliburton's satirical *Clockmaker* series of 1836. Haliburton, a conservative Nova Scotian judge who wished to warn his countrymen about their

base democratic neighbors, portrays in Slick, the clock peddler,
a shrewd, garrulous parasite with an inherent love of barter.
Like all marginal figures, however, the Yankee peddler could
also represent the dangerous side of cultural values and be
viewed as a trickster exploiting confidence.[3] The stage was set
for the appearance of a native American *pícaro* when the
Yankee Peddler, real and fictitious, traveled South, and in the
frontier region between the southern Appalachians and the
Mississippi River, then called the Southwest, underwent a literary transformation as the poor-white squatter.

Suddenly in the 1830s conservative lawyers, doctors, and
journalists in the southwestern region began to write local-
color sketches for the widely distributed New York sporting
paper, the *Spirit of the Times*.[4] These relatively cultured writers,
aware of the older tradition of the East and seaboard South,
were roused to fear and to laughter by the rampaging frontier
environment. On the one side were the gentlemen (themselves) and on the other were the rogues (Jacksonian rabble
variously depicted as loafers, pickpockets, cardsharps, actors,
impostors, and confidence tricksters). One southwestern
writer, Johnson J. Hooper, was to create an American rogue
with a dimension as symbolic *pícaro*. In *Some Adventures of
Captain Simon Suggs* (1845),[5] Hooper all but removes himself
from the narrative as a mediating influence between the confidence man and the reader. The author-gentleman having
retired behind a curtain of irony, the world represented
through the warped mind of Simon Suggs, forerunner of
William Faulkner's Flem Snopes, is dark and degraded, and
moral standards are dissolved in Simon's favorite motto, "It's
good to be shifty in a new country." Indeed, *Simon Suggs*
unfolds as the story of civilization running amuck. Son of an
itinerant frontier preacher, Simon takes early to cards, tempts
his father to "cut Jack," secures the family horse—that closely
resembles Don Quixote's Rocinante—and hits the trail. When
Simon next appears, he is married, the father of a large
pinewoods family, and known all over Tallapoosa County as an

unscrupulous speculator in Indian lands. Specializing in confidence tricks, Simon in successive episodes outwits greedy strangers by posing as a rich planter, a senator, and a wealthy Kentucky hog-drover. In later episodes, Johnson broadens the social landscape to include the whole morally degraded frontier society. With his fellow citizens Simon joins in a cruel swindle of the Creek Indians. Then, as rumor spreads that the Creeks plan revenge, Simon, privately informed of the rumor's falsity, fans the fears of the ignorant villagers into a drunken blaze, has himself named captain, declares martial law, and turns the hysteria to his own profit by fining those who stumble across the sentry lines. The hysterical—and significantly Jacksonian—mob is even more grotesquely revealed when Simon attends a revivalist meeting. Singled out by an ecstatic congregation as a well-known sinner, he pretends to undergo miraculous redemption, then passes a collection plate among the tear-stricken crowd and disappears into the swamps. It is not Simon's last, but it is his most memorable trick, and forty years later Mark Twain imitated this camp-meeting scene for similar reasons in *Huckleberry Finn* (1884).

The *Adventures of Captain Simon Suggs* combines several elements of the picaresque idea. It is concerned with the disintegration of reality, goodness, and trust. It represents evil on two planes, individual and social, because the confidence man fulfills the degraded desires of society, in this function appearing ironically as the people's true representative. Through the typical picaresque technique of unreliable first-person narration, Hooper is able to show a violent splitting apart of society from culture and of materialism and opportunism from the control of an older order of American democratic ideals. Although its episodes, originally sketches in the *Spirit of the Times*, are insufficiently integrated as novelistic art, *Simon Suggs* is the first lengthy picaresque fiction in American literature, its protagonist the prototype of later American *pícaros*.

By the 1850s, the American rogue was well entrenched in the popular consciousness, and a favorite stage for acting out his role had become the deck of a Mississippi steamboat. This was his stage in Herman Melville's *The Confidence-Man: His Masquerade* (1857), a complexly orchestrated fictional masterpiece that explores and exposes the picarism of modern life. The action of *The Confidence-Man* takes place from sunrise to midnight (and possibly beyond) on April Fool's Day aboard the steamer *Fidèle* (*Faith*). The titular hero is a composite of all the various passengers, and their presentations of masked selves, in terms of costume, gesture, and role, constitute the bulk of a narrative with little progression save that between the appearance at sunrise of a Christ-like deaf-mute and his exposure at midnight as a savage young peddler in collusion with a diabolic cosmopolitan who apocalyptically extinguishes a "solar lamp" in the gentlemen's cabin.

The ingenuity of *The Confidence-Man* is that Melville discovers a way to reexpress his familiar tragic themes in a picaresque schema. Whereas the protagonists of *Moby Dick* (1851) and *Pierre* (1852) destroy themselves in efforts to make moral absolutes fit the practical conditions of everyday life, Melville himself in those novels speculates that life is a hoax, a comedy of thought, or a vast practical joke founded on man's confidence in gods that fail. In *The Confidence-Man* the supernatural jokers are no more than petty con men—as it were, Yankee peddlers made as one cosmic *pícaro*—engaged in the symbolic action of picaresque myth in which the world heads blindly toward annihilation, all human beings unable to abandon eschatological hopes or the illusion that gods are made in man's image. Believing God and human nature to be past finding out, Melville exposes as fraudulent pretense all dogma, philosophy, and myth that present them in clear light. The man who is tricked by rational explanations of the universe is soon apt to believe that God is Satan. Melville's *pícaro* has cosmic pretensions to credit he does not possess, and in the form of all the characters in the novel he appears as an impostor and usurper of identity. The Ship of Faith has been man-created out of an inherent need for confidence in life. Yet this very human aspiration of faith represents its greatest danger. What is created by man may be destroyed by man; a swindling faith may lead to the disintegration of reality, goodness, and trust; and such a disintegrating world is the *pícaro's*, conceived in the image of the confidence man, loveless and unreal as a dream.

The Confidence-Man is a picaresque novel in a non-autobiographical symbolic form. Some of its characteristics relate it to central picaresque tradition. *The Confidence-Man*, like *Lazarillo de Tormes*, parodies heroic and epic literature, specifically the Bible from Genesis to apocalypse; presents life as a series of encounters between the *pícaro* and society; presents *pícaro* and society, as well as good and evil, as mutually reflective aspects of the same reality; shows reality functioning as an illusion; is structured to reveal disintegration into chaos and spiritual death; makes the world's lack of love desperately apparent; and has a *pícaro* for protagonist. Like the Spanish *pícaro*, Melville's confidence man is both a failed identity and a half-outsider. Behind his masks he is neither a true god nor an adequate human. Through the world's lack of Pauline charity, he has become deformed in a shifting, dehumanized nonself. He is another dead soul, another invisible man. Nevertheless, he has a kind of character as a stranger who seeks by means of imposture to enter in to the human community. In terms of his function vis-à-vis his victims, he yearns to be accepted by and necessary to them. An outsider with respect to humanity's need for confidence, he is doomed to the outside because, like the mature Lázaro of *Lazarillo de Tormes*, he conceals a heart of stone.

Mark Twain's *Adventures of Huckleberry Finn* is both a conventionally bad boy or trickster story and a continuation, at the core, of picaresque myth. The thrust of the narrative is non-picaresque in the sense that Twain apparently believes in a life of freedom, love, and moral choice. However, Twain is aggressively anti-historical, viewing culture as implacably determined by the corrupt past. In *Huckleberry Finn*, as in *Lazarillo de Tormes*, readers are deceived into approval of the protagonist and of his apparent, but empty, social success and moral regeneration. On the surface, it is a novel in which an apparent *pícaro* discovers right uses for his trickery and comes to oppose the symbolic confidence men, the King and Duke, with whom he becomes involved. But Huck's deceptive triumph over what Twain describes as "a deformed conscience" is negated by Tom Sawyer's evasion, in those chapters in which Huck loses humanity and approximates the deformed identity of the confidence men. Therefore, because there is disparity between Twain's intention (a bad boy grows morally) and execution (the soul of the boy is deformed), it can be argued that *Huckleberry Finn* is truly picaresque, its hero a *pícaro*, not just another light-hearted roguish vagabond reminiscent of Gil Blas in Lesage's eighteenth-century novel of manners.

Beneath the surface of Twain's novel there is evident an interest in the *pícaro* as a lonely child confronted and trained by an unsympathetic, enslaving society. Huck has some of the *pícaro*'s sensitivity about inferior social status. He is alienated from home and tends to become involved with persons existing precariously on social frontiers. For a while, he fosters charitable actions, finding in Jim, the runaway slave, a true father. But when the King and Duke take over their raft, Huck reacts passively. The con men symbolize a deformed part of Huck that is in conflict with his natural goodness, and hence Huck is reluctant to save himself. By the time of the Wilks fraud, Huck has sickened of the imposters' fake sentimentality and decided to rescue Jim from their scheming. But it is a barren commitment. Precisely at this moment of what seems positive virtue, Huck surrenders to *conscience*, always for Twain the over- layer of prejudice and false valuation imposed upon all members of society in the name of religion, morality, law, and culture. Having resumed status in Tom Sawyer's complacent world of games-playing and moral sentiment, Huck soon joins forces with Tom to torment Jim as if the slave's humanity had never existed for him. No longer an outcast, Huck has entered into debased civilization as surely as Lázaro de Tormes finds social success—at the price of the soul. By the end of *Huckleberry Finn*, Huck's future course is a Guzmán-like extension of an ascetic's despair. He is going to "light out for the territory" so that Aunt Sally can't "sivilize" him. That is, he seeks more bad boy adventures that, far from representing his freedom from bondage to civilization, must, according to Twain's logic, confirm his petrifaction at the heart of convention.

Because a *pícaro* takes his formal character from a hollow imitation of the corrupt society in which he struggles for existence, the *pícaro* may symbolize that society. Just so, the King and Duke symbolize society, conscience, civilization, and history. To reject such symbols is extreme, requiring absolute self-reliance, even escape from time—an impossibility according to Twain's own deterministic view of history whereby man's life is at best a long delaying action against corruption.[6] So Huck cannot escape the confidence men; he reflects them. His failed humanity can never be redeemed by freedom or by love. In *Huckleberry Finn*, as in the classic Spanish novels, there is no catharsis of roguery.

Ralph Ellison's *Invisible Man* (1952) seems often to conform closely to novels in the picaresque tradition. Mock-autobiographical in form, it is the episodic story of an innocent social outcast who for most of his life has masqueraded in identities given him by others and whose own will to illusion has maintained these masks at the cost of achieved identity, reality, and humanity. The nameless narrator of the title is acutely conscious, at last, of the transparency of any selfhood superimposed by society, yet, because he is literally living underground in a state of total isolation from others, he seems to resemble the loveless *pícaro* reduced to a mechanical personification of the negative, rather than a person preparing to surface to a new life of responsibility. Distinctions between right and wrong are exposed as ambiguous, another picaresque motif. Even at the end, Invisible Man still embraces trickery, enjoying the joke of making society bear the expense of its failure to penetrate his confidence man's disguise.

But if Invisible Man enjoys his joke, he knows, unlike the *pícaro*, that his life is far from hollow. In fact, after all his violent experiences as a victim of racial stereotyping, he has achieved, not lost, his form and brought his soul boldly into the light. As he declares in the prologue, "Without light I am not only invisible, but formless as well; and to be unaware of one's form is to live a death. I myself, after existing some twenty years, did not become alive until I discovered my invisibility." Thus the actual form of Ellison's novel is an antipicaresque journey toward personal freedom and the eventual recovery of a soul left uncontaminated by society. Like Huckleberry Finn, with whom Invisible Man identifies himself, the archetypal American struggles against patterns of conformity. These are inimical to democracy and personal passion. Identity is won when the individual self is freed from the definitions of others. Thereafter, real life begins as a personal destiny "of infinite possibilities," as Ellison has his hero observe in the epilogue. Invisible Man's refusal to accept limits means he is no longer either an outcast or a tragic victim. His self-creation is salvation from disintegration. His role-playing, like the *pícaro*'s, enables him to survive by manipulating the illusions of society, but he, himself, has an uncompromising sense of who he is and where he has been. As soon as a *pícaro* is free to create his own reality, reconstituting out of experience a common and responsible humanity, he is no longer truly a *pícaro*; he is, rather, a rogue-survivor, one of the many permutations of the contemporary American confidence man.

The hero of Saul Bellow's novel *The Adventures of Augie March* (1953) is also a rogue-survivor. Like Invisible Man and like Yossarian in Joseph Heller's *Catch-22* (1961), Augie is playfully self-aware of the need for psychic survival in a world of heavy, overly serious people who cannot recognize the games they play. Like Huck Finn, he usually appears in a passive relation to others. They command him, punish him, dupe him, create roles for him. Constantly subject to outside influences, Augie tells more about them than about himself. Instead of trying to flee or to change the world around him, he accepts it as it is, risking little and disengaging easily, even from love. Nothing is a destiny good enough, nothing deserves his full enthusiasm or commitment. His is a healthy pliancy, a force of opposition. Shape-shifting, adaptation, and impersonation are thus the styles with which Augie confronts the world, and the more or less aimless sequence of his adventures bears close resemblance to traditional picaresque narrative. But Augie is not fully a *pícaro*. He remains stubbornly himself, with exhilarating readiness to engage in the world, piece by piece. His adaptability, unlike the true *pícaro*'s, is a mode of being and essence of identity and discovery.

Nevertheless, Augie March, somewhat like Lázaro de Tormes, is to a degree an unreliable narrator and betrays a *pícaro*'s lack of belief in the reality of the human condition. "A man's character is his fate," he asserts at the outset of his story, conjuring up an image of a vast world of possibilities for making something of himself in life. But by the time he actually has come to writing his memoirs, he is still only a traveling man, tied to a less than fully devoted wife, and engaged in less than honest work on the Continent as the agent of the shady lawyer Mintouchian. The revelation of Augie's final position comes after a life of vicissitudes partly determined, in typically picaresque psychology, by low origins and early negative influences. As he is walking across a frozen Belgian field with the maid Jacqueline, his efforts to sing for warmth fail miserably. He can only retreat from her reality into a world of cold negation, not the world of bright prospects and genuine human feeling previously recounted. There is, in sum, a diminution, if not quite a disintegration, of Augie's sense of reality, goodness, and trust. A fatalistic despair links this American part-*pícaro* to Spanish precursors.

Elements of the picaresque idea can be found throughout American literature. Life presented as essentially a game is evinced in works from Benjamin Franklin's *Autobiography* (1868), Thoreau's *Walden* (essays, 1854), and Poe's tales of hoaxes and diddles to Jack Kerouac's novel *On the Road* (1957), John Barth's *The Sot-Weed Factor* (1960), and Ken Kesey's *One Flew Over the Cuckoo's Nest* (1962)—and in many other works past and present. If an artist adopts the quasi-picaresque strategy of acting, as a sort of confidence trickster, human life may be exposed as a set of tricks and defective rituals. For example, in Nathanael West's novel *Miss Lonelyhearts* (1933) a tormented, cheated mob forces a man to attempt to fashion an authentic self that will make his role effective in giving the mob authenticity in turn. Robert Coover, in *The Public Burning* (1977), also recalls the old picaresque pattern of relationship between a trickster and his world of trickery. In that novel the original Yankee trickster is recreated as a supernatural character called "Uncle Sam," advisor and instigator of another character named "Vice-President Richard Nixon." Obviously, with the growing relativism about moral codes in contemporary life and the widespread loss of deference to official public beliefs, authors are less tempted than in the past to disguise the fictional and actual shiftiness of the confidence man. The spread of official collective con games leads to a new imperative to be shifty in a new country. Where reality and appearances are inverted for the sake of self-performance, the people's primary duty can be seen as reinforcement of their mutual illusions. The outlook is playful rather than cynical, but it is clear that the *pícaro* remains a latently potent archetype in the national life.

III. West

HIGHER ELEVATIONS

Back in the old days, the 1940s, when imaginative literature was welcomed by publishing houses and when editors and writers could still regard the printed word as almost holy, Robert Frost cheerfully told a group of student writers at Duke, "Your teacher is paid to love you, and your editor is paid to hate you." In other words, the teacher of writers would encourage talent, and the editor would put it to the test. Hate it properly, so to say. The teaching and editing of literary composition represented two necessary sides of the same cultural coin minted from language and tradition. New writers surfacing from discoveries in the buried self had to find understanding somewhere, especially in America, a puritanical country where art is a concupiscence with the devil seldom forgiven except by a blessed issue of dollars; new writers needed nurturing and fortifying of the spirit against the day of editorial hating, the chastening of style, the ordeal of learning how hard it is to write, but also that good writing earns a place and, once in a while, an audience, even a living.

Well, those were the days. Whereas teachers of writers are everywhere now, a hard editor is good to find. Now, like as not, your editor is not paid to hate you but to ignore you; that is, if you write fiction or poetry and have some dreamy notion of a national literature which endures, not easily disposed of, not Kleenex. Perhaps what such writers now must fear most is not a failure of nerve and talent before the criteria of lucidity, force, and exactitude, but exclusion from access to readers. And that is a condition of intolerable silence, silence of the voices of truth and beauty, silence that is insidiously enervating to a nation's soul—its literature. Faced with the prospect of such silence, then, many thousands of gifted writers, not only the new but also the experienced, have turned for the love and hate, the encouragement and chastening, the renewal of pride in their work, to what used to be called the "little" magazines, the literary magazines that rarely pay, rarely have a circulation

over 1,000, but can play a caretaker role with respect to literature.

In 1974, I became editor of *Writers' Forum* in order to
become one of the caretakers. I confess to evangelical zeal in
the proceedings, perhaps by inheritance of folly. My grandparents tried to convert the Persians (of all people!) to a weird form
of Christianity, and my father's cousin wrote 2,000 hymns such
as "Throw Out the Lifeline, Someone is Drifting Away."
Righteousness, however, is of no use to teachers, who are paid
to love, or to editors, who, even if unpaid, must hate you properly. The missionary drive is there without, I hope, the objections. Still, where money is concerned, few literary editors
whom I know ever seem to have much for their magazines. It
must be faith that fuels us. Every so often I recall Grandpa
Blackburn's assertion, "The Lord will provide," and think, He
better. And lo! we go to press with another thick volume of
Writers' Forum, and miracles happen. For instance, a few years
ago, when I didn't have $1,900 to pay a typesetter, he complet-
ed his job, suffered a nervous breakdown, left town, and oblig-
ingly never submitted a bill. Similarly, when I noted the dis-
crepancy between the $2,000 in my account and the $7,000
required to produce our tenth volume, a local literate, clearly
prescient tentacle of a huge international publishing house
offered to compose and print the book for $3,000, as a charita-
ble contribution; and a remarkable increase in book sales more
than made up the difference. Like Wilkins Micawber, I became
doggedly optimistic.

From the beginning, I conceived of the magazine as a congregation of and forum for writers, editors, teachers of writers,
and critics. Once in the early 1950s, myself an inchoate and
floundering writer, I had joined an audience of hundreds at the
University of North Carolina at Greensboro to hear William
Blackburn and Robert Penn Warren deliver public critique of
student stories printed for the occasion in a campus magazine.
The idea was simple: a love feast where everyone present had
read the stories and could participate in what my father, with

characteristically heavy sigh, liked to describe as "a civilized dialogue that has been going on since Aristotle." The results of that forum were superb. Quite a few new writers were encouraged, the most famous being Mac Hyman, who a few years later would write *No Time for Sergeants*. Thus *Writers' Forum* came about, though the Rocky Mountains did not seem the right place for Aristotle's *Poetics*. (Later, I knew I was dead wrong about this. When Pike's Peak looms over your psyche, catharsis of excessive humility and fear just comes with the territory). I would send out a call for stories and poems throughout the Rockies, publish the best of them, distribute the magazine to writers and others, and, on a day in March 1974, assemble them to hear a discussion led by John Williams, John Edgar Wideman, and James Yaffe, who would then award cash prizes. So it came to pass, with 150 excited people coming to Colorado Springs from as far away as Albuquerque, New Mexico, and Laramie, Wyoming. The First Prizes went to Yusef Komunyakaa for poetry and to Russell Martin for fiction, both writers who have gone on to establish for themselves national reputations.

The conference was held annually for four consecutive years. Each time, a volume of *Writers' Forum* was readied in advance. Among distinguished writers to speak at a conference were Richard Hugo, John Nichols, Max Steele, Rudolfo A. Anaya, and one Pulitzer Prize-winning poet whose name I won't mention because he was drunk and contemptuous of aspiring writers. After his departure for the province of Manhattan, the conference was abandoned, but the magazine was retained, its pages opened to writers everywhere, unrestricted by region and now figuratively bringing writers together, new writers with contemporary masters, among them Fred Chappell, Reynolds Price, Paul Engle, William Stafford, and Frank Waters. We continued to make "discoveries," sometimes "firsts," including work by minority persons whose problems with the Great Silence can be greater than those of graduates from creative writing programs. *Writers' Forum* was first to publish stories by Craig Lesley and Bret Lott, both of whom later served the magazine as editorial advisors in fiction and as talent-spotters, so to say, on the west and east coasts. All in all, over twenty years, out of tens of thousands of manuscript submissions, we have selected and published more than 150 fiction writers and 300 poets.

Having learned not to restrict the magazine's pages to those writers available to attend a conference, I nevertheless continued to emphasize the role of *Writers' Forum* as publisher of new American literature about or from the West. There are good reasons for this emphasis. One, serious western writing (opposite of the "Western" of international fantasy) has not always fared well in the East, and, two, the West may well be the most vital literary region in the United States today. Rich in writing but poor in publishing, the West cannot long remain misrepresented or unknown. A region as vast as Western Europe, the West is the ancient heartland of the continent, has a deep and tragic history, and in spite of suffering many of the ills that afflict the nation elsewhere, offers through its towering mountains and harsh deserts a spiritual wonder that ignites passions and lifts the heart. The stories of this magnificent land are being told— some have been told for thousands of years—and *Writers' Forum* was specifically dedicated to listening to and publishing them.

When I joined the English faculty of the University of Colorado at Colorado Springs in 1973, it was a small campus accommodating 1,200 students of all ages in a few scattered buildings, the most imposing of which had once been one of the world's greatest tuberculosis sanatoria. One of the Pulitzers had rested in this building, an event that was the closest I had come to a literary tradition when, during spring break of 1974, *Writers' Forum One* went to press, if that's the word. Most of my budget of $300 had been expended on the typing, on stencils, of 192 8-by-11 inch pages and on reams of mimeograph paper sufficient to produce 300 copies; the remainder of the money would go to a bindery. The university—which, by the way, now has 7,000 students and capacious new buildings—had no Xerox copying and collating machines, nor could it provide secretarial or "work-study" assistance. One simply ran projects on empty. There I was, going to press in the basement of a building haunted by the ghosts of departed lungers, on a deserted campus, and with three days to go to meet the bindery's deadline. I did the mimeographing myself, for thirty consecutive hours cranking up and feeding a ga-thunking A.B. Dick machine until pages grew into stacks, stacks into columns reaching to the ceiling like the legendary manuscripts of Thomas Wolfe. Late Saturday night the job was done, or so I foolishly believed, and I went home with my clothes soaked in ink and my head ringing in a sort of rapture. Collating the pages next day by hand *did* seem a bit formidable. I called one of my students, Dan "Duck" Pond, a retired Marine colonel who had hit the beaches in three wars. He volunteered to help me next morning. I poured myself a double Jack Daniels, saluted Parnassus and the gods of little magazines, and fell into fitful sleep with visions of millions of sheets of paper blowing in the wind like bleached autumnal leaves.

Sunday morning was gray with the threat of snow. Duck showed up at ten. Together we lugged 57,600 sheets of paper from the basement to a large room that had once been the sanatorium's morgue. On tables that might once have been slabs for stiffs, we assembled 192 stacks, each 300 sheets thick. Then Duck made the first-ever *Forum* book, bending over 192 times in a sort of automatized agony. I made the second book. When we were done, twenty minutes had passed, and a metaphorical lightbulb had become incandescent above my wrinkled millimetric brow.

"Duck," I said in a half audible croak, "it's impossible."

Duck laughed. He probably laughed at Iwo Jima and Porkchop Hill. "Yup," he nodded after a pause.

"What are we going to do?"

"Call more grunts," Duck said.

We did that. After dialing a dozen numbers without result, I got through to Michelle's Restaurant ("World Famous Ice Cream Creations as Featured in *Life* Magazine") where the girlfriend of another one of my students worked as a waitress on Sunday. Sure, she'd come after work. And call Mark. And Mark would call his friends and they would call theirs and.... No problem.

An hour later, several platoons of volunteer book collators might have been observed in the morgue going happily round and round, bobbing and straightening. Big pregnant hippies down from the communes. Mountain men with shovel beards. Poets, cowboys, high school dropouts who began every utterance with "man," waitresses still in uniforms splotched with hot fudge sundae, Snow White and the Seven Dwarfs. Someone brought coffee and sandwiches. Someone else brought six-packs of Coors. At the stroke of midnight the last copy of *Writers' Forum One* had been assembled and stowed in the trunk of my '64 Dodge. Those wonderful princes and princesses departed on their motorcycles and pumpkins as a quiet snow drifted across them, like a benediction.

Humanity today, having no unifying worldview, is experiencing universal, destructive unrest. Certainly such unrest seems to be a feature of the contemporary American short story, which is apt to manifest neither faith nor a stable sense of moral order. A possible result of this situation is that form is given precedence over content. Like as not, the story writer today—to judge only from the thousands of manuscripts that have come to the attention of only one editor—relies upon technique rather than vision, upon "voice" (usually a first-person self lamenting an unlived life) rather than substance. We have a technical knowledge, a horizontal and "sociological" deployment of fictional strategies as opposed to a vertical and mythological one. Yet it is obvious that we live in a revolutionary age in which awareness is opening on all fronts, psychological, moral, ethnic, ecological. If, so far, few writers seem to recognize the interrelatedness of a living universe or reveal themselves at home in a world culture, there are still many writers who are honest, for whom the world of nature is not designified and for whom the world of humanity renews the traditional American sense of wonder. Here in the shadow of Pike's Peak

where a "little" literary magazine was born, the higher elevations of the human spirit suggest themselves as a beacon for
endeavor and perhaps, who knows, as a prophecy of new con-
junctions of feeling with form.

THE INTERIOR COUNTRY

"Beautiful my desire, and the place of my desire,"[1] wrote Theodore Roethke in "North American Sequence," a series of poems depicting the soul's journey spatially into the interior of the continent, temporally into the interior of the past to effect redemption through acceptance, and spiritually into self-transcending depths of interior landscape. It is through place that one exceeds place. One comes to stand outside self with a heightened awareness obtained by relationship with the external world and to the mystery of life, itself. The what and the how of Roethke's poetry of place, then, may serve to introduce the serious literature of the various "wests" of the modern American West—truly the heartland, truly the interior country. For the literature of this region is a genuine literature of place, of a real place or series of places inhabited by real people, neither a mythical "country of the mind" (as Archibald MacLeish dismissed it) nor a cultural province existing for the sake of national fantasies or of historical exploitation. The interior country is in fact a place of beautiful desire, a symbolic landscape with a power to revitalize the continental soul.

To approach this interior country, we must first remove the shrubbery of capital-W "Western" literature and film that stands between us and the truth that is beautiful. The shrubbery is not easily cut down. It is stubbornly rooted in morality plays about cowboys and Indians and in stereotyped chivalric romances about hard-riding, fast-shooting heroes who have a kind of messianic ego-identity. Fabulous as the West may have been from the time of the Spanish conquistadors to, roughly, the start of the present century, serious writers want little of this Buffalo Billing. In *Pike's Peak*, an authentic novelistic epic first completed as a trilogy in the 1930s, Frank Waters told the story of New Westerners struggling and failing to attune their psyches to a rightness with the land. In this novel, comparable to Herman Melville's nineteenth-century classic novel *Moby Dick*, the protagonist's materialistic egotism turns to madness as he

seeks the heart of a Great White Mountain.[2] Here, the leg-
endary virtues of western pioneers disintegrate when not balanced with nature's living mystery. Then in *The Ox-Bow
Incident*, Walter Van Tilburg Clark's novel published in 1940, the
stripping down of frontier fakelore continued in earnest as,
behind the façade of retributive justice, the tragic consequences
of wrong-minded self-reliance and mob violence lay exposed.
And so it has been since then, western writers continuing to
feel the need of making a clearing, of turning stereotyped characters and situations on their often nakedly imperialistic heads,
without at the same time discarding the real achievements of
individualism, the lingering authenticity of innocence, and the
possibilities still for realizing the American dream in a land that
likes to live in the shape of tomorrow. Whereas some of this
effort has been and is the result of a "mock-Western," negative
stance, the commitment of anger, like as not, yields a positive
force in the attitude of love and respect for a land long-violated
yet magnificent and capable of touching us at the core of being.
For this reason, the classic capital-W "Western" hero such as
Jack Schaefer's Shane, who is solid and separate and alone in
his sense of individuality, cannot be brought down merely by
social humiliation—society in the West being still in process of
formation, Native American and Hispanic communities aside.
The fabulous Western hero has to be humbled in his whole relationship with the universe, that his egoistic will-to-power may
be brought into balance with nature and humanity, not assert-
ed too far, not seeking to possess the land or to extract from the
world of nature more than nature will allow.

The antiromantic and realistic approach to the interior
country has led some western writers of fiction to a conception
of personality different from the one found in traditional
European and Eastern American literature with its centuries-
old emphasis upon the subtle nuances of manners and morals.
To be sure, that traditional perspective, often expressed in satirical vein, has not gone dry. Today's Californian and Sun Belt
culture called forth the steady gaze of such powerful moralists

as Wallace Stegner in the Pulitzer Prize-winning novel, *Angle of Repose*, and Edward Abbey in the hilariously fulminating novel, *The Monkey-Wrench Gang*. But the traditional perspective may not serve the western writer out in the metaphorical lunar landscape beyond the Sun Belt. So he or she may not be writing traditionally at all, a view championed by such contemporary scholars as Thomas J. Lyon, for many years editor of *Western American Literature*. The reader who approaches all western fiction from the traditional perspective will argue that western writers, overpowered by landscape, neglect the complexity, depth, and realism of characterization one should expect, and create, instead of subtle fiction, something akin to moral fables. In other words, inferior fiction. And, it is true, western stories often have an ethical and philosophical import that suggests a regional imperative. However, where some of the greatest of western writers are concerned, there is apt to be *more*, not less, subtlety of characterization than one finds in manners-and-morals fiction. To view character as weighed in the balance between the sense of the individual self and the sense of its being a part of nature, of the timeless and indivisible whole, demands skill of the highest order.[3]

Whereas European and Eastern and (usually) Southern American fiction has flourished in hierarchic society and tends to rest its case upon individual action in the social sphere, western fiction sometimes goes beyond the social nuances of interpersonal relationships to the nuances of the interior life, where true subtlety lies. It is as if a western writer has to envision something like the whole range of our lives in society, in history, and in nature and to dramatize the effect, like that of ever-widening ripples on a pool, of the microcosmic individual on the macrocosm at every level from the family to social group to the land and, ultimately, to the cosmos itself. Out West, where the individual consciousness is spatially forced to come to terms with a macrocosmic universe oblivious to its presence, the personality may be formed between polarities of reason and intuition, between conscious and unconscious forces. If the polarization prove constructive, a fictionalized character may become attuned to place and discover at-one-ness with it and with humanity. On the other hand, if the polarization prove destructive, a character may destroy the land, its ancient inhabitants, community, and his own humanity. Western fiction at its best is a call for living within the emerging process of creation. A western writer, far from being artistically limited by place, may move through it and from it in a kind of ritual catharsis to therapeutic vision.[4]

What, then, is the West? It comprises the region beyond the 100th meridian, an arid region fragile both socially and ecologically. The West is principally the Rockies—New Mexico, Colorado, Wyoming, Montana, Arizona, Utah, Nevada, Idaho, and the eastern areas of California, Oregon, and Washington— with subregional borders from West Texas to the Dakota Badlands and from Baja California to Puget Sound. This region represents more than half of the continental United States. It is sparsely populated save for patches of wildly growing cities, especially along the Pacific littoral, and aridity limits future population growth. A region half-owned and not infrequently exploited by the federal government, the West has wilderness areas into which urban civilization has been allowed to expand, but the social and economic structure of major cities is likely to remain tentative and shifting.

Wallace Stegner calls the West "an oasis civilization,"[5] its history since the arrival of New Westerners one of the importation of humid-land habits into a dry land that will not tolerate them, of the indulgence of personal liberty in a country that experience says can only be successfully tamed and lived in by a high degree of cooperation. In short, the West lives precariously close to a reality that warns of the collapse of its eco-systems and of the consequent physical and psychical impoverishment of its inhabitants. The sheer beauty and mystery of the West are vulnerable indeed.

Yet vulnerability elicits the response of cherishing, as if the West is a child requiring constant care and protection. When this child-like land and the children of it are, unremittingly, raped by the forces of materialism—and metaphors of rape, violence, and mutilation are strongly present in stories of the modern West—then it is easy to understand why western writers often reveal their love through outrage. Here, though, is some explanation of a surprising fact: writers need not be native to the West nor long resident in it to care about it, to derive actual substance from it, and to write about it at depth of import. The same literary phenomenon is less true, if true at all, about other regions. Southern literature, for example, reflects a special historical experience of land and people and of a language shared from the Carolinas to Mississippi. Consequently, nonsouthern writers have contributed little to the South's letters. By contrast, Spanish and Native American languages excepted, "western" English has few deeply shared meanings, and its vernacular is in part a fabrication of popular culture, in part an importation from other regions and nations. Freed of linguistic restraint, the newcomer may feel and express solidarity with native writers born with wild rivers, lonely plains, and towering mountains in their blood. This freemasonry among new and native writers may be accounted for, too, by the nature of experience of the interior country: the subtleties not always being traditionally social, they may come readily to the soul's grasp and the heart's concern. A correct compassion, in sum, may be sufficient credentials for a writer to become western and to participate in the West's history.

It may be argued that the West has no history, or rather, as Gerald Haslam puts it, it has been assigned "a permanent, ossified past without a present."[6] Where, indeed, are the connections, and how to recover them? The problem is a serious one for western writers, whatever their racial and cultural backgrounds. Anglos of the dominant culture may yet be nostalgic about the "winning of the West" in the past century, whereas Hispanics and Native Americans feel victimized by this conquest, their traditions enervated. Meanwhile, as eastern assumptions persist that the West is a historical vacuum, nuclear devices will be detonated in the deserts, water and mineral resources will be exploited regardless of human needs, and wilderness will suffer urban encroachment. Because these events have already happened, a restored and properly focused history is a concern for all writers in the modern West. From such restorations as are currently available, a picture emerges not only of relentless plunder but also of the past and continuing genocide against the Indians.[7] In other words, there is a *burden* to western history with profoundly tragic implications, a tragic awareness opening up on two fronts: that of the attempt of New Westerners to comprehend the land psychically, failing which comprehension they subdue it to European and Eastern American patterns; and that of encounter with the Indian, whose enduring presence undermines notions of a heroic Manifest Destiny. As Dee Brown shows in *Bury My Heart at Wounded Knee: An Indian History of the West*, the West was not won but *lost*. This sense of burdensome history continues in Peter Matthiessen's *In the Spirit of Crazy Horse*, an analysis of how a defiant group of Indians has been "neutralized" since the early 1970s by government forces working to clear the way for progress—that is, for multinational energy corporations that will mine the vast mineral resources and pump down water resources from reservation lands as well as from public lands. Once Americans understand the true nature of western history, writers of the modern West will have found their audience.

Western writers often share in and express tragic vision. Tragedy, which is the inevitable result of taking a complete view of the human situation, makes the richness and beauty of life depend on a balance. The basic tenet of this world-view is that all life is maintained by observance of the natural order, that is, perception that what goes on in one sphere affects what goes on in other spheres. Both Greek and Shakespearean literary tragedy reveal that a disorder in the human system is symbolically paralleled by a disorder in the social system and by a disorder in the cosmic system. The core of tragedy's idea of order, by contrast, is the sacredness of the bonds which hold human beings together and establish mutuality between their lives and the natural order.[8] It is at this juncture that western experience and the idea of tragedy are apt to meet. The experience of the New West—a civilization largely made possible through technological achievements such as construction of Hoover Dam in the mid-1930s—is that the power of tragedy's destructive principle has been admitted and constitutes a general threat. Although the industrial, military, agribusiness, and governmental infrastructure has now stretched western development to the breaking point, particularly in terms of resources and of the problems associated with "instant cities,"[9] the Great Western Boom continues with visions of projects larger than the pyramids, of excavations rivaling the Panama Canal, of trillion-dollar military projects, of Sun Belt expansions, and of forced relocations of Indians from ancestral lands. Thus at the very moment of the region's greatest rise to power, unless there is a dramatic return to the ethics of balance, a hubristic civilization of the New West may be headed into decadence, catastrophe, and silence.

Part of the evidence of a tragic vision in western writers lies in their questioning of the ideology of individualism, which has had a heyday in the West. The historian Frederick Jackson Turner was its most influential and enthusiastic proponent. The West, he wrote in 1920 in *The Frontier in American History*,

> was another name for opportunity. Here were mines to be seized, fertile valleys to be preëmpted, all the natural resources open to the shrewdest and the boldest.... The self-made man was the Western man's ideal, was the kind of man that all men might become. Out of his wilderness experience, out of the freedom of his opportunities, he fashioned a formula for social regeneration—the freedom of the individual to seek his own.[10]

Well, that thesis rings a historical freedom bell all right. But its peal is increasingly hollow now that a metropolitan West is destroying what's left of the frontier. The national, indeed international, myth of a West of rugged individualism triumphing over a decaying East has proven itself, in part, a denial of humanity. In terms of tragic vision, the ideology of individualism throws the natural order out of balance, negating tragedy's complete view of the human situation by vesting authority in the atomic individual regardless of the effects on the social system and the cosmic system. Of course, the great open spaces of the West may still enforce an isolation that can make people independent and resourceful; may call forth a saving, intuitive reluctance to surrender themselves to the blind ethics of an imperfectly formed, excessively masculine society; may make it possible to escape from the moral claustrophobia of ideology, and to open emotional doors to forces of the natural order that can nurture western civilization without demanding that it be repudiated altogether.

Journeying to the interior of historical experiences in the full light of tragic consciousness, Anglo, Hispanic, and Native American writers may and sometimes do discover that the connections between past and present are to be found not in a span of centuries, but in millennia. At the Sun Temple at Mesa Verde in southwestern Colorado we begin to comprehend the antiquity of the heartland; and in witnessing the unique mystery plays enacted in Hopi, Pueblo, and Navajo ceremonies we may realize that an ancient American civilization is a living presence— and more. The symbols of this civilization are pertinent to the future survival of the human species. Historical orientation locates the pulse of the heartland in pre-Columbian Mexico among Mayan and Aztec cultures, the center being the sacred city of Teotihuacan, at the mythic heart of which lies the Temple of Quetzalcoatl, the "plumed serpent," symbol of the union of heaven and earth, matter and spirit, a self-sacrificing God-Redeemer who taught that the Road of Life is within man, himself. An ethic based upon regard for all forms of life, the Road is a psychological affirmation of an evolutionary emergence of mankind to a new stage of increased awareness of our responsibility in the cosmic plan. Astonishing as this deep meaning of western history may seem, it is true to say that Ancient America has power stored up for the redemption of Modern America. Accordingly, some writers of the West, among whom there is the genius of Frank Waters, are able to render the modern world spiritually significant and to fulfill the prime task of mythology, which is to carry the human spirit forward.[11] The West is a region of myth vitalized by the relationship of peoples to the land. For Native Americans especially that relationship is sacred. Other westerners, drawn to similar regard, move spiritually from the damaged terrain of exterior landscape to the interior country where place is important because it is timeless and self-transcending—where, in Roethke's mystical vision, "all finite things reveal infinitude."[12]

The modern West is the modern world. This beautiful country, though, is not as benighted or as chaotic as a Waste-Land, its special poignancy being that it remains a place of the soul's desire. Western writers confront with urgency and insight and with remembered anguish some of the most tortured racial, moral, and spiritual questions of our time, and some find answers to them. Waters envisions a coming world of consciousness of the timeless essence of both the exterior and the interior country. Stegner calls for an ordering principle that will allow modern culture to stop its drift toward decadence. Other writers assert our needs for less wilfulness and for a return to humanity, to love and community. Still others remind us that, our earthly tenure being brief if not illusory, we should not take the world too seriously, but take it nonetheless, honestly, responsibly, and wholeheartedly. And even when the world seems to have lost all meaning—when, like Edward Abbey's Will Gatlin, we have descended in our quest for meaning to the very pit of the Grand Canyon of our microcosmic selves—there spreads before us the prospect of endurance and the knowledge that we could not imagine doing anything else, any less.[13] In the final analysis, stories of the modern West have the power to lift the gaze of our hearts to a larger sky. "Everything is held together with stories," concludes Barry Lopez in one of his stories. "That is all that is holding us together, stories and compassion."[14]

A WESTERN RENAISSANCE

More than a quarter of a century ago, I moved to the West, fulfilling an old dream of mine, pulling up family roots in the Carolinas and New England. Until then the family's only western pioneer of sorts was a great-grandfather, William Maxwell Blackburn.

He was born in Carlisle, Indiana, in 1828. Having been trained at the Princeton Theological Seminary for a career as minister and educator, and eventually having published a colossal, now superseded *History of the Christian Church from its Origin to the Present Time*, he accepted a call in 1885 to become founding president of tiny Pierre College, now Huron University, in South Dakota. According to the *Dictionary of American Biography*, he must have presented a formidable figure. He taught "mental, moral, and political science" and was, we are told, "dignified and even courtly, producing the impression of one who was a forceful thinker but was indisposed to impose his thoughts upon others." He was bearded, of course, this patriarch, and I assume he believed in the literal truth of the Bible. There is one family memory of him that I find quite touching. When he discovered fossils in the Badlands, he had the intellectual honesty to begin taking seriously Darwin's theory of evolution. Good for you, Great-Grandpa! Still—the point I would make here—he doesn't seem to move to a visible West. Behind the mask of this gentleman, so indisposed to impose his thoughts upon others, there is someone who could be living just about anywhere. I doubt that he thought of himself as an exile in the West or that he ever intended to move back east. He died in Pierre in 1898. In my imagination he is perpetually stooped over a fragment of dinosaur, his eyes burning with curiosity, his feverish brain pondering how to fit the monster into mental, moral, and political science. It would be ridiculous to think of him as an eastern gentleman who, upon arrival in the West, suddenly degenerated into a culturally and intellectually inferior yahoo. Yet there is precisely this attitude that many people have. Instead of being regarded as Americans who just happen to live in the West, westerners are apt to be regarded—and treated—as drop-outs from significant history and culture. It does little good, if one resists this attitude, to put in a word for common sense. Euro-Americans, Native Americans, Hispanic Americans, African Americans, and Asian Americans—peoples of the West—may break their hearts, create lasting works of art, build families and institutions, but they're going to be seen as living in a blank spot between New York and Hollywood (to borrow a phrase from William Eastlake). Where literary achievement is concerned, the writers in the West may be shunned as "regionalist," their very real experiences—in one culture, experiences from a living past that is several thousand years old—denied access to universality. For some reason, western writers are supposed to write "Westerns," even though William Faulkner never wrote "Southerns" nor Melville "Pacificans." A blank spot which comprises as much as half of the continental United States must apparently be subdued, poisoned, and over-populated before serious civilization can begin. Never mind that this "region" has vast plains, towering mountains, abysmal gorges and flashing rivers to tell us, in the words of Robinson Jeffers's "Credo," that "the beauty of things was born before eyes and sufficient to itself; the heart-breaking beauty/ Will remain when there is no heart to break for it." Never mind that the West has an ancient history and a long and burdensome modern history. Someone who in all other respects might be considered intelligent is going to call the West merely "a state of mind" and dismiss it from reality.

Some westerners share this attitude. Instead of looking for and into the depths of western life they look eastwards like abandoned souls with a collective crick in the neck. They are wasting their careers in a wilderness. "Culture," for them, is epitomized by the slick smallness, the self-satisfied emptiness, and the withered humanity that once characterized writing of *The New Yorker* school. Perhaps there is more than a trace of puritanism in this outlook. When the Puritans sailed west to New England, their intention was not to settle permanently but to be ready for return to England as soon as Oliver Cromwell summoned. He promptly and happily forgot them. So, now, our isolated westerners must sometimes wonder if they can ever get back to grace.

Test your own attitude. For example, did you know that Raymond Carver was born and raised in the West? If you did know, do you believe that the fact makes any difference in our understanding of his sensibility?

From 1976 until his death in 1988 at the age of fifty, Carver published dozens of original and compelling short stories that established his New York reputation as a major American writer of fiction. What we talk about when we talk about Carver is an imaginative artist of complexity and depth, a master in the tradition of Chekhov and Hemingway. Most critics have emphasized Carver's obsessions with social malaise and its terrors, with loneliness, failures of communication, voyeurism, infidelity, exhibitionism, and the like. Consequently, he is mistaken for an easterner with "eastern" concerns and quiet desperations, with the celebrated minimalist style—which, incidentally, he repudiated—perceived as a clever trick for handling themes of alienation. On close inspection, however, Carver's vision of humanity is not narrowly minimalist. It moves from the alienated to the potentially redemptive and is controlled by compassion. In short, his imagination tends toward the opening of systems of enclosure—and that, according to A. Carl Bredahl, Jr., in *New Ground*, is a defining tendency of the western imagination.[1]

If a western writer such as Carver is rightfully celebrated as a master because he is wrongfully identified as an eastern writer, what about western writers who are not celebrated, back east, at all?

For most of this century there has existed in New York an institution that I shall call by its former name, the American Academy (until recently, the American Academy and Institute of Arts and Letters). Its brochure in 1989 claims that election to the academy "has for many years been considered the highest formal recognition of artistic merit in this country." The academy, it would seem, takes a comprehensive look at American artists. And yet western writers are rarely elected to membership. The 1989 roster of the academy's Department of Literature is only 5% western writers (Wallace Stegner, Wright Morris, Paul Horgan, Gary Snyder, possibly Robert Bly, Evan S. Connell, and Susan Sontag, though their "western" affiliations are slight); with the death of Stegner, that gives us in 1994 three, or a vaguely possible six, out of 128. Several years ago, when I urged nine members of the Academy to place the name of Frank Waters in nomination, or at least to have him recognized for his titanic literary achievements, one of those members courteously replied that recognition of Waters is indeed long overdue—but absolutely nothing has happened.

Although one does not have to be elected to membership in the Republic of American Letters, there is plenty of evidence that western writers are beneath the salt when it comes to the canon of American literature. Some years back, I surveyed some anthologies and Big Mac textbooks in this field and discovered that "American" means mostly northeastern, some southern, little western. Of the 51 poets represented by 571 poems in F.O. Matthiessen's 1950 edition of *The Oxford Book of American Verse*, Robinson Jeffers with 19 poems is the only westerner included. The often reprinted *Short Story Masterpieces* edited in 1958 by Robert Penn Warren and Albert Erskine has 36 stories, only three of them by westerners (John Steinbeck, Jean Stafford, H.L. Davis). R.V. Cassill's 1600-page *Norton Anthology of Short Fiction* (third edition, 1986) includes stories by Steinbeck, Stafford, Carver, Morris, Willa Cather and Ursula LeGuin. Random House's *The American Tradition in Literature* (fifth edition, 1981) lines up Bret Harte, Cather, Steinbeck and Jeffers and adds a few poems by Theodore Roethke, William Stafford, and Snyder. Macmillan's *Anthology of American Literature* (third edition, 1985) offers Roethke, Jack

London, and Tomás Rivera and prints Steinbeck's *Of Mice and Men* in its entirety, surely a minor work. To bring this survey up to date, I've looked at the table of contents of *Harper American Literature* (second edition, 1994), a two-volume block-buster with 4,500 pages—enough, one would think, to accommodate a generous selection of great western literature. The *Harper Collins Book Review* robustly claims that *H. A. L.* "continues to cover virtually every recognized American literary classic. It also celebrates the wide-ranging literary, regional, ethnic, and gender diversity the selections represent." Celebrate diversity? Good. The West is rich in diversity. Some twenty westerners are represented in *H. A. L.*, out of 250 selections. We have here Steinbeck, Cather, London, Roethke, Snyder, Carver and William Stafford, also Ambrose Bierce and Katherine Anne Porter; and some "new" names are showing up, Chief Seattle, Chona, Andre v Garcia, N. Scott Momaday, Rudolfo A. Anaya, Leslie Marmon Silko, Louise Erdrich, Ishmael Reed, Joy Harjo and Alberto Rios. There is no coverage of western literary classics.

Then there is the "case" of Jeffers. Back in 1949 Gilbert Highet wrote in *The New York Times Book Review* that the critical neglect of Jeffers constituted the greatest shame in American letters. Now there are a number of critical books, most notably William H. Nolte's *Rock and Hawk: Robinson Jeffers and the Romantic Agony*, that make it clear what a great poet Jeffers was. Yet a funny thing is happening to Jeffers on his way to the anthologies: he is disappearing. *H. A. L.* reprints only four of his poems. *Prose & Poetry of the American West* omits him altogether.

But I do not want to pick a quarrel with the establishment, when the establishment stands every chance of winning. Besides, sooner or later, the West will be perceived as it is, not as a "region" in a pejorative sense but as an integral part of the United States—and in contemporary literary culture probably the most vital part. I think of my great-grandpa and the fossils in the Badlands, and I remember that it takes time for people to shake off received ideas and to accept the evidence that is right in front of their eyes.

When I first visited the West, I was looking for adventure, not a home. It was the summer of 1948, and I had just completed my sophomore year at Yale. I sweated in a grain elevator in Alva, Oklahoma, in explosive, pressure-cooker heat. I drove a John Deere from dawn to dusk in the wheat fields near Oberlin, Kansas. For a jam factory near Minneapolis, I unloaded sugar from box-cars, throwing 100-pound sacks around as if they were beanbags. I visited the Evans Ranch at the 9,000-foot elevation beneath Mt. Evans in the Colorado Rockies. Frequently broke and, in-between jobs, hungry, I worked with ex-GIs, ex-cons, migrant laborers and other non-Yalies. I became tanned and strong. Best of all, I discovered the wonder of immeasurable America. I saw gigantic webs of heat lightning silently spun on Kansas nights like black foil rippled. I watched red combines easing, like toy submarines, through oceans of golden wheat; wild deer grazing among putty-colored aspens; timberline mountain waters jinking through wind-trembled grasses; snow-flanked ranges scintillant in the sun beneath skies of cobalt blue. Standing on the Continental Divide, I vowed to return to the West some day. When I was back in New Haven, I found life in the Ivy League somehow effete and impertinent.

But if I wakened early to the West as a spiritual home, I was tardy in discovery of its great literature. I had read, while still a teenager in Durham, North Carolina, Cather, Steinbeck, Jeffers, A.B. Guthrie, Jr., and especially Walter Van Tilburg Clark. I knew that *something* was "out there." Still, my southern pieties went unchallenged. I subscribed to the sentiment that William Faulkner's great period from 1929 to 1942 stands unmatched in American literature, and that he alone in the twentieth century equaled Melville's genius in range, energy and power. As recently as 1981, when I gave a paper at the Faulkner and Yoknapatawpha conference in Oxford, I regarded the "Southern Renaissance" as the crowning achievement in the century's letters. What a galaxy of writers! Could any other region boast writers as good as Faulkner, Wolfe, Welty, Warren, Tate, Price, O'Connor, Wright, Styron, Chappell, Percy and others? Of course not.

Then came the shock. I chanced to read a novel by a western writer hitherto unknown to me, Frank Waters. This novel, *The Woman at Otowi Crossing* (1966; revised edition, 1987), was, I realized, "up there" with such classics as *The Scarlet Letter*, *Moby Dick*, *Huckleberry Finn* and *The Sound and the Fury*. Then I read Waters's *The Man Who Killed the Deer*. Another great, great novel. I was stunned, thrilled. And worried about leaping to conclusions. After all, western writers are not supposed to be major American writers, and it is certainly a heresy in our academic gradgrindery to talk of "unknown" writers in the reverent breath reserved for Faulkner and Melville. I read on—and on. *People of the Valley*, *Pike's Peak* (and the trilogy of novels preceding it, *The Wild Earth's Nobility*, *Below Grass Roots*, *The Dust Within the Rock*). On to the superb prose of *The Colorado*. On to the profound philosophy of *Masked Gods*, *Book of the Hopi*, *Pumpkin Seed Point*, *Mexico Mystique*, *Mountain Dialogues*. Finally, there was no backing down from critical judgment: Frank Waters is the West's greatest prose writer and one of the two or three most important American writers of this century. Waters stands in relation to the civilization of the West as Faulkner did to that of the South. That is how the notion of a "Western Renaissance" suggested itself, with this literary giant at the center of the upsurge of cultural energy.

The evidence of a flowering is now easy to find.

First, there is the evidence of regional anthologies and textbooks, that is to say, to collections with serious critical and historical intent. In the 1970s there had been a few slap-dash paperback collections featuring southwestern and West Coast writers, but little sense in them of a literary heyday. Then came Russell Martin's *Writers of the Purple Sage*: *An Anthology of Recent Western Writing* (Penguin, 1984). This was followed by *The Interior Country*: *Stories of the Modern West* (Swallow/Ohio,

1987), which I edited with the help of Craig Lesley and Jill Landem. That same year James and Denise Thomas began to edit *The Best of the West: New Short Stories from the Wide Side of the Missouri*. In 1991, Craig Lesley broke new ground when he edited for Laurel his magnificent 385-page anthology, *Talking Leaves: Contemporary Native American Short Stories*. In 1992, Martin issued with Penguin another collection, *New Writers of the Purple Sage: An Anthology of Contemporary Western Writing*. Two more hefty anthologies saw publication in 1993: *Higher Elevations: Stories from the West, A Writers' Forum Anthology* (Swallow/Ohio), which I coedited with C. Kenneth Pellow; and the 532-page *Dreamers and Desperadoes: Contemporary Short Fiction of the American West*, which Lesley has coedited with his wife, Katheryn Stavrakis, for Laurel. With forty-three writers represented, *Dreamers and Desperadoes* places needed emphasis on western humor, on stories about workers, and on neglected Asian American and African American writers of the West.

Other, recent anthologies have ethnic and territorial concerns. Some of these are, as follows: *Voces: An Anthology of Nuevo Mexicano Writers* (1987), edited by Rudolfo A. Anaya; *The Last Best Place: A Montana Anthology* (1990), edited by William Kittredge; *New Growth: Contemporary Short Stories by Texas Writers* (1989), edited by Lyman Grant, and *New Growth/2* (1993), edited by Mark Busby; *Many Californians: Literature from the Golden State* (1992), edited by Gerald W. Haslam; and *Where Past Meets Present: Modern Colorado Short Stories* (1994), edited by James B. Hemesath. There is also a curiously uninformed but readable collection, *Best of the West: An Anthology of Classic Writing from the American West* (1991), edited by Tony Hillerman. James Work's 733-page textbook, *Prose & Poetry of the American West* (Nebraska, 1990), provides still further evidence that there is in the West—and has been for some time—an enormous surplus of literary talent.

Second, where establishment of canonical texts and writers is concerned, there has been a large increase during the past twenty years in the amount, range, and quality of research on western literature and history. Now more than three decades old, *Western American Literature* is established as an authoritative journal, one, moreover, with awareness of a vast region rich in writers. Members of the Western Literature Association have helped to produce *Fifty Western Writers: A Bio-Bibliographical Sourcebook* (1982), and *A Literary History of the American West* (1987), a bold, 1153-page, unwieldy but well-written attempt to show us what has gone on since 1492, and goes on, and the 1081-page *Updating the Literary West* (1997). Book-length critical and biographical studies of Waters, Jeffers, Steinbeck, Cather, Clark, Momaday, Harvey Fergusson, Mary Austin and Wallace Stegner are among those now available; Ann Ronald's *The New West of Edward Abbey* (1982) is an invaluable critical barometer for gauging the temper of the contemporary literary scene. Finally, westerners no long have to feel irritated by the eastern orientation of *The New York Times Book Review* and *The New York Review of Books*: *The Bloomsbury Review*, edited in Denver by Tom Auer, not only gives ample attention to western writers but also has emerged as one of the best critical reviews of books in the United States.

Third, small presses and literary magazines out west are increasingly being joined by university presses and large eastern publishers in the recognition and publication of western writers. I encourage readers to consult the copyright acknowledgements and biographical notes in the regional anthologies already mentioned.

Fourth, the West is beginning to recognize its own writers by means of awards, not keeping them waiting for the infrequent Pulitzer. The Western Writers of America Golden Spur Award is no longer reserved for the spurious genre of "Westerns." The Pacific Northwest Booksellers Awards for Excellence have gone to writers such as Craig Lesley and William Kittredge, not just to the commercially successful. In 1971, the Premio Quinto Sol brought prominence to Rudolfo A. Anaya. The Texas Institute of Letters gives annual awards.

Establishing a canon for Western American literature as a whole or for a Western Renaissance in particular is beyond my intention and capability. In what follows, I limit myself to western writers since the 1930s, give emphasis to those who seem "modern" or "new," and am necessarily selective even of these. "The West seems to be coming of age," Russell Martin writes in *New Writers of the Purple Sage*. This same sense that something has happened and is happening is conveyed by Katheryn Stavrakis in her introduction to *Dreamers and Desperadoes*. When she and Lesley started the project, she writes,

> we knew there was a great deal of talent, but we were taken aback to find out how much. The discovery confirmed our feeling that writers of the West are on the cutting edge of literature in this country, mining a deep vein of energy and vitality.

Lesley and Stavrakis are particularly drawn to imaginative writers whose hearts and minds have been empowered by the greatness of western landscape, who have a sense of history and tradition, who represent the diversity of western races and cultures, and who explore a West of real people with real experiences. Having emphasized the Native American "storyteller" tradition in *Talking Leaves*, they show in *Dreamers and Desperadoes* that the contemporary West has many styles and stances, all expressive of energy and vitality.

As a Western Renaissance emerges from the background of western letters, many of the writers included in the anthologies are going to give it definition. Here is a tentative list, with overlapping that points to some general editorial agreements:

> From *Writers of the Purple Sage*: Richard Hugo, N. Scott Momaday, Leslie Marmon Silko, John Nichols, Rudolfo A. Anaya, Edward Abbey, William Kittredge, James Welch, Ivan Doig.

From *New Writers of the Purple Sage*: Joanne Greenberg, Rudolfo A. Anaya, James Welch, N. Scott Momaday, Gretel Ehrlich, Tim Sandlin, William Kittredge, Ron Carlson, Ivan Doig, Barbara Kingsolver, Linda Hogan, David Quammen, Terry Tempest Williams.

From *The Interior Country*: Frank Waters, Edward Abbey, Walter Van Tilburg Clark, Craig Lesley, Rudolfo A. Anaya, John Nichols, William Kittredge, Jean Stafford, Gladys Swan, Raymond Carver, Clark Brown, Barry Lopez, Leslie Marmon Silko, Wallace Stegner, James B. Hall, Joanne Greenberg, William Eastlake, David Kranes, Max Schott.

From *Higher Elevations*: Ron Carlson, Gladys Swan, Clay Reynolds, Robert Roripaugh, Peter LaSalle, Julian Silva, Miles Wilson, Robert O. Greer, Jr., Craig Lesley, Susan Lowell.

From *Talking Leaves*: Paula Gunn Allen, Louise Erdrich, Joy Harjo, Linda Hogan, N. Scott Momaday, James Welch, Mary TallMountain.

From *Dreamers and Desperadoes*: Rudolfo A. Anaya, Rick Bass, Ron Carlson, Ivan Doig, William Kittredge, David Kranes, Craig Lesley, Barry Lopez, James Welch, Terry Tempest Williams, Elizabeth Tallent, Ursula LeGuin.

From *Prose & Poetry of the American West*: Frank Waters, Thomas Hornsby Ferril, A. B. Guthrie Jr., John Steinbeck, Walter Van Tilburg Clark, Wallace Stegner, Wright Morris, William Stafford, Edward Abbey, N. Scott Momaday, James Welch, Leslie Marmon Silko, Gary Snyder, Ann Zwinger.

From *New Growth 1 & 2*: Clay Reynolds, Rick Bass, Carolyn Osborn, Miles Wilson, Peter LaSalle, Donley Watt, Paul Scott Malone.

From *Best of the West*, 1-4: Peter LaSalle, Joy Harjo, Rick Bass, Rudolfo A. Anaya, Gladys Swan, Ron Hansen, Louise Erdrich, William Kittredge, David Kranes, Elizabeth Tallent, Gordon Weaver, Ron Carlson, Richard Ford.

This is a much more reliable list than one might compile from *Best American Short Stories*, which is edited in Boston and has commercial leanings, but one should not depend entirely upon anthologies. The names of new and experienced writers can be gleaned from literary magazines such as *South Dakota Review*, *Puerto del Sol*, and *Writers' Forum*, to name several with a western emphasis. Finally, there being no comprehensive anthology of western poetry, one must be wary of well-known names and look for excellence among the lesser known such as Walter McDonald, Simon Ortiz, and George Keithley. Still, all in all, we've already come up with enough names to bring an honorific like "renaissance" into play.

In *The Interior Country* I argued, following Stegner and others, that in important ways we did not win the West at all; we lost it. The distinguishing sign of the modern, serious, post-romantic West is precisely that recognition, and an attempt to "win" the area truly—to be worthy of it. In other words, a certain tragic vision of history is necessary to literary maturity and is suggested when the writing, along with a revised awareness of history, evokes certain deeper, positive, and universal values. While few modern writers of the West have inscribed reality as deeply as Waters, Jeffers, Stegner and Clark, most at least signal sophistication and reassessment and embody in their writing new ways of looking at life in the West.

The term "renaissance" means, of course, rebirth or reawakening. In American culture the term is used as an honorific to refer to a more or less historically definable upsurge or awakening of regional literature. The context of occurrence is generally one in which the region is making the transition from traditional to modern forms of life. A cultural movement of the kind is usually characterized by a sharing of a common body of values and is both an expression of and a reaction to modernization. These important generalizations, which clarify what we should be looking for in defining a Western Renaissance, come from Richard H. King, author of *A Southern Renaissance: The Cultural Awakening of the American South, 1930-1955*.[2]

King shows that a renaissance can be understood historically as a dynamic of transition between two worlds. Thus the New England Renaissance was discovered/invented with Lewis Mumford's *Golden Day* (1926) which focused on five major writers between 1830 and 1860, Emerson, Thoreau, Melville, Whitman and Hawthorne; was continued through Van Wyck Brooks's *The Flowering of New England* (1936); and reached a sort of critical (and imperial) apotheosis in F. O. Matthiessen's *American Renaissance* (1941). The Southern Renaissance, though its prestige rests to a considerable extent upon the achievement of Faulkner, refers to activity by a cluster of writers and intellectuals from the 1920s to the 1950s.

In a mood of measured appreciation, I think it is time to announce a Western Renaissance. In making this announcement, I am aware that John R. Milton of *South Dakota Review* and Thomas J. Lyon of *Western American Literature* have for decades been calling attention to the phenomenon of literary vitality in the West. Here, I suggest some approaches.

If the focus is on major writers, I propose Waters, Jeffers, Stegner, Steinbeck, Clark, and Abbey, in that order. If the focus is on masters, I would add Eastlake, Ferril, Hugo, Momaday, Carver, Welch, Anaya, Roethke, Doig and Greenberg. But there are more than a hundred masterful writers involved in the movement, and nominations remain open. If the focus is on classics, I propose the following novels: Waters, *The Man Who*

Killed the Deer and *The Woman at Otowi Crossing*; Clark, *The Track of the Cat* and *The Ox-Bow Incident*; Stegner, *Angle of Repose*; Abbey, *The Monkey-Wrench Gang*; Steinbeck, *The Grapes of Wrath*; Momaday, *House Made of Dawn*; Anaya, *Bless Me, Ultima*; Guthrie, *The Way West*; Nichols, *The Milagro Beanfield War*; Doig, *Dancing at the Rascal Fair.*

Finally, what are the historical dimensions of a Western Renaissance? As we've already seen, there is a tremendous flowering of western literature happening right now. But if we look back sixty-five years, we may discern what I believe is the beginning of the awakening, before Jeffers's *Selected Poetry*, before Ferril's *Westering*, before Clark's *Ox-bow Incident*. Quite specifically, I see the beginning of the renaissance in Frank Waters's *The Wild Earth's Nobility* (1935):

> "HEE-YAH!"
> The sharp guttural cry roused Rogier from his rever-
> ie in the shadows of the porch where his heavy
> square-built body lounged motionless in a chair, his
> gaze enmeshed in the vast web of twilight translucent
> between the row of cottonwoods before him and the
> imponderable barrier of mountains rising farther
> west to cut off his world of thought.[3]

On the surface this novel is a regional history stocked with what might be called documentation of mining. Actually, mining is but a metaphor for psychological excavations—Rogier's "world of thought." When he succumbs to gold fever, it is not gold he is seeking in the depths of the earth. It is no less than the secret of the supreme universe that he seeks, which is to say the secret of himself in relation to nature, symbolized by the barbaric yawp of the Indian and by Pike's Peak. The story of Rogier is, in short, a paradigm of Euro-American history in its New World inflections on the frontier. Historical experiences of exile, conquest, and colonization, of dreams of a better life, and of belief in the atomic individual's unchurched and immediate access to the revelations of God are gathered here at the heart of the continent where the peak is a beacon of promise and a numinous source, like Melville's white whale. And this whole experience is found wanting. For the first time that I know of in western literary history, materialism, rationalism, and the cult of individualism are dramatically revealed as underlying causes of American tragedy.

Waters is also going to be the first western writer—and surely one of the few in modern world literature—to guide us through a vast historical transition from the dead-end of the Waste-Land to a new world of the mind. It is this spiritual quest that so elevates *The Man Who Killed the Deer* and *The Woman at Otowi Crossing* to the heights of universality. The quest of Waters also exemplifies something spiritual to be found in western American literature generally, something that supersedes the angst and nihilism so prominent in nonwestern literature. We may now fairly claim that a Western Renaissance signals not just the extension, numerically and geographically, of our national culture, but its revitalization and transformation.

IV. Novelists

FAULKNER AND CONTINUANCE OF THE SOUTHERN RENAISSANCE

Generally, I believe, it is agreed that the memorable southern literature of the twentieth century appears at a time when the older South's moral order, the old notions of certainty and belief, has ceased to suffice as an explanation of and an adequate basis for daily experience. C. Vann Woodward, following Allen Tate, defines the Southern Renaissance as "literature conscious of the past in the present"; this consciousness disdains nostalgic myths and romantic dreams of the South's past and turns instead to the South's real experience with history, with defeat and failure, with long periods of frustration and poverty, as well as with human slavery and its aftermath of racial injustice.[1] Similar conclusions are pressed by Cleanth Brooks in *William Faulkner: The Yoknapatawpha Country* and by Louis D. Rubin, Jr., in *The Faraway Country: Writers of the Modern South*, two books published the year after Faulkner's death and still invaluable studies of the relationship of modern southern letters to a view of man as an inextricable part of a living history and community. Brooks emphasizes the pastoral mode in Faulkner's fiction, what man has done to his fellow man and to nature, a kind of Wordsworthian lament for an Edenic world lost as irrevocably as Benjy Compson's pasture and Ike McCaslin's wilderness. Rubin discerns in such various writers as Faulkner, Thomas Wolfe, Robert Penn Warren, and Eudora Welty a spiritual detachment from values of community, history, and society and an emotional emigration from the geographical South into a country of the mind—not Asheville but Altamont, not Northern Mississippi but Yoknapatawpha—and emphasizes a tragic sense of the literature, one born out of the feeling that an old order is passing away. At all events, the pastoral and the tragic combined give southern writing much of its gravity of tone.[2] What I want to do here is raise some questions as to boundaries. In what ways, if at all, has a southern tradition in literature been continued since, say, 1950?

First, who qualifies as a southern writer? John M. Bradbury's *Renaissance in the South: A Critical History of Literature, 1920-1960* deals with 700 writers, thus bringing us perilously close to admitting what we've long suspected, that every hamlet in Dixieland shelters more inglorious rustic bards than Gray's "Elegy" ever contemplated. Clearly, this kind of approach won't do, this *renaissancing* of every southerner not demonstrably illiterate. Do we swap non-southerners for those who de-camped, recalling that it was recently fashionable to give T.S. Eliot for W.H. Auden at an arbitrary rate of international poetic exchange? We are of course traditionally hospitable. Take, for instance, Hervey Allen of Pennsylvania. One of the few distinguished American writers who actually served in the gas-green trenches of France and survived, he recuperated in Charleston, helped DuBose Heyward found there the Poetry Society of South Carolina in 1921, and wrote of southern mood and history in his poetry, in his biography of Poe, and in two of his historical novels, *Anthony Adverse* and *Action at Aquila*. Or take Sherwood Anderson of Ohio whose sojourn in New Orleans provided young Faulkner with some encouragement. But neither Allen nor Anderson, welcome as their presence may have been, qualifies as a southern writer. Southernness has to be bred in the bone, has to do with roots. And it excludes no one on the basis of race: Richard Wright and Ralph Ellison belong to southern tradition.

As long as we are talking about a general cultural manifestation of the literary imagination, we are probably safe in assuming that a writer need have spent only his or her formative years in the region—until the age of twelve, say—to become forever a southerner. For instance, in William Styron's *Set This House on Fire* (1960) the Virginia-educated Peter Leverett declares he is "estranged from myself and from my time, dwelling neither in the destroyed past nor in the fantastic and incomprehensible present" (18-19).³ Such estrangement is peculiarly rooted in southern experience. But roots also have to do with a whole complex of values bodied forth in language. To write as a southerner, seriously that is, one learns early-on the emptiness of the old rhetoric of Cloud-Cuckoo-Land (as W.J. Cash called it), of innocence and success and invincibility, and one also learns early-on to contract out of our All-American, urban, anti-pastoral values of imperial politics and flash merchandise. On your own and not because of a literary influence, you come upon the richness and variety of southern speech. For instance, long years before I read *As I Lay Dying*, I knew that countryfolk in Moore County, North Carolina, 800 miles from Lafayette County, Mississippi, say "right well" and "right smart" and "studying up them Ten Commandments what taken the Lord forty days when he done done the world in seven." Southern writing is the outgrowth of an early collective experience of a certain kind of people spread over a land bigger than France, a marrow-deep experience of land and blood. From childhood, Wordsworths all, we inherit the real myth of our dispossessed and dispossessing land, with both wonder and irony, coming the hard way up to our common heritage and our common toil.

There is, I surmise, no intrinsic reason to believe that a vigorous southern tradition in literature should cease with the passing of its first geniuses. True, the so-called extended family may be breaking up in the South, as elsewhere, and small towns get larger. True, television wreaks philological havoc. I don't suppose you could go now to the Outer Banks of North Carolina and hear one of Blackbeard's descendants say, "When's hoigh toide on the'oiland, goin oot in me bo-at." True, the assumptions of permanence, out of which Faulkner's great art arises, no longer come with the territory; that is, now, with the memory of the territory. On the other hand, we can readily recognize the durable strength of our emotional pieties when these are tested by the flip conceptions of non-southerners. To hear them tell it, you would think southern literature is a sort of parody annunciation: thus once, amidst magnolias and wild grits, the deity disguised as Poe's raven ravished, still unravished, Dixie, and in that lethargic rush engendered there the burning shacks of Atlanta and Elvis Presley dead. Whatever else they know, southerners know what it's like to feel insulted. A literature of outrage and defiance is certainly a continuing possibility.

If there is no intrinsic reason to doubt the continuance of southern literary tradition, there is nonetheless evidence that it continues in a mode differing from that of the elder generation of writers. This, I take it, is why Rubin describes a boundary between the Faulknerian mode of novel and the kind of novel William Styron began writing in *Lie Down in Darkness* (1951). Styron's extraordinary first novel, written in New York in his early twenties, owes more than echoes to *The Sound and the Fury* and *As I Lay Dying*. I have no desire to rehash the matter here. Rubin, among others, has performed that function admirably and demonstrated beyond any lingering doubt that Styron did not exhibit the "derivative imagination" once so absurdly attributed to him.[4] Loveless families are *not* all alike, nor are funeral processions, nor are southern girls lost for the same reasons; and the uses of interior monologue did not grow stale after Faulkner's. Styron *couldn't* have written as Faulkner did. Absent from *Lie Down in Darkness* are the historical dimension and community perspective of Faulknerian tragedy: "Where Faulkner created a Greek-like tragedy reminiscent of the fall of the House of Atreus," writes Rubin, "Styron produced a domestic tragedy that had no element of fated dynastic downfall about it."[5] Quentin Compson's alienation from Yoknapatawpha County is *em*blematic of his failure to cope with the modern world; Peyton Loftis's alienation from Port Warwick is *symp*tomatic of her parent's selfishness and weakness. Moreover, where *The Sound and the Fury*'s juxtaposition of Compson decadence and Dilsey's theologically validated compassion gives a powerful sense of living myth, in *Lie Down in Darkness* only the semblance of such juxtaposition exists, there being no authenticity either to Carey Carr's or to Daddy Faith's versions of Christian ethics. Styron's positives lie elsewhere, implicitly in *Lie Down in Darkness*, explicitly in his second novel, *Set This House on Fire*: the way to human survival lies through personal choice and maturation. Cass Kinsolving, hero of the later novel, creates his own salvation and brings to the community his own stability. Southern attitudes toward history and society have been tested and finally made to depend for their reality on Cass's own inward acceptance of them. This proceeding would certainly seem to evince a new mode in southern writing.

Somewhat parenthetically I might say at this point that the most "Faulknerian" moment in Styron's writing occupies four pages of *Set This House on Fire* (88-92). The rich, sleazily corrupt boy, Mason Flagg, has been sent home from school for seducing (in the school's chapel!) the witless thirteen-year-old daughter of a Chesapeake oyster fisherman, who, outraged and hellbent on retribution, suddenly appears outside the Flagg family's Virginia mansion. Then, just as suddenly, Mason's father commands the oysterman to put down his murderous lead pipe. He does so. End of scene. Styron of course is foreshadowing how Mason's later life leads to the rape of an Italian peasant and to Cass Kinsolving's more or less remorseless murder of him. But just think what Faulkner might have done with these materials! Our oysterman might have founded a dynasty in order to avenge himself upon the Flaggs; and we can see the poor ravished but unwoebegone daughter riding in the last mule-drawn wagon toward Jefferson through the quiet dust of the world's last worthless, umbrageous twilight, she thinking, *My mother is an oyster*.

Although Styron himself evidently rejects the idea of a new mode, his novels dispose one to think otherwise.[6] A rejection of "southernness" is a protest, quite wholesome, against being tagged as a regional writer. But a modal proposition, one that involves differing affirmation of possibility, impossibility, necessity, or contingency, is not a limiting tag. Thus a new mode of southern writing may easily accommodate an extension of the South's experience with history stretching beyond geographical frontiers. The South, more than any other American region except the West, has a common bond "with the ironic and tragic experience of other nations and the general run of mankind."[7] This, Woodward's fine observation of universality in southern thought and feeling, may help to explain why Styron, among other writers of the post-1950 era, has refused to limit his "faraway country" to Virginia. Of course, he makes in *Set This House on Fire* some memorable imaginative excursions to "Port Warwick" and to the Carolinas, but New York is in there, too (as it had been in *Lie Down in Darkness*) and above all Paris and parts of Italy. *The Confessions of Nat Turner* (1967) takes place in the Tidewater, to be sure, and what Styron calls a "meditation on history" could have meant, but doesn't mean, a renewal of Faulknerian meditations on race in *Absalom, Absalom!* and in *Go Down, Moses*. The publication of *Sophie's Choice* (1979) clarifies what Styron has been doing: it is a southerner, and no surrogate Albert Camus, either, who confronts the hardest existential choices wherever his imagination may lead him, to the despair of a Black revolutionist in nineteenth-century Virginia or to the despair of a Holocaust survivor in New York. Styron remains a representative southern writer when he views the hell of dehumanization anywhere and everywhere, the special vantage point being the tragic-pastoral poet's. Like Virgil in the *First Eclogue*—sometimes called "The Dispossessed"—a southern writer (like western writers), sees an alien world of dehumanizing power encroaching on the ideal landscape, and he or she faces, behind the masks of contemporary Arcadians, the prospect of unending deprivation and despair.[8]

Although Styron does not create a Yoknapatawpha on native soil, he extends his vision of the South to a country quite literally faraway—Poland—as in this passage from *Sophie's Choice*:

> Poland is a beautiful, heart-wrenching, soul-split country which in many ways ...resembles or conjures up images of the American South—or at least

the South of other not-so-distant times. It is not alone that forlornly lovely, nostalgic landscape which creates the frequent likeness—the quagmiry but haunting monochrome of the Narew River swampland, for example, with its look and feel of a murky savanna on the Carolina coast, or the Sunday hush on a muddy back street in a village of Galicia, where by the smallest eyewink of the imagination one might see whisked to a lonesome crossroads hamlet in Arkansas these ramshackle, weather-bleached little houses, crookedly carpentered, set upon shrubless plots of clay where scrawny chickens fuss and peck— but in the spirit of the nation, her indwellingly ravaged and melancholy heart, tormented into its shape like that of the Old South out of adversity, penury and defeat. (*SC*, 246-47)

In both Poland and the American South, Styron continues,

the abiding presence of race has created at the same instant cruelty and compassion, bigotry and understanding, enmity and fellowship, exploitation and sacrifice, searing hatred and hopeless love. While it may be said that the darker and uglier of these opposing conditions has usually carried the day, there must also be recorded in the name of truth a long chronicle in which decency and honor were at moments able to controvert the absolute dominion of the reigning evil, more often than not against rather large odds, whether in Poznan or Yazoo City. (*SC*, 247-48)

In speaking, then, of the possibility of the continuance of southern tradition, I would lay stress upon universality. Writers like Styron continue to affiliate with the victims and dispossessed of this world, to withdraw with them from the world's mad society, and to shape their quest for renewed life by first,

Prospero-like, mastering nature through mind, through the kind of civilized control that makes possible the growth of love. Literature, as Solzhenitsyn said in his Nobel lecture, is a nation's soul. The long sad memories of the southern writer compel a change of wording: literature is the world's soul.

Every artist revolts against a previous form of possession. Axiomatic as this saying is, a good deal of criticism over the past forty years has seemed impervious to the fact of revolt where southern writers are concerned. We are supposed to be mesmerized by Faulkner's style, cowed by his stature. Yet one doesn't receive the impression that Styron, Flannery O'Connor, Reynolds Price, Walker Percy, Fred Chappell, Elizabeth Spencer, and a host of other writers have been writing in a daze or lying down on the tracks waiting for the Dixie Special to come helling along. We—they—must usually answer to two charges of "influence": Faulkner's language and techniques did a trick on us, and we all came trailing clouds of Gothicism.

Reynolds Price issues a correct defiance: "Serious writers of fiction born in the American South, setting their work in the region which they possess and must comprehend, do not imitate the obsessive themes of the private language of a single distinguished elder, William Faulkner; they imitate the South, their South, as Faulkner imitated his South, his private relation to a public thing, a place ...inhabited by millions of people united by an elaborate dialect formed in syntax and rhythm (like the people themselves) by the weight of land, climate, race, religion, history."[9] It is a case, in other words, "of southern writers, almost to a man, *not* being involved in an imitation or mimicry of Faulkner but of Mr. Faulkner and other southern writers being involved in an imitation of a given original, of a common original—which is the way men and women have talked in the South in the last fifty or sixty years."[10] Having read the work of Eudora Welty when he was in high school, Price feels that she, not Faulkner, is the one who revealed to him possibilities for fictionalizing landmarks of his own world. This is self-discovery through a writer, not imitation of one.

As for the charge of Gothicism, Flannery O'Connor refuted it wonderfully: "I have found," she wrote, "that any fiction that comes out of the South is going to be considered grotesque by the Northern critics, unless it is grotesque, in which case it is going to be considered realistic."[11] And it is not to Faulkner but to Mark Twain and Nathanael West that one must turn to find her literary precursors.[12]

The impact of Faulkner on other writers cannot be simply assumed. His first encounter with Faulkner's works left Reynolds Price cold, and many writers nowadays have probably not read them at all. Although Faulkner's reputation is in a solid state, the fact of the matter may be that his impact on other writers may have just begun. Few of us born in the 1920s and 1930s ever heard of Faulkner until Malcolm Cowley brought out the Portable Edition in 1946, and even then, I strongly suspect, most of us strung out our reading of the novels—not all of them either—over the next thirty years, a period almost as long as that which elapsed between the publication of Shakespeare's First Folio and the appearance of Dryden's criticism. Perhaps Faulkner's star is just now looming in our previously unfocused lens.

The post-World-War-II generation of writers felt distanced from Faulkner. Wright Morris, commenting on the Nobel Prize speech about the ding-dong of doom, observes, "It is the *nature* of the future, not its extinction, that produces in the artist such foreboding, the prescient chill of heart of a world without consciousness."[13] William Styron's *Esquire* article on "My Generation" has something similar to say: "We were traumatized not only by what we had been through and by the almost unimaginable presence of the bomb, but by the realization that the entire mess was not finished at all.... When at last the Korean War arrived, ...the cosmos seemed so unhinged as to be nearly insupportable."[14] So the new generation's doubt over humanity, over the survival of the humane within humanity, became an intense preoccupation.

This sense of distance from Faulkner has led and might still lead to serious parody, a literary stance definable as both a compliment and a deliverance, a testament of real and loving devotion to *il miglior fabbro* but also a ceremony of disaffiliation. It is as if the imaginative power, far from being derived from the artist parodied, derives him from itself—reproduces him through a process of refictionalization. Thus Faulkner's techniques, themes, settings, and presumed style can be approached and imitated *as if* they symbolize a whole culture, the Old South, old, that is, to a writer from the urbanized New South. Styron's *Lie Down in Darkness*, for example, exploits the Faulknerian mode in the fashion of parody: Styron obtains his visa from the Old South, so to speak, in order to travel to the new southern presence, now an urbanized landscape that brings Virginian shipyards, country clubs, and fraternity houses into easy conjunction with New York subways and flats.[15]

To explain how a parody-intention comes into play, there being a lack of testimonials, I will have to risk indulgence and a kind of presumptuousness by disclosing what I myself did in a novel called *The Cold War of Kitty Pentecost* (1979).[16] It was a composition that took many years and various drafts to complete, but in the final draft I was more or less fully conscious of a partial Faulknerian parody. I wanted to juxtapose New South and Old, contriving to exhibit the latter as pseudo-Faulknerian, a world of strong-willed and violent people accursed by racial fears. At several points I even put Faulkner himself on the scene. I had seen him in Virginia, nattily attired, head held dreamily high, walking along the highway between Charlottesville and Farmington, so when I first introduce the reader to Mrs. Pentecost, representative of the Old South, I fused that image of Faulkner into the portrait, pictured her walking along a highway, and let the description echo "A Rose for Emily":

> Transcontinental eighteen wheelers were expresstraining past this figure in black mourning clothes of a bygone era, this figure with head and

shoulders almost as stiff as a waxwork at Madame Tussaud's, sounding horns at her, raking her with cyclones of diesel exhaust, yet there she was walking, a scarecrow in black whose flesh, he remembered, sagged off high gaunt cheekbones like drippings of candlewax and was of that pallid hue—a figure fragile, indomitable, ludicrous, haughty, and mad. (*KP*, 32)

Faulkner is not Mrs. Pentecost—good grief! But I confess to a ghostly presence. At a later point in the novel I wanted a character who would sum up its theme; I needed a sort of disembodied voice with sepulchral tones, a Melvillean Dansker, the *Agamemnon* man. I gave the speech to a lawyer from Charleston named Buck McKay. That passage reads:

The voice of Buck McKay was communicative in a reserved way. "Extending sympathy with the mind is easy, and it's not enough. Besides, it can be dangerous to liberty. But, as for the other, extending sympathy with the heart, the glacier-slow movement of man towards some frail kinship with his kind—kinship of his own desiring and making from love and hope and sacrifice—it also may well not be enough. Nevertheless it is now the only movement in which his liberty has meaning. What is needed is a change in the human weather, atonement, compassion. But what we are likely to have instead is a kind of spiritual Stone Age in which whatever fire first stirred in whatever brutish and fetid cave our nearer ancestors to cherish and to fear the new god of themselves will be gradually extinguished and finally forgotten, and then our cold, lonely, unsupported souls shall be set adrift, like the planet itself, among myriads of unknown stars." (*KP*, 107-08)

In this scene Buck McKay is addressing and consoling a highly sensitive, potentially revolutionary black student from the modern industrial city of Poe's Hill, North Carolina; the distant shade of Faulkner is his Virgilian guide to an old Inferno but capable of hinting at the New South's hope for redemption from ways of the past. There are deliberate echoes from *Go Down, Moses*—the love-hope-sacrifice incantation, the brutish cave, the ancestral self-worship—but the full weight of the passage falls upon the rather unFaulknerian conceptual word, "unsupported." The image of our drifting planet owes much, in fact, to a photograph, taken from the Apollo spacecraft, of Earth shimmering and blue-green in a black void of space. As for the two kinds of possible human community, that of the intellect and that of the heart—their conflict forming the "cold war" of the narrative and title—such a theme runs so deeply in American literature that I can feel comfortable in presenting a personal variation. I recognize in my first novel "southernness" and continuance of tradition, and I confess that such limited knowledge of Faulkner as I possess played a part in the writing. But I feel no need to apologize for the connections, for they are fewer than appearances might suggest.

I have argued that the southern tradition in literature continues in a new mode emphasizing individual salvation and accommodating the tragic experience of outsiders everywhere. Further, I have observed how a reductionist criticism, with stress upon "influences," produces misunderstanding of the South and of the nature of narrative art. Now, I wish to present the view that Faulkner the *artist* belongs to a literary tradition that reaches back to antiquity—the tradition of verse drama.

Needed here is Denis Donoghue's definition of verse drama: "A play is 'poetic' when its concrete elements (plot, agency, scene, speech, gesture) continuously exhibit in their internal relationships those qualities of mutual coherence and illumination required of the words of a poem."[17] By these terms even a silent film may achieve a high style in both tragedy and comedy. The poetry inheres in the structure of a drama as a whole and in the manner in which, and the degree to which, all the elements act in cooperation. As Donoghue noted as early as 1959, a novelist like Faulkner succeeds as verse-dramatist where so many poets, confined to theatrical conventions, have failed. Those conventions prove recalcitrant to the poet's efforts to discover a form commensurate to the depths of individual modern experience. On the other hand, the novelist, released from theatrical conventions, may present large dramatic actions that focus a civilization in all its complexity.

T.S. Eliot believed verse has advantages over prose; there were possibilities of reinforcing and deepening the dramatic effect by the musical effect of a varied pattern of style. Tension would be slackened, though, when, for example, a character has to come off the high style and order a cup of coffee. Eliot tried in his plays to give characters credible speech that would also, almost surreptitiously, remain heightened. But, because actors look like real people, radical departures from credible speech are difficult to sustain. Finally, Eliot and other modern drama-tists struggled to construct, however artificially, a code that could be broken and affirmed, that would set limits to a hero's conduct. That is to say, to achieve an authoritative style, one must establish without showing one's hand a decorum of cere-mony, to dissolve realistic terms into a self-subsistent universe wherein the values of human choice and action can be assert-ed. One would have to affect the sublime, the elegiac, or the apocalyptic—and "get away with it," as Donoghue remarks. And to get away with it is to seize the opportunity of "framing one's own rules." Yet modern verse drama has discovered no truly satisfactory convention "by which the dramatist may indicate more of the truth about an agent than that agent may be expect-ed to know."[18] The omniscient dramatist cannot step forward to comment and expect to get away with it.

Faulkner's verse dramas, secured from theatrical conven-tions by the novelistic convention of authorial omniscience, get away with it. The Sole Proprietor of Yoknapatawpha County enjoyed the privilege of making an internally consistent world;

of defining human action against a convincing background of communal code and ceremony; of creating characters with a force of will behind their words and acts; and above all of devising strategies to establish and maintain a high style of epic, tragic, and comic decorum. He consistently *sees* his material as mythical. His poetics carries and lends necessary distance to events of tragic, mythical grandeur. His characters wear masks larger than life, and for them he contrives, as Albert Guerard observes, a "notlanguage" that tells you what is in a character's soul: "what the whole personality (conscious, preconscious, unconscious) would say if it could speak."[19] Indeed, Guerard surmises that Faulkner's view of his characters may well have been Mr. Compson's in *Absalom, Absalom!*: "people too as we see, and victims too as we are, but victims of a different circumstance, simpler and therefore, integer for integer, larger, more heroic and the figures therefore more heroic too, not dwarfed and involved but distinct, uncomplex who had the gift of loving once and dying once instead of being diffused and scattered creatures drawn blindly limb from limb from a grab bag and assembled."[20]

Realistic novels are usually submerged in the stream of time, the aesthetic equivalent of formlessness, but anti-realistic dramatic art demands that time be made important through ideas of order. Some sense of the timeless, of the sacred, is called for. Belief in (or merely the adoption of) the eschatological, that is, the doctrine of judgment and historical consummation, gives daily happenings an unrusting patina, and this, however mysterious, does fulfill a profound human need for family and corporate continuity. In the eschatological view, the past flows into the present, the timeless is co-existent in time, so that a person may incorporate into himself what is scattered and passing and give it a meaning and an identity. What we love, we become—other persons, the land—renewing without change what is free and growing as well as what is old and past.

Here, where it is not necessarily a question of Faulkner's belief in Christianity, we discern that his greatest works, taken singly or as a whole, dramatize the act of the mind in *defining* the relations of man to himself, to society, to history, and to the cosmos. His typical strategy is a *juxtaposition* of negative and positive polarities; he suspends dramatic illumination and choice until what is *not* (not-love, not-life) has exhausted its power in outrage and despair and then what *is* (love, life, no-time) returns us to wonder.[21] The defining mind produces dramatic structures so remarkably unified as to seem Aristotelian. In *The Sound and the Fury*, Dilsey's numinous reality defines the mad loveless world of the Compsons. Her positives are fourth after three prior negative sequences of narrative. So we have a reversal except that it is *our* peripeteia, the audience's. In *As I Lay Dying*, the positives of family and of community are defined by the negative of Addie Bundren's strategically located soliloquy from death-in-life and life-in-death. Addie's revealed wilful vindictiveness looks ahead to the "not-love" of characters in later books. In *Light in August*, the stories of Lena and Joe Christmas are juxtaposed throughout: timeless and time, life and death, community triumphing over alienation, comedy over tragedy. But these juxtapositions precipitate the climactic dramatic action whereby Gail Hightower defines and comes to knowledge of his own selfishness and is prepared to believe in the good of himself. The whole structure of *Absalom, Absalom!* is poised as powerfully and as delicately as the cornerstone of a Gothic arch on the moment of Quentin's surprised definition. "But that's not love. That's still not love." Self-love had established the matrix for Sutpen's tragedy and for the tragedy that eventually lost him both sons, in that moment when one son lay dead and the other became a fugitive from justice. And in *Go Down, Moses*, in Part IV of "The Bear," Ike McCaslin discovers why his family and the wilderness are accursed and consequently chooses to relinquish all forms of possession. Ike is "juxtaposed ...not against the wilderness but against the tamed land which was to have been his heritage," and he is "juxtaposed" against his kinsman and heritage; like the bear, who is "widowered childless and absolved of mortality," Ike paradoxically recovers the "nothing" of sacred earth and the "anonymity" of human brotherhood. Nevertheless, the peripeteia of *Go Down, Moses* is reserved for "Delta Autumn" when old Isaac realizes one cannot repudiate the inheritance of guilt: he is astonished and diminished by the fact that the old ritual of incestuous miscegenation has repeated itself in the white great-grandson and the part-black great-granddaughter of Carothers McCaslin. Such summaries as these leave much untold, but it is clear that Faulkner's structures of definition are a component of his poetics and provoke insights into moral values in human relationships.

Faulkner's rhetoric, it should be self-evident, reinforces the structures of definition. Reality is constantly being forced into corners in order to reveal its "uncomplex" and irreducible terms, usually by means of absolutes such as timeless, motionless, soundless, immemorial, eternal, indivisible, infallible, indestructible, and so on. This rhetoric, rightly available to him as novelist, has eluded the verse-dramatists *per se*.

We arrive, then, at a conclusion more surprising than we might have anticipated from our initial discussion of the historical consciousness in the literature of the Southern Renaissance. Faulkner's elevation of that consciousness into the poetics of verse drama means that his art, as all great art, transcends its time and place. We might expect the continuance of the southern tradition not only in the South but also in parts of the world where artists feel the need of "faraway country" to focus civilization. And, indeed, Faulkner's influence has helped a Colombian to write a masterpiece of "magic realism". I refer to *Cien Anõs de Soledad* or *One Hundred Years of Solitude* (1967) by Gabriel García Márquez.[22] The next Faulkner will appear, like as not, in China, Nigeria, or Peru.

Yet to speak of a "next Faulkner" is misleading. That is why, I believe, the concept of a Southern Renaissance is validated as an ongoing expression of literary vitality. If we may allow comparison of Faulkner with Shakespeare, let us welcome a William Styron as, say, an American and Southern John Donne.

Just as Shakespeare and the younger Donne represent different aspects of their times, so do Faulkner and the younger Styron. Faulkner creates the world of Yoknapatawpha and rules it omnisciently; Styron's voice is more intimate than Faulkner's and calls to mind the John Donne of playful and passionate lyrics, disconsolate elegies, urbane satires on human corruption, and, above all, of vehement, compassionate, and doom-haunted sonnets and sermons. Donne's world is no longer the fixed, timeless, sacramentalized one of the Middle Ages and Renaissance but a world that has lost the old coherence and, under pressure of that loss, has twisted itself into all kinds of restless and elaborate shapes connoting the fellowship of terror.

William Styron's sensibility seems remarkably similar to Donne's. Ostensibly Styron's novels address the tragic existential condition of victimization—by Freudian complexes, by systems of enslavement—and invite our feelings of pity and terror by making the central action (save in *The Long March*) one involving the persecution and death of a beautiful young woman. Yet the poetic urgency of these novels derives, Donne-like, from the refusal of God to reveal Himself, from, in other words, a metaphysical dilemma. How, Styron repeatedly inquires, can there be personal redemption in a world without God? "*Then what I done was wrong, Lord?* I said. *And if what I done was wrong, is there no redemption?*" Nat Turner's cry at the end of Part I of his *Confessions* (115) and toward the end of the novel (423) evokes a final Donne-like response as Nat experiences remorse at having killed the gentle, potentially loving Margaret Whitehead. To be purged of moral blindness, of self-absorption, and of the self-destructive element is, in Styron's world, to achieve a measure of salvation. Cass Kinsolving's retribution, Nat Turner's revolt, and Sophie Zawistowska's sexual rejuvenation together represent not only existentialist life-values but also, out of a victim's long subjugation by others and self-conviction of guilt, a form of spiritual reconstitution. Styron's affirmations of unity, though, are as precariously poised as Donne's—which is to say, more precariously than Faulkner's.

A southern writer is compelled to confront his inheritance of guilt and the historical loss of parental and social authority. Faulkner in one generation and Styron in another have made of their confrontations quite different fictions, but they share with one another and with other southern writers—and, curiously, with writers of seventeenth-century Europe—a refusal to abandon the notion of guilt or the quest for atonement. For them, the human drama still unfolds from a necessary correlation of the individual with society and of both with God. For them, mankind still desperately needs to be battered back into human wholeness.

ON READING FRANK WATERS

The protagonist of Frank Waters's novel, *The Man Who Killed the Deer*, is a Pueblo Indian caught between two worlds. Having been schooled in the White man's outlook—individualism, rationalism, and materialism—he is now recovering some Indian values such as intuition, the power of the unconscious, the sense of the sacredness of nature, and of the interconnectedness of all life. Rather than rejecting one culture in favor of another, the protagonist is actually reconciling duality and emerging into a higher consciousness. This emergence gives his story its representative quality. He is not an Indian boy returning to the blanket so much as he is a paradigm of modern man's evolution toward a new world of the mind.

The alternative to emergence, in Waters's view, is the prolongation of tragedy on a world scale. Our individualism, rationalism, and materialism, left unchecked and unbalanced, make us think of life as separation. There is even a long religious tradition to support this outlook, as for instance in Genesis 1:28, "Be fruitful and multiply, and replenish the earth, and subdue it." Created in God's own image and divinely commanded to subdue nature, man in the Judeo-Christian mythology is separated from nature. Yet, if we regard nature as an inanimate treasure house existing solely to be exploited for the material welfare of mankind, tragic consequences follow. Subjugation of nature has caused irremediable damage to earth, air, and water. Our own inner nature, consisting of unconscious forces, has often been repressed, and repression has produced a tragically disordered personality. Thus Waters observes in *Pumpkin Seed Point*:

> Our own minds and bodies became the battleground of man against nature, man against God, and man against himself, divided into two warring selves: reason and instinct, the conscious and the unconscious. [1]

Social, economic, political, and technological expedients cannot remedy this disorder. The remedy lies within the mind—if,
as Waters believes, we open it to "all the voices, shapes, and symbols through which intuition speaks to our inner selves."[2]
Consider a sentence from *Deer*: "So little by little the richness
and the wonder and the mystery of life stole in upon him." The
richness and the wonder and the mystery of life that steal in
upon the protagonist's awareness are his own intuition speaking
to his own inner self, healing divisions of man and nature, man
and God, and man against himself. In sum, Waters envisions values that could redeem modern culture, rescue our humanity,
and ultimately save us from ourselves.

A redemptive vision of this order lifts Frank Waters out of the
relative obscurity of the American Southwest into a position of
significance globally at the present time and in the immediate
future. Of course, we ask, why isn't he better known, why hasn't
he been recognized? I recall that as late as the 1950s Mark Twain
was not widely regarded as great enough for the literary canon.
Still, I don't know the answer to the question. But I do know that
some readers recognize him, perhaps several million to date. I,
myself, never heard of Frank Waters until 1982. Then, however,
on reading him, a recognition took place, a *shock* of recognition.
Why me? What experiences prepared me for this shock? In offering here a few personal anecdotes and reflections pertinent to
the dialogue that can take place between a reader and books, and
between the author of those books and a reader, I do not mean
to pretend that "my" discovery, so to speak, is of any more importance than discoveries by others. We all of us bring to a dialogue
perceptions and viewpoints shaped by different experiences,
influences, and circumstances. I can testify only to my own, for
what they might be worth.

I grew up ignorant not only of Waters but also, largely, of the
West. I didn't think of the West, until recently, as the heartland
of an ancient, complex civilization, nor did I think of it as a
region of high culture capable of producing great literature.
Where I grew up, the West seemed a cultural backwater, a

vague state of mind, or just something violent and empty that you saw at the movies. It so happened that I did, fortuitously, discover a western writer, Walter Van Tilburg Clark, one of the great ones. But the discovery of *The City of Trembling Leaves* when I was sixteen years old probably appealed more to my viscera than to the intellect. I had been prowling around the stacks of Duke Library in search of pictures of naked women. What I found were a few dogeared medical textbooks on anatomy, showing cadavers. The nomenclature was interesting, but the pictures were less than satisfactory for a teen-age sex-fiend. So, drifting to shelves of fiction, I seized and took home with me that big, new novel by Clark and became absorbed for a week in the story of a man's growing up in a weird place called Reno and his courtship of a pretty girl, their marriage and honeymoon camping out on the shores of Lake Tahoe. The honeymoon hooked me on the West. It seemed a different, sort of sexy place after that.

Nothing in my education prepared me to take a mythological approach to literature. Not until 1968, when, again quite by chance, I found in Blackwell's Book Shop in Oxford a four-volume study of world mythology, Joseph Campbell's *The Masks of God*, did I realize what I had missed. Those books so revolutionized my understanding of literature and of, in particular, the archetypal imagination, as to make my previous literary education seem obsolete. Undoubtedly, the discovery of Joseph Campbell contributed to my recognition of Frank Waters's myth-making genius. Still, growing up, I did have the fortune to learn enough about modern depth psychology to draw up a respect for it. Mind you, in those days Freud was fashionable, Jung a dirty word. But there were at Duke University two Jungians, the world's foremost parapsychologists, inventors of such household words as extra-sensory perception, or E.S.P.— Dr. Banks Rhine and his wife Louisa. They were family friends. I didn't learn much about psychology from them, but I did come to meet one of Dr. Rhine's former students, Dr. D.D. Holt, a Methodist minister, and Dr. Holt was a spiritual goldmine.

There in his church office were shelves loaded up with books on psychology. Many a summer's afternoon Dr. Holt devoted to explaining to me such esoteric notions as the collective unconscious and the integrated personality. We also discussed religion. Since I was incapable of swearing to a belief in the literal truth of the Apostles Creed, Dr. Holt persuaded me that its truth could be understood figuratively and psychologically. The Virgin, for example. Could it be that Dr. Holt prepared me to understand the Goddess Mother archetype so evident in Frank Waters's novels?

To my father, William Blackburn, I owe two teachings that have become passions with me: one, that the imagination is the essential creative spirit; two, that artistic and intellectual integrity must never by compromised. Since I am talking about myself as a reader of Frank Waters, I should say a few words about imagination and integrity.

It seemed to my father and it has always seemed to me that the recognition of imaginative power in a literary work is an indispensable criterion for any critical assessment of it. When it comes to deciding what sort of literature really matters to us, I believe we should award recognition on the basis of imaginative excellence, which is self-validating regardless of gender, race, culture, or nationality, and on the basis of vision as well as competence, wisdom as well as delightfulness, fullness as well as relevance. Moreover, in my belief, imaginative literature is the most reliable access to reality that we can have. My father's early lessons about the power and validity of the literary imagination kept open for me this possibility of a literature of vision. On reading Frank Waters, the possibility was confirmed.

My father taught me how precious the academic spirit is, how rare, even in academies, the disinterested love of truth may be, and how deprived a society forced to live without it. I am a person, I freely confess, who can be moved to tears by the evidence of integrity. I admire writers who risk all for truth, who dedicate their lives to a quest for truth, and who have no truck with sentimentality, which means to pass off on yourself feelings you don't really have. Many American writers, many of our best-known and popular writers, I am sorry to say, do not always meet the test of integrity. Insofar as I can tell, Frank Waters always meets it. Whether he is debunking the legend of Wyatt Earp (in *The Earp Brothers of Tombstone*) or he is interpreting the oral histories and religious symbols of an ancient and elusive people (in *Book of the Hopi*), he aims for truth, well-documented. He doesn't sentimentalize characters in his novels. An old woman (in *Pike's Peak*) is fond of chewing on her wart; Maria del Valle (in *People of the Valley*) clamps a cigarette with her single tooth; Inocencio (in *Flight From Fiesta*), though he will redeem himself, is one Indian who *is* usually drunk; Helen Chalmers (in *The Woman at Otowi Crossing*) is a saint, so sensitive she cannot bear to see a mushroom destroyed but so exuberant she loves to swim in the nude. Such realistic details and balanced portrayals constantly remind us of our common humanness and enhance, rather than subvert, Waters's dramatization of the richness and the wonder and the mystery of life. His open-minded quest for truth has made him the primary and often solitary literary voice for western America for most of the last half of this century.[3]

Why isn't he better known? I raised this question a while ago and said I didn't know the answer. But a partial answer lies in the integrity of his own approach to art. *The Yogi of Cockroach Court* was revised various times over a period of twenty years before its publication. The 1500-page Colorado trilogy of the 1930s was revised in the late 1960s as the 750-page *Pike's Peak*. *The Woman at Otowi Crossing*, begun in the early 1950s, was revised four times before its publication in 1966, and the definitive edition was not published until 1987. Although the conversion of *The Man Who Killed the Deer* into a film might have made Waters famous, out of respect for his Native American friends and for their way of life, he did not pursue the matter.

Ironically, millions of people who see Kevin Kostner in *Wyatt Earp*, a Lawrence Kasden film released in 1994, will be unwittingly getting some sense of Waters's *The Earp Brothers of Tombstone* in terms of narrative structure and dramatis personae.[4]

My first reading of *Otowi* in 1982 convinced me that Waters, previously unknown to me, was at the time, when it comes to breadth and depth of vision, America's greatest living writer. A couple of personal experiences prompted my special interest in that book. Permit me to relate them.

Quite early one afternoon in 1949, when I was a student in New Haven, Connecticut, I was suddenly seized by a feeling that my mother, then living in Richmond, Virginia, was in mortal danger. I had never before been possessed by such a strange feeling, and my mother, insofar as I knew, was in excellent health. The feeling embarrassed me, but it wouldn't go away. Finally I telephoned my mother's landlady in Richmond. She informed me that my mother was seriously ill with pneumonia and had been rushed to the hospital that very morning. Without further inquiry I took a Greyhound bus overnight to Richmond, went directly to the hospital, and found my surprised mother recovering nicely. But from what she told me, it was obvious that she had been close to death at the very moment, early the previous afternoon, when I had that overwhelming feeling. In Jungian psychology, this "ordinary" experience of a meaningful, acausally related coincidence in time would be called synchronicity. According to that theory, there is a ground of unity revealed in meaningful coincidence, a timeless reality that exists apart from our rational, linear perception of the dimensions of past, present, and future. A sense of this timelessness is wonderfully evoked in *The Woman at Otowi Crossing*, the protagonist of which experiences synchronicities.

The other experience happened after I graduated from Yale in 1951 and had volunteered as a private in the United States Army. Months later, precisely at the crack of dawn on October 29, I was lying in battle fatigues on a cold patch of desert sand in Nevada just as, six miles behind me, an atomic bomb exploded, fusing jagged mountain ranges over a hundred miles away with a white light, like billions of magnesium flares simultaneously ignited. I counted to five, then turned my head. There it all was, an obscenely beautiful fireball so large in diameter as to stretch from one end of the valley to another, and then the mushroom cloud. On an immediate level, *The Woman at Otowi Crossing* is the story of an "ordinary" middle-aged woman, Helen Chalmers, who has mystical visions, a fusion of self into the complete pattern of the universe, and terrifying precognitive dreams, the content of which appalls her—nothing less, as we know through dramatic irony, than A-bomb and H-bomb explosions. On another immediate level, the story chronicles the Atomic Age from the Manhattan Project through the Trinity Site explosion, Hiroshima, experiments in the Nevada desert, and the H-bomb explosion in the Marshall Islands.

I trust it can be seen from this summary that *Otowi* produced for me that shock of recognition.

When I included that novel in my "Great Books" course, many students responded to it more enthusiastically than to works by Homer, Dante, and Dostoyevsky. And consider this: just as I was gaining confidence in assessment of Waters as a great writer, there arrived in my mail a call for papers from The Frank Waters Society, of which I had never heard! After correspondence with its founder, Dr. Charles L. Adams, I was encouraged to submit an essay. A cautious lot, we academicians. When we have an unorthodox opinion, no matter how soundly conceived, we are apt to conceal it. So it was, when I joined the company of literary scholars who are seriously devoted to objective studies of Waters, I hesitated to speak, lest I find myself enveloped by flames. Finally in a stage whisper I declared to a colleague that I considered Waters a great writer. He was startled and looked me up and down quizzically. Then his face relaxed. "I'm so glad you said that, Alex," he said, "because that's exactly what I think, too. You know," he went on, "Frank Waters is probably the best-kept secret in twentieth-century American letters."

Mr. Waters came to Colorado Springs in 1983 to receive an honorary degree. That was when I first met him. As anyone can tell you who met Frank, he was the warmest, most friendly, unassuming person one is ever likely to encounter. But on this occasion I felt apprehensive. Once before I had met a writer of Mr. Waters's stature, William Faulkner, and Mr. Faulkner had been about as monumentally friendly as a face on Mt. Rushmore. I had dropped in on Mr. Faulkner one afternoon at the University of Virginia. As part of his duties as writer-in-residence there, he kept open office hours. One was encouraged by the English department to speak with the Nobel laureate. I found Mr. Faulkner seated in a swivel chair, smoking his pipe. After motioning me to a seat, he turned his back on me and said nothing. I waited, expecting him to say something eventually. After all, writers being dreamers, we permit them social license. After this silence continued for at least five minutes, I coughed and ventured a stupid question. "Sir," I asked, "what do you write about when you write?" There was a pause. Slowly Mr. Faulkner removed his pipe, swiveled around to blink at me and spoke in a low, weary Mississippi drawl. "Man in his eternal dilemma," he replied to my question. He pronounced it *dee-lee-muh.* Then he swiveled away from me and resumed smoking. This procedure repeated itself for an hour. Ask Mr. Faulkner's back a question, wait for the 180-degree turn, get the beauty of the oracle hot, watch the dreamer return to his mountain.[5] Now I was meeting Mr. Waters. Would he say, "Man in his eternal dee-lee-muh"? He wouldn't. He didn't. We were friends from the word go.

From 1984 through 1988, encouraged by Mr. Waters as well as by Dr. Adams, I familiarized myself with the Waters canon as well as I could, wrote tentative essays, and set about the task of overhauling my education. Now for the first time systematically, I was reading Jungian psychology, primitive, oriental, and occidental mythology; ancient Mesoamerican symbology; Native American cultural anthropology; Tibetan mysticism and the like. It became evident that a scientific movement in the direction of mysticism is extremely active, its basic assumption being that the universe *is* unfolding according to a hidden, dynamic, and "enfolded" order. The idea that matter is alive suddenly made sense of passages in Waters where he writes of living stones and great breathing mountains. The idea that matter is not only alive but shares with the human mind a common background source suddenly made sense of psychic landscape in all of Waters's novels from the time he began to write them in the 1920s: what he calls the "spirit of place" has a component in consciousness. After these discoveries, I no longer doubted the essential validity of Waters's prophetic vision. In 1988, I began to work on the book that was published in October, 1991, as *A Sunrise Brighter Still: The Visionary Novels of Frank Waters.*

There were ups and downs. Once while struggling to create a title for an essay to convey an image of Waters's originality, I whimsically proposed to him, "Homer of the Heartland." He wrote me as follows:

> Dear Alex: You poor guy, struggling to find a title! I know what that is, it's always been a problem to me. But now I've come up with the perfect one for you: THE BARD OF THE BOONDOCKS....

A couple of my "discoveries" turned out to be moonshine. Although Waters clearly belongs to the American literary tradition of Emerson and Melville, I seemed to find evidence that he was also influenced by, of all people, Edgar Allan Poe. The last line of Poe's *Narrative of Arthur Gordon Pym* yields the title of Waters's novel, *The Dust Within the Rock.* Moreover, Waters's first novel, *The Lizard Woman,* is an imaginary voyage like Poe's *Narrative.* But when I asked Mr. Waters about this work by Poe, he responded that he had not only never read it, but also he had never heard of it! Where the title of *The Dust Within the Rock* came from, he could not recall. Scratch Poe. Then, another time, I thought I could prove that Waters was influenced by Jung as early as 1938—a significant date inasmuch as two of his masterpieces, *People of the Valley* and *The Man Who Killed the Deer,* were composed after that. The evidence? Mr. Waters had made a remark to me about having had access, in Taos, New Mexico, to Mabel Dodge Luhan's library, which contained volumes by Jung, "after 1938." But I had jumped to conclusions. Mr. Waters soon clarified the matter. True, the Luhan library had been opened to him in 1938, but he had never read Jung until the mid-1940s, after publication of *People* and *Deer*. Fortunately, once the supposed "influences" were cleared off, the case for Waters's originality was dramatically improved. He had, so to say, anticipated the findings of modern depth psychology, even gone beyond them.

The day came when I mailed Mr. Waters a completed manuscript. This is what he wrote:

> Congratulations, Alex, on finishing your study of my books. A long and tedious job, and a work of love and intuitive perception. I often am sorry I didn't help you more, but I think I might have got in your way & wanted to give you full rein.

Pleased as I am by the publication of the book and by its favorable reviews—the reviewer in *American Literature* suggested that Waters is indeed as important a writer as Faulkner.[6] I could ask no finer reward than that of Mr. Waters's letter.

The thought that characterizes and informs Waters's books has been far from the mind of the literary and cultural establishment these past fifty years. But now it is on the cutting edge of just about everything we take seriously in this country: multiculturalism, the natural environment, and our political, ecological, and spiritual relationship with the future. Dr. Adams and I nominated Frank Waters continuously from 1985 to 1993 for the Nobel Prize in Literature, but his death in 1995 at the age of 92 means that recognition of his greatness will come posthumously, as it did for Melville. One day, though, his name will be known to untold millions of readers, not least because, in the middle of the twentieth century, he projected the shape of what is now tomorrow, with a feeling called hope.

WATERS AND MODERN FICTION

There are at least three levels of response to the novels of Frank Waters. On the first level, Waters is identified as a regional writer whose subject matter is confined to western history and cultural anthropology. Thus, for example, *The Man Who Killed the Deer* is read as if it were an "Indian" novel of a certain time and place, whereas in fact it is a universal allegory that never presumes to perceive the world from within a Native American consciousness. On a second level, Waters is identified as a mystical philosopher for whom fictional form is merely a convenient containment of an order of intellect and an order of morality that have not been organized in the order of art. The fallacy of this response is the belief that ideas in fiction have a foreknown existence and can be smuggled into narrative as a preconceived set of themes. Ideas in art, however, do not exist at all except in some predetermined order of art. A third level of response is therefore needed, and it is the critical one. Waters is a novelist whose vision has its source in the creative spirit of the archetypal imagination and its achievement in art. When his novels are read as works of art, Waters assumes his rightful place in the great tradition of modern fiction.

Not so long ago there was general agreement about the great tradition of modern fiction. It began with Gustave Flaubert, whose *Madame Bovary*, published in 1856, was held rigorously to an ideal of artistic objectivity and accepted as the triumph of realism in French literature. The tradition then passed, as it were, to Henry James, whom Flaubert had befriended in Paris in 1875-76. Flaubert, for James, was "the inspiring image"[1] and "the novelist's novelist,"[2] and much of what James wrote about the art of fiction and put into practice in his own novels remained indebted to the Flaubertian ideal. The bond of friendship between James and Joseph Conrad then helped to inspire Conrad in the theory and practice of the art of fiction. Thereafter the great tradition gathers in its sweep James Joyce,

Virginia Woolf, E.M. Forster, William Faulkner, and others, including F. Scott Fitzgerald, who re-read *Madame Bovary* every year with a devotion that other believers might reserve for the Bible. From the point of view of this tradition, at least in the 1950s, some writers did not measure up to its ideals. H.G. Wells spurned "art" in favor of journalism, D.H. Lawrence only occasionally mastered his emotions, Thomas Wolfe simply disgorged the raw material of his experience, John Dos Passos desperately attempted to control his materials through structural manipulation, and John Steinbeck used lyrical interruptions to disguise the limitations of his methods. Clearly, the demands upon the artist in fiction are great, for he or she must have a devoted fidelity to the medium, that we, the readers, may discover the subject matter and the meanings of which the matter is capable. But the rewards, too, are great. The journalists and the sentimentalists and the autobiographers with their bulletproof egoism are soon forgotten, whereas artists loom larger with the passage of time. They do indeed forge in the smithy of the soul the uncreated conscience of the race.

Summarizing the ideals of modern fiction, Mark Schorer in "Technique as Discovery" (1948) holds it as axiomatic that technique alone objectifies the materials of art and alone measures them, defining the values of experience by means of selection, structure, and language, itself, as used to create larger meanings beyond ordinary speech. When we speak of technique, then, we mean something more exacting than the arrangements of events to create plot; or, within plot, of suspense and climax; or as a means of revealing character motivation, relationship, and development; or as the use of point of view as some nearly arbitrary device for the heightening of dramatic interest through the narrowing or broadening of perspective upon the material, rather than as a means toward the positive definition of theme. Technique, of course, is all those obvious forms that are usually taken to be the whole of it. But modern fiction insists upon technique that separates the artist from his material, thereby not only containing intellectual and moral implications, but also discovering them—"values in an area of experience which, for the first time *then*, are being given."[3] A technical virtuosity of the surface cannot rival the technique that achieves as its subject matter all the untractable elements of spirit beneath the surface of experience, for the discovered subject matter of modern fiction is "not some singleness, some topic or thesis, but the whole of the modern consciousness."[4] A novelist inevitably utilizes experience, but he utilizes it in such a way that it is transformed into a pattern, and that pattern *is* the novel, something that has pulled away from the purely social and secular contexts of the life out of which it was coming. In sum, what Schorer is saying about the way meaning enters and is rendered in fiction requires that technique be viewed as the texture of metaphors which, by their quality, determine the theme and even the structure of a novel, its symbolic properties, and ultimately the special character of the mind behind it.

Implied by Schorer but not emphasized is the religious, mystical, and mythic mode of consciousness that has sometimes shaped modern fiction. The search of Flaubert and James for beauty through form was, at bottom, an attempt to transcend spiritual and cultural disabilities and to re-connect with the most central meanings of human life. Where Flaubert is concerned, it was the romantic, the idealist, the mystic who was driven to the representation of material reality in order, somehow, to get beyond it. Consider these excerpts from his letters:

> L'auteur, dans son oeuvre, doit être comme Dieu dans l'univers, present partout, et visible nulle part. (It is necessary for the author in his work to be like God in the universe, everywhere present and in nothing visible).[5]

> La vérité matérielle (ou ce qu'on appelle ainsi) ne doit être qu'un tremplin pour s'élever plus haut.

> (Material truth, or what might be called that, ought to be an inclined plane for lifting us higher).[6]

> Sans l'amour de la forme, j'eusse êtê peut-être un grand mystique. (Without the love of form, I perhaps would have been a great mystic).[7]

> Dans l'Art aussi c'est le fanatisme de l'Art qui est le sentiment artistique. La poésie n'est qu'une manière de percevoir les objects extérieurs, un organe spécial qui tamise la matière et qui, sans la changer, la transfigure. (In Art also it is the fanaticism of Art which is the artistic sentiment. Poetry is only a manner of perceiving exterior objects, a special organ that extracts matter and that, without changing it, transfigures it).[8]

Expression is creation, and technique makes reality, transfiguring "matter" or external objects into something else that assumes a life of its own. That is why, contrary to what one might expect of the so-called realism of *Madame Bovary*, its heroine, victim of romantic illusions, comes through to us on a grand scale of dignity. Flaubert as omniscient author and ironist has so powerfully communicated his hatred of the "real," that is, the *bourgeoisie*, that poor Emma, muse of the imagination, is elevated in value. As structured, that novel has a double consciousness, that of a central figure who suffers from a lack of fine awareness of reality and that of a concealed narrator who knows all that Emma could not possibly know and who reflects her fate in its full spiritual dimensions. In the critical language of Flaubert's day, the thematic conflict of *Madame Bovary* consists in the tension between the "real" and the "romantic," and while romantic illusions are exposed and ruined, the moral and spiritual possibilities inherent in creativity have not lost their validity. Flaubert, far from reducing the range of fiction, showed us how to *extend* it honestly, how to include, in a proper structure, both the exposition of the naturalistic surface of life and the invocation of a "higher" reality, the creative spirit itself, whether we call it the romantic, the ideal, the mystical, or the visionary.

James thought to improve upon Flaubert's art through the technique of a center of consciousness. Unlike Emma Bovary, his central figures would have the intelligence to *see* reality, after which disillusionment they would seek a personal salvation adopting a moral code based upon tragic knowledge acquired from experience. James's method, as distinct from Flaubert's, was to present the dramatic conflict of the romantic and the real from within a restricted point of view and to place a central character, such as Lambert Strether in *The Ambassadors*, where he would undergo most intensely a "process of vision."[9] The fascinating aspect of this procedure is that the culmination of a character's perception is so contrived as to bring the *reader* to the same moment of truth. Percy Lubbock describes the procedure in *The Ambassadors*:

> To bring his mind into view at the different moments, one after another, when it is brushed by new experience—to make a little scene of it, without breaking into hidden depths where the change of purpose is proceeding—to multiply these glimpses until the silent change is apparent, though no word has actually been said of it: this is Henry James's way, and though the *method* could scarcely be more devious and roundabout, always refusing the short cut, yet by these very qualities and precautions it finally produces the most direct impression, for the reader has *seen.*[10]

What this means, apart from James's desire to share a complex vision, is that the dramatically structured novel offers the greatest opportunity for revelation of the "hidden depths" where life suddenly opens up to some fateful realization of where *we* are. True, James's vision is largely social and moral—

and Conrad's would make it entirely so, as would Hemingway's—but there are moments in James when, like his brother William, he envisions the possibilities of which our minds, operating in society, are capable.

So here we have in Flaubert and James, early masters of the technique of modern fiction, the high aim of reaching beyond material reality and its alienating effects to reveal a new world. And that is the high aim of the visionary novels of Frank Waters, an aim realized in a technique remarkably similar in its methods to that of the masters in the achievement of its subject matter.

Waters's essays on literature show him preoccupied with fiction that reveals universal order as a cause-and-effect relationship. Two of these essays are pertinent here, "Relationships and the Novel," published in 1943, and "Visions of the Good: What Literature Affirms and How," a lecture presented in 1986 at a writers' conference in Winona, Minnesota.[11] In the 1943 essay, Waters rejects adherence to orthodox form and declares the main function of the novel to be "to reveal the relationship between man and his surrounding universe" (105). This relationship is "continually increasing, expanding" in a revolutionary world wherein modern man "finds himself alone in a vaster space with the debris of all his former securities, comforts and beliefs tumbling about him" (106). When the artist catches the "vital inter-connectedness" of characters, or that between people and the conditions of their place and time, "this relation builds up its own inherent, proper form" (107). Waters illustrates his theme with George Stewart's *The Storm*, a novel that reveals the cause-and-effect relationship between a force of nature and the people and things affected by its destructive passage. *The Storm* is thus a "significant" novel because it reveals "a relation to something pertinent in all our lives that we have formerly ignored as nebulous and abstract" (107). Something as impersonal yet as alive as a force of nature fulfills the "essential purpose" (105) of a novel, truly universalizing its meaning. In other words, our connection to the universe, not

the traditional interplay of character and society, is the ultimate concern of the novelist.

In the unpublished 1986 lecture Waters defines the function
of literature in its higher forms above entertainment and
escape as visionary and prophetic, "something that reveals the
purpose of our existence, gives us a vision of our potential creativity, and helps to raise our level of consciousness." Literature
is both "a repository of the past" and a "glimpse, as it were, of
something beyond our temporal existence." A vision "affirms or
suggests that the world and man, matter and spirit, are one, and
that some strange power helps to direct the course of our lives."
Waters sees this vision reflected in myths of all races, in the
plays of Shakespeare, in the novels of Dostoevsky, D.H.
Lawrence, Faulkner and Isak Dinesen, and in "America's greatest novel," *Moby Dick*. Visionary works of literature "possess the
common quality of awakening in us a sense of something transcendental somewhere 'out there' beyond us or 'in there' within us." But in what literary manner is the transcendental communicated? Specifically, it is communicated as "the nebulous
influence of fate, destiny, nemesis, karma, whatever we call it."
This influence can be personalized, as in the Fates of Greek
mythology, objectified, as in *Moby Dick*, or impersonalized, as
in the East's concept of karma, but its essence is "that every
intent and action causes eventually a compensating effect."
Representation of the influence is a perception of a "law of universal moral order that guides our continual 'becoming' ...and
our development to a higher level of consciousness...." Because
intuitive awareness of a purposive law guiding our existence
"lies in each of us," the higher forms of literature and myth can
bring that law's influence to "conscious recognition."

At first glance, Waters's idea of a transcendental function of
literature may seem better suited to myth and drama than to
the modern novel. However, if we return for a peek at
Flaubert's letters, we find that the novelist's novelist considered
as the artist's highest and most difficult goal his awakening of
our intuitive and unconscious sense of life:

> Ce qui me semble, à moi, le plus haut dans l'Art (et le plus difficile), ce n'est ni de faire rire, ni de faire pleurer, ni de vous mettre en rut ou en fureur, mais d'agir à la façon de la nature, c'est-à-dire de *faire rêver*. (It seems to me, myself, that the highest effect of Art, and the most difficult to achieve, is neither to make us laugh nor to make us cry nor to arouse our rage and fury but to produce an effect after the manner of nature, that is to say make us *dream*).[12]

We recall, too, that the whole effect at which James aimed in dramatizing a process of vision was also to be an awakening of our sense of meaningful life. The most beautiful works of art, these masters of fiction are saying, convey a serene and pitiless aspect, a kind of imperturbability that is effected by an idea of order.

Waters's novels communicate an idea of universal moral order. In *The Yogi of Cockroach Court* the idea is translated as karma and in *The Man Who Killed the Deer* as conscience; in *Pike's Peak*, the idea of order is represented as Self, or Absolute Consciousness, and those terms also can be used to describe the protagonist's experience of totality in *The Woman at Otowi Crossing*. The idea of order in *People of the Valley* is conveyed by an intricate pattern of imagery that resolves the contradiction between technological civilization and the values of a rural microcosm.

The technique that creates vision in these novels depends upon double consciousness: an omniscient point of view and a center of consciousness. When these viewpoints collide, ironies are released, as for example when Tai Ling, Rogier, and Martiniano are searching for selfhood in the wrong manner. When the viewpoints coalesce, as they eventually do in every Waters novel (even in *Pike's Peak*, with the introduction of March Cable as a new center), Waters lets us glimpse, as he says, "something that reveals the purpose of our existence, gives us a vision of our potential creativity, and helps to raise our level of consciousness."

Although some current critical theories hold in disfavor—if not in contempt—the idea that imagination is an essential power and quality of spirit and would like to regard as either willful or nostalgic the critic who speaks of "vision" in literature, it seems to me self-evident that vision is a force in which a writer feels implicated. It is the power, as Denis Donoghue asserts, "of making fictions and making sense of life by that means."[13] Colin Falck, who sees as our most urgent current need in literary theory the restoration of the concepts of truth or of vision to our discussions of literature, goes further. Literature and literary criticism, he argues, "may need to be prepared to embrace, and to subsume, religion and theology if they are to discover or to rediscover their own spiritual meanings."[14] Through myths or imaginative archetypes, Falck believes, art can reach beyond the appearances of ordinary life into reality, itself, and restore to its dignity the notion of ontological truth.

Jungian and Campbellian aesthetics support this view of vision. Jung warns us against reducing the visionary to personal factors or dismissing as illusion the vision that defies rational understanding. The vision, he writes, "is not something derived or secondary, and it is not a symptom of something else. It is true symbolic expression—that is, the expression of something existent in its own right, but imperfectly known."[15] Joseph Campbell discerns four functions of a mythology: mystical, cosmological, sociological, and psychological. The first function is to reconcile waking consciousness to the mystery of the universe as it is. The second function is to render an interpretative total image of the same. The third function is to shape the individual to the requirements of his social group. And the fourth function is to foster the centering and unfolding of the individual in integrity, in accord with himself, his culture, the universe, and the "ultimate mystery which is both beyond and within himself and all things." According to Campbell, the failure in modern centuries of the sociological function of a mythology has put the individual on his own. Consequently it is lived experience, not tribal or dogmatic authority, which leads to "creative symbolization." A creative mythology restores to existence the quality of adventure, at once shattering and reinterpreting the fixed, already known, in the sacrificial creative fire of the becoming thing that is no thing at all but life, not as it *will be* or as it *should be*, as it *was* or as it *never will be*, but as it *is*, in depth, in process, *here and now*, inside and out.

Creative myth, Campbell continues, "springs from the unpredictable, unprecedented experience-in-illumination of an object by a subject, and the labor, then, of achieving communication of the effect," by calling upon the "world's infinitely rich heritage of symbols, images, myth motives, and hero deeds." Ultimately, the art required is to make sounds, words, and forms

> open out in back, as it were, to eternity, and this requires of the artist that he should himself, in his individual experience, have touched anew that still point in this turning world of which the immemorial mythic forms are the symbols and guarantee.

The creative energy of the whole is in each of us, bare of egohood, and the individual is thereby mythologically considered as "Lord of the World Center," a *kosmogonos*, creator of all higher consciousness by means of "cosmogonic power."[16]

The connection between creative mythology and literary form now needs to be made. Many years ago, G. Wilson Knight, the British critic and novelist, proposed that the way to read Shakespeare is to regard each play as a visionary whole and then to work into the heart of each play:

> Each incident, each turn of thought, each suggestive symbol throughout *Macbeth* or *King Lear* radiates inwards from the play's circumference to the burning

central core without knowledge of which we shall miss their relevance and necessity: they relate primarily, not directly to each other, nor to the normal appearances of human life, but to this central reality alone.[17]

This, it seems to me, is a sound critical procedure for the reading of any creative artist whose vision of reality has carried him or her beyond the confines of superficial appearances. The remarkable aspect of Knight's approach, however, is not the distinction between appearances and reality but the assumption that certain literary forms are geometrical, having a central core, like the hub of a wheel, enveloped by circumstance. For, in mythological symbolization, the spoked wheel is the turning world, and the hub is like Self, or Emerson's eternal ONE, holding all fast. Such a geometry of the spirit helps us to visualize not only the form of a particular play or novel but also the form of an entire *oeuvre*, the sum of an artist's work. The focus of such visualization is on the hub ("the burning central core"), on a Power which is the apriority of space and time in the Here and Now that, radiating outwards, becomes Everywhere and Always.

Campbell identifies this power in world mythologies as the Goddess Mother of the universe. "It is into and through her," he writes, "that the god-substance pours into the field of space and time in a continuous act of world-creative self-giving."[18] The power is ontological, that is, having to do with the essence of things, and cosmogonic, that is, having to do with creative evolution. It is not, this power, "out there," to be sought and found in transcendence, but is to be recognized in oneself, in every individual and in all things.

The search for beauty through form in modern fiction, we can repeat, was an attempt to transcend spiritual and cultural disabilities and to re-connect with the most central meanings of human life. I believe that there is a core of such meanings in the novels of Waters and that it can be identified in the affairs of humankind as Creative Man. The human individual in these novels is constantly and truly visualized as seated at the hub of life, at the *axis mundi*, at the intersection of time and space. The seat of true religiosity, Waters writes in "Mysticism and Witchcraft,"

> is not the great formalized church but the human heart. Only here is lit that spark of mystical apperception which illuminates, if only for an instant, the darkness of our inner selves and the totality of the universe about us. By it we will realize that in the human atom resides all the creative power and all the time we need to transform this catastrophic era into an age more fruitful than any we have known.[19]

The human heart (meaning, of course, the mind) is the center, not unlike James's center of consciousness. Around it are ever widening circles of relationship and finally the cosmic circle itself. This is the geometrical figure with which, for example, *The Man Who Killed the Deer* begins and ends. When Palemon is seeking Martiniano on the mountain, he sees a boulder "marked with the strange signs of the Old Ones—a circle enclosing a dot...." Then at the end of the novel, as Martiniano is watching the Indian pilgrims dance in a circle, he reflects, "A man drops but a pebble into the one great lake of life, and the ripples spread to unguessed shores, to congeal into a pattern even in the timeless skies of night." As John R. Milton has shown, the large space and the small space have been brought into juxtaposition, and then, after Martiniano has at last grasped the meaning of the Deer, these spaces are congealed into one pattern.[20] And we see Martiniano *in* the center of the larger spaces of earth and stars. As Creative Man he unifies everything in the picture—and in the novel.

But this unifying function of Creative Man is more than a spatial form horizontally or one-dimensionally perceived as in the image of the dot within the circle or of the individual as centered within the cosmos. Creative Man is perceived in depth, the third dimension of space that translates into time, the fourth. As Quay Grigg observes about Waters's time-space, here-and-now, "Einsteinian" geometry of spirit, there is at its core a vertical image akin to a mountain peak. Waters's *oeuvre* is modeled, Grigg finds, "not on our rational, separate perception of time *and* space, but upon those denizens of the unconscious who point both backward and forward in time, and who float like mountain peaks above the dimension of space."[21] In other words, our usual perception of dimensions—past, present, future, length, breadth, depth—is configured as, instead, a mythic timelessness that, far from being static, is in paradoxical process of standing still and of being vertically heightened. It follows, I think, that at the visionary core of a novel by Waters the creative powers of the universe are centered in an individual and are therein emergent.

Creative Man, who is center of consciousness and the creator of all higher consciousness, is a composite of these individuals. In *Yogi* the horizontal plane of mundane consciousness is crossed by the vertical plane of supramundane consciousness, the plane of Tai Ling's search and eventual illumination. In *People*, Maria del Valle's hawk-like eyes survey the world from a mountain top, and her life integrates the vertical plane from it to the womb-valley below. The tragedy of Rogier is that, in the psychological sense, he seeks selfhood *in* the mountain when his own inner self *is* the peak, the world's center. The experience of Helen Chalmers in *Otowi* is her breakthrough into the fourth dimension and her realization, in the words that begin the novel, *"There is no such thing as time as we know it. The entire contents of all space and time co-exist in every infinite and eternal moment."* Helen exists for us in a time-space continuum, a centering and a towering of the human spirit. All of these characters, including Martiniano but with Rogier excepted, represent Creative Man, Helen above all. She is the most fully realized and warmly beautiful manifestation of Creative Man, and the mystical, cosmological, and psychological functions of creative mythology have in her been brought into masterful focus in depth, in process, here and now. Creative Man reconciles waking consciousness to the mystery of the universe as it is, renders a total image of the same, and fosters the centering and unfolding of the individual in accord with self, culture, the universe, and that ultimate mystery which is both transcendent and immanent. Hence there is in most of Waters's visionary novels an immediacy and emotional power of mythical happenings, a power that can only be conveyed as a sense of Creative Man's ever becoming within a duration of time which has no beginning or end and within a continuum of space which is boundless.

Creative Man—this composite of Lee Marston (in *The Lizard Woman*, Waters's first novel), Tai Ling, March Cable, Maria del Valle, Martiniano, Palemon, Edmund Gaylord, and Helen Chalmers—is artistically achieved subject matter, a projection through original flesh-and-blood characters of a new world of the mind. The Emergence of this Creative Man brings a vision of new, higher consciousness to American and modern world literature. One might say that this vision is a culminating instance of the trajectory of modern fiction. Waters's vision of our common humanity in process of creative enlargement engenders a feeling of hope for modern mankind and a sense of new and authentic beginnings, bringing to fruition the aspirations of the modern masters that what must emerge from the art of the novel would be more intensely alive than the naturalistic surface of life.

V. Atomic Age

ARCHETYPAL PROMISE FROM APOCALYPTIC PREMISE

It seems strange to me now that when I first arrived I was not conscious of the myth beginning to take form. Not only the myth of the Project on top of the mesa, but the myth at its foot, at Otowi Crossing. Only now can one realize they were two sides of the same coin, neither of which could have existed without the other. Both growing, as all myths must grow, with agonizing slowness and in secrecy. Forming one myth as we know it now—perhaps the only true myth of these modern times.

[*Otowi*, 74][1]

This statement attributed to Dr. Edmund Gaylord, an atomic physicist who has awakened from his sleep in conscious will and instinctive behavior and who seeks a new world of the human spirit, is part of Frank Waters's most original fictionalized attempt to resolve the apparent contradiction between science and mysticism, matter and mind, reason and intuition. The myth of the Project, which is based on the discovery of a New World of enormous physical energy locked inside the atom, is evidently one polarized to consciousness, with its credo of rationalism, materialism, and the concept of linear time. The myth of the Woman at Otowi Crossing, which is based on the discovery of a New World of enormous psychic energy locked inside the mind, is evidently one polarized to the unconscious, with its powers of perception of and being within the wholeness and timelessness of Creation.[2] These myths are said to be "one myth," complementary and united or reconciled, "perhaps" a single psychophysical energy—Absolute Consciousness, or Irreducible Reality—that may be realized once humanity has evolved to a new and higher stage of awareness. *The Woman at Otowi Crossing* presents Waters's mature novelistic vision of Emergence.

What might be surprising is Gaylord's earlier misconception of his own intellectual powers and of the methods of science that he has applied in helping to bring about atomic and thermonuclear explosions. But it is a historical misconception deeply engrained in our thinking, not easily remedied; and it is shared by many scientists still today who, while conducting experiments based on the matter-energy equation and on the relativity theory that events occur in a space-time continuum, are reluctant to discard the outmoded Newtonian view of a mechanistic universe. This situation, reported by such scientific philosophers as Arthur Koestler, Fritjof Capra, and F. David Peat, may well have its source in the Western idea of "mind."[3] When science is properly conceived, it is creative, its processes of thinking vividly intuitive, subjective, and irrational until after the experimental event. Science, like mysticism, depends on the unconscious mind. Scientific thought, properly conceived, is compatible with mysticism and a principal manifestation of individual, unenforced spiritual experience. But of course scientific thought is seldom so conceived: science is believed to be a branch of knowledge that operates predominantly with abstract symbols whose entire rationale is objectivity, logicality, and verifiability.

From this a paradox arises. Should the creative act emerging from unconscious mentation be regarded as depthlessly conscious? It arose with modern science, itself, under the influence of Descartes, who identified "mind" with consciousness alone, as if conscious and unconscious experiences belong to different, opposed, and irreconcilable compartments. Although the concept of the unconscious is an ancient one, it has for more than three centuries evoked a feeling of wary skepticism that, in turn, blocks the way to psychic integration with our individual selves and to comprehension of a worldview of everything in the universe being interrelated and interdependent. That has long been Eastern mysticism's worldview, and Einsteinian physics and Jungian psychology have only in the twentieth century begun to approximate it and to synthesize the insights of East and West. At the present time, at the end of the twentieth century, there are signs of change indicated in the titles of popular scientific books such as *The Tao of Physics*, *The Dancing Wu Li Masters*, and *Synchronicity: The Bridge Between Matter and Mind*—and in the characterization of an atomic physicist in *The Woman at Otowi Crossing*. For the most part, however, modern science has ignored and continues to ignore the grave and the constant in human affairs: the unconscious and its archetypes.

And now this same one-sided, materialistic, and hubristic science has bequeathed to the world since 16 July 1945, when the first atomic bomb was detonated in New Mexico, the apocalyptic premise to survival, the possibility of annihilation of all life as we know it.[4] Although Waters does not personally believe that such a dire catastrophe awaits us, the development of this power of destruction has occurred when, by all accounts, modern culture has reached a highly alarming stage of crisis of social, ecological, moral and spiritual dimensions.[5] Today there are no boundaries, and the old ethnically oriented mythologies which centered authority in gods "aloft" rather than in the individual human spirit are dying except in archaic cultures. Humanity faces man-made apocalypse at the very moment in history when the archetypal promise of myth, individually centered yet universal in meaning, has only begun to announce itself through creative minds as if urgently summoned to our aid from the depths of the unconscious psyche.

Therein, I think, lies the prophetic greatness of *The Woman at Otowi Crossing*. Begun in 1953, though not published until 1966 and even then not brought out in a definitive edition until

1987, the novel carries forward and enlarges on a comparison-contrast developed in 1950 in Waters's *Masked Gods*: the atomic reactor at Los Alamos and the Sun Temple of Mesa Verde, considered as allegories about physical and psychic energies, reveal that "both the transformation of matter into energy, and the transfiguration of instinctual forces into creative energy depend upon the reconciliation of the primal dual forces of all life" (*Masked Gods*, 421-22).[6] By preempting the fission-fusion language for nuclear energy as a metaphor for a psychological conflict resulting in release of new energy, Waters was prepared within a few short years after the Hiroshima bombing on 6 August 1945 to accept the Atomic Age as a revelation of reality (albeit an age tragically introduced in a destructive form) and to confront the apocalyptic premise—that one nuclear war forecloses the future—with the archetypal promise of the creative myth of Emergence. If we evaluate an author's achievement not only with respect to the ordinary recalcitrance of his materials but also with respect to the magnitude of conflict imaginatively confronted and artistically contained, *Otowi* will have to be considered as perhaps the supreme visionary novel in world literature at present. Although many modern novelists have confronted the facts of death in the self and in the heart of culture, it is Waters who convincingly invigorates the primal powers constituting hope.

While he was writing *Masked Gods*, Waters was influenced by aspects of Jungian psychology and was in particular drawn to Jung's idea of a "reconciling symbol" as explained in M. Esther Harding's *Psychic Energy* (1947). According to the theory, a solution to conflict will not appear in the form of an intellectual conclusion or in a change in conscious attitude, such as might be brought about by education or precept, but will develop spontaneously in the unconscious, arising as an image or symbol that has the effect of breaking the deadlock. The potency of the reconciling symbol "avails not only to bring the impasse to an end but also to effect a transformation or modification of the instinctive drives within the individual. This corresponds in the personal sphere to that modification of the instincts that, at least in some measure, has been brought about in the race through the ages of cultural effort."[7] Almost incredible as this proposition seems, the psychological imperative to bring about a radical change in the instincts and a promotion of human development has long been believed to be possible in the East, in the various forms of yoga, for instance. The reconciling symbol leads, Waters feels, "whole races, nations, and civilizations in great bursts of creative energy to another Emergence, a new stage of consciousness" (*Masked Gods*, 410). He speculates that such a symbol might be the circle: just as in relativity theory "a ray of light-energy travelling from the sun at 186,000 miles per second will describe a great cosmic circle," so the "evolutionary Road of Life completes its circuit by returning to its source" (*Masked Gods*, 434). He further speculates that a phenomenon such as telepathy points to the possibility of future emergence, through the unconscious, to a psychological fourth dimension in which past, present, and future are "coexistent" (*Masked Gods*, 431).

These speculations would help to shape the theme of *The Woman at Otowi Crossing*. Through an imperative of the unconscious, the protagonist breaks through to a mystical experience of timelessness, finds a solution to conflict, and emerges to an awareness that is, so to say, the paradigm for cultural transformation. Likened to a mandala-shaped kiva, the protagonist is, herself, a kind of personification of a reconciling symbol. By counterpointing the myth of the Project and the myth of the Woman at Otowi Crossing and unifying these in the myth of Emergence, Waters shapes for those who can respond to it a vision for the future, in which world crisis is resolved on a higher plane of at-one-ment with the cosmos.

The rediscovery of the unconscious mind and of its capacity for spontaneously releasing the energy of archetypes as solutions to crisis is of the highest interest in contemporary consideration of the "death of mankind."[8] The unconscious mind has power to effect alteration of our inner life and of the outer forms in which life finds expression and support. The promise of the unconscious mind lies in its creativity.

But if creativity may free us from a plunge into world catastrophe, is it not also a form of human motivation? Early twentieth-century psychology, influenced by Freud, reduced motivation to escape from anxiety and tended to leave out of account activities that might be self-rewarding and urges that might be independent of such biological drives as hunger, sex, and fear. Nowadays, nonreductionist theories have dramatically revealed the deleterious effects of protracted stimulus starvation as well as the organism's need for more or less constant stimulation, or at least a steady flow of information—a hunger for experience and thirst for excitation probably as basic as hunger and thirst, themselves. In other words, living organisms exhibit an exploratory drive and demonstrate an essential creativity. It follows that what is self-rewarding can be at the same time self-transcending and other-rewarding, and here, at the psychological rather than at the consciously ethical level, we encounter our gift for empathy. In the manifestations of the unconscious, such as in dreams, the boundaries of the self are fluid. One can be oneself and somebody else simultaneously. The gift for empathy then activates our participatory emotions, those that answer the human need for meaning whereby the self is experienced as part of a totality, which may be God, nature, and mankind. Therefore, the full human self is a power for human survival because in its most developed representatives—in mystics, for example—a whole new body of possibilities is brought into the field of experience, breaking the crust of closed societies and opening them to the perception of dimensions in which all life is timelessly incorporated as a unity.[9]

And so we come to see that a process of emergence to a higher consciousness, in which rational consciousness is reconciled with the unconscious, becomes the realization of a common humanity and an orientation in the direction of world culture. Mankind's development is then not determined by catastrophe but by, in Waters's philosophy, "the periodic synchronization of human and cosmic rhythms" (*Mexico Mystique*, 274). As consciousness expands to relate the inner life of man to his material outer world, the cataclysmic changes that many people have predicted since the release of atomic energy may prove instead to be transformation into a new world of the mind, due to the release of psychic energy.

If we grant that transformation is validated by mystical experience, we may still think that visionaries are people close to the edge of neuroticism. And they are, in the sense that they have moved out of society into the area of original experience, where they must interpret life for themselves. The actual crux of the matter where mysticism is concerned is not that it seems antisocial and not that all symbolic expressions of it are faulty but that mystical experience is the *function* of life. Campbell makes this point in one of his television interviews with Bill Moyers:

> MOYERS: In classic Christian doctrine the material world is to be despised, and life is to be redeemed in the hereafter, in heaven, where our rewards come. But you say that if you affirm that which you deplore, you are affirming the very world which is our eternity at the moment.

> CAMPBELL: Yes, that is what I'm saying. Eternity isn't some later time. Eternity isn't even a long time. Eternity has nothing to do with time. Eternity is that dimension of here and now that all thinking in temporal terms cuts off. And if you don't get it here, you won't get it anywhere. The problem with heaven is that you'll be having such a good time there, you won't even think of eternity. You'll just have this unending delight in the beatific vision of God. But the experience of eternity right here and now, in all things, whether thought of as good or as evil, is the function of life.[10]

What Campbell is saying in *The Power of Myth* (the interviews published posthumously in 1988) is what Waters has been saying in his visionary novels all along, but pointedly in *Otowi* because its protagonist is a mystic. It is she who is normal, who is functioning within the vision of eternity. The other characters—with the exception of an old Indian and eventually with the exception of Gaylord, who has a mystical experience of his own—only think of themselves as "normal," when in fact their thinking in temporal terms cuts them off from reality. We have a protagonist who has been nudged into the realm of the paranormal, but who is nonetheless truly normal, a paradox for those who haven't broken through into the mystery dimensions or been pushed into the interface between what can be known and what is never to be discovered.

Yet modern science, itself, has been pushed precisely into such an interface, unable, for example, to decide whether an atom is a wave or a particle, when it is both and therefore the manifestation of a transcendent energy source. Again, it is the thinking in temporal terms that creates the problem, for we are accustomed to regard events in nature as a causality of pushes and pulls to connect them. Now that scientists are beginning to postulate that events arise out of the underlying patterns of the universe, the similarities between the views of physicists and mystics are being acknowledged, and the possibility of relating subatomic physics to Jungian psychology and to parapsychology is being seriously studied. With such studies, the classical notion of causation is being modified to make room for what Jung called an "acausal connecting principle," or synchronicity.[11]

Synchronicity is the term employed by Jung to explain the coincidence in time of two or more causally unrelated events that have the same or similar meaning. According to the theory, archetypal energy could be manifested both in internal imagery and in external events, and the meaningfulness of this coincidence of a psychic state and a physical event is emphasized by the connection with archetypal processes.

Synchronicities act as mirrors to the inner processes of mind and are thus to be associated with a profound activation of energy deep within the psyche. As described by F. David Peat, the very intensity of synchronistic happenings suggests their profile:

> It is as if the formation of patterns within the unconscious mind is accompanied by physical patterns in the outer world. In particular, as psychic patterns are on the point of reaching consciousness then synchronicities reach their peak; moreover, they generally disappear as the individual becomes consciously aware of a new alignment of forces within his or her personality.[12]

It seems that one cannot describe the advent of this psychic energy without using the language of explosiveness, of something that reaches a peak, like the critical mass within an atomic reactor, and then bursts, like a bomb. Indeed, Peat believes that synchronicities tend to occur during periods of personal transformation, when there is a burst of psychic energy: births, deaths, intense creative work, falling in love, and the like. As we shall see, the synchronistic happenings that occur to the protagonist of *Otowi* fit into this profile exactly. As her old way of life is dying, as she herself is dying, she "explodes" into visions that are meaningfully precognitive of nuclear explosions, and then, as she becomes aware of a transformed personality, the synchronicities disappear and her Emergence—the myth made manifest—consolidates itself in the new world of consciousness.

Significantly, I think, Jung first contemplated synchronicity at the time when Einstein, a guest on several occasions for dinner in Jung's home, was developing his first (or special) theory of relativity.[13] In relativity theory we can never talk about space without talking about time and vice versa. When all things are seen as interdependent and inseparable parts or manifestations

206 ～ ATOMIC AGE

of an ultimate, indivisible reality, with opposite concepts unified in a higher dimension of space-time reality, there is no
"before" and no "after" and thus no causation. Accordingly then,
phenomena such as telepathy, clairvoyance, and precognition,
all of which suggest an explanation beyond the merely coinci-
dental, might also point to the unfolding of an order that is neither matter nor mind. Indeed, the theory of synchronicity leads
to the proposal that "mind and matter are not separate and distinct substances but that like light and radio waves they are
orders that lie within a common spectrum." What may be
reflected in a synchronistic happening such as precognition
are, according to Peat, "the dynamics of the macrocosm as it
unfolds simultaneously into the mental and material aspects of
a person's life."[14] Synchronicity, in short, proposes a bridge
between mind and matter and admits a spiritual element into
the philosophy of science. Hence Erich Neumann wrote in
1955 in a eulogy to Jung, "If the premise of synchronicity ...can
be validated, this would mean no more nor less than that phenomena which have hitherto been described in theological
terms as 'miracles' are in principle contained in the structure of
our world."[15] Jean Bolen, another Jungian psychologist,
declares in *The Tao of Psychology*:

> With the idea of synchronicity, psychology joined
> hands with parapsychology and theoretical physics
> in seeing an underlying "something" akin to what the
> mystic has been seeing all along. The important ele-
> ment that synchronicity adds is a dimension of per-
> sonal meaning that acknowledges what a person
> intuitively feels when a synchronistic event is direct-
> ly experienced. Theories and laboratory experiences
> make thinkable the idea of an underlying invisible
> connection between everything in the universe. But
> when it is an intuitively felt experience, a *spiritual*
> element enters. The human psyche may be the one
> receiver in the universe that can correctly apprehend

the meaning underlying everything, the meaning that has been called the Tao or God.[16]

When Jung studied Richard Wilhelm's translation of the Taoist *I Ching* or "Book of Changes," he recognized that an acausal synchronistic principle had long been known in Chinese mysticism, which is primarily concerned with nature's Way, or Tao. The Chinese, like the mystics of India, believed that there is an Ultimate Reality which underlies and unifies the multiple things and events we observe, and Tao, in its original cosmic sense as the undefinable, Ultimate Reality, is thus equivalent of the Hinduist *Brahman* and the Buddhist *Dharma-Kaya*. The Tao differs from the Indian concepts, however, by virtue of its intrinsically dynamic character. As explained by Capra, the Chinese "not only believed that flow and change were the essential features of nature, but also that there are constant patterns in these changes." The Taoists, specifically, "came to believe that any pair of opposites constitutes a polar relationship where each of the two poles is dynamically linked to the other."[7] From this belief, so difficult for the Western mind to grasp, that contraries are aspects of the same thing, there was derived a further belief that any extreme development becomes its opposite within the limits for the cycles of change. When, for example, a culture consistently favors yang, or masculine values and attitudes—analysis over synthesis, rational knowledge over intuitive wisdom, science over religion, and so on—and has neglected the complementary yin, or feminine, counterparts, such a one-sided movement reaches a climax and then retreats in favor of the other polarity. Thus, where synchronicity is concerned, the coincidence of events in space and time not only points meaningfully to a ground of unity but also suggests a dynamic web of patterns according to which the synchronistic event may signal a change of polarities of transpersonal significance.

We have reached the juncture where Jung's theory of synchronicity and Waters's myth of Emergence mingle to form the dynamic worldview of *The Woman at Otowi Crossing*. Waters, in 1950, had read Wilhelm's translation of the *I Ching* and Jung's foreword to it explaining synchronicity and realized "the universal significance of this profound book" (*Mountain Dialogues*, 114). It helped to confirm his speculations about the Mesoamerican symbology of life as a continuous transformation of opposites through movement, a movement mythologized in Indian America as Emergence through successive "worlds" when a civilization reaches a verge of extreme development and is replaced by another one on the Road (Tao, "Way") of Life. To Waters, that ancient myth of Emergence was and is an allegory for man's ever-expanding consciousness, and here in Jung's theory of synchronicity, although it represents phenomena on a lower temporal plane than Emergence, was a link: parapsychological phenomena occur mainly in the surroundings of an individual whom the unconscious wants to take a step in the expansion of consciousness. A fictionalized individual represented as having authentic mystical experiences, including synchronistic events, might be projected into the vanguard of a new age that is coming to birth as an old age has reached its climax in an apocalyptic premise. Assuming that every event in the visible world is the noncausally related effect of an archetype in the unseen world, one would have a fiction revelatory of a dynamic process in history. And that fiction is *The Woman at Otowi Crossing*.

On an immediate level, *Otowi* is the story of an "ordinary" middle-aged woman, Helen Chalmers.[18] As the story opens, she and her lover, Jack Turner, are waiting at a railroad whistle stop for the arrival of Emily, Helen's twenty-year-old daughter by a previous marriage. It is soon apparent that Helen, who abandoned Emily in infancy, has accumulated psychological dynamite—guilt, shame, and fear of financial failure—during almost twenty years of lonely isolation in a remote area of northern

New Mexico called Otowi Crossing, where she manages a tea-room in a small adobe house. Emily does not arrive that day, but an army colonel does, to inquire about a school called Los Alamos on the mesa above Otowi Crossing. Soon after experiencing a faint premonition, Helen discovers that she has breast cancer. Realizing that she cannot marry Turner, she contemplates the seeming futility of her life. Just then she has the first of her mystical visions, a "fusion" (21) of self into the complete pattern of the universe. After many misgivings and resentments about this awakening, she courageously accepts the power of destiny that drives her, commits herself to its fulfillment, and painfully sacrifices intimacy with the two persons she most loves, Turner and Emily. Doomed and yet reborn, with only Facundo, an old Indian from the nearby pueblo, to understand her integrity and psychic power, she has terrifying precognitive dreams, the content of which appall her—nothing less, as we know through dramatic irony, than A-bomb and H-bomb explosions, even planetary disappearance. She nevertheless grows in spiritual power and becomes a benevolent influence on many who know her, including physicists from the secret city of Los Alamos, who are experimenting with another, seemingly opposite kind of power. Helen influences one of these physicists, Gaylord, so much that, as he is observing the first H-bomb detonation over the Pacific, he has telepathic knowledge of the moment of her death and transfiguration, the triumph of spirit over matter.

That is the story on one immediate level. Waters never permits us to lose sight of Helen as a flesh-and-blood woman who suffers into wisdom; who swims in the nude and responds exuberantly to the natural world; who enjoys sex and friendship; who cooks and who nurses the afflicted. Waters, however, counterpoints the four parts of her myth—breakthrough to hidden reality, learning to live in a new world of freedom, exercise of released psychic energy, and its constructive influence on others—to the myth of science, whose hierophants successively break through to the new world of subatomic energy, release it, and victimize themselves and masses of humanity with radioactive fallout. So another immediate level of the story is a history of the Atomic Age from the Manhattan Project through the Trinity Site explosion, Hiroshima, experiments in the Nevada desert, and detonation of the H-bomb in the Marshall Islands. The interaction of the immediate levels of the story leads to a distinction between Helen Chalmers, the vessel of worldly experiences, and the Woman at Otowi Crossing, the personification of the myth of Emergence. Lest the woman in her mythic role seem to impose on modern sensibilities, Waters allows various characters to raise our objections for us, a strategy of an ironist. Turner believes Helen is a neurotic recluse in danger of becoming a psychotic lost in a meaningless dream state. Emily, an anthropologist with intellectual pretensions, is upset by her mother's mythological interpretations of historical signs. Throckmorton, a rich but puerile politician, sees Helen as easy prey for his manipulation. All these characters get their comeuppance. Turner's pragmatism is a betrayal of trust that loses him any chance for a complete relationship with Helen. Emily's science is of no emotional help. After aborting her child by Gaylord, she comes to an academic dead end in a Mexican university. Throckmorton's goose is cooked when Turner tricks him into making public a proposal for bombing America's enemies. While the fates of these characters may not remove all objections to the myth of Emergence, they do indicate some validation of Helen's normalcy and moral wholeness.

The most convincing validation of Helen's mysticism comes from the story of Gaylord, to whom focus shifts in the last third of the novel. Repeating the pattern of Helen's emergence, but with a terraced crescendo, he inherits her archetype as a moving principle of life. Thenceforth his spiritual effort is to hold to the experience in loyalty, courage, and love beyond fear and desire. In mythological terms this "gay lord" is like the questing hero from Grail legends: an impotent Fisher King of the Atomic Waste-Land is cured of his wound and given reign over a regenerated world. When we first encounter him, he is dedicated to science at the expense of emotional development. He is little more than a dehumanized robot isolated from his Jewish family and the teeming life of New York City. In spite of his duty to science, though, he feels drawn to Emily shortly after his arrival at Los Alamos. Therein lies his dilemma, for security regulations strictly forbid courtship. When Emily becomes pregnant, Gaylord promises marriage but procrastinates, betraying the dictates of his heart at the very hour when a historical Klaus Fuchs is passing atom bomb secrets to Harry Gold—*that* big a betrayal. Gaylord gets his bomb at Trinity, *his* secret; Emily gets an abortion, *her* secret. Gaylord, unaware of the abortion and beginning to mature emotionally, no longer feels alienated from his family and neighbors in New York. When he is apparently sterilized by radioactivity during an accident at Los Alamos, the tragic irony of his apparently irreversible fate—as guilt-ridden as Helen's had been—is his belated feeling of compassion for humanity. The climax of Gaylord's story occurs in Nevada when a "shot" fails to explode after countdown, and it is his duty to climb the tower to defuse the bomb. At this moment he experiences disassociation from the instinctual pattern of fear and guilt that has constituted his emotional field. Having attained spiritual detachment, Gaylord disconnects the jinxed bomb and, later in Las Vegas, finds the courage to "connect" his presumably lost manhood with a willing "show-biz" goddess, allusively a lunar deity named Monday Willis. In a wonderfully comic scene, Monday breaks down the barriers of Gaylord's isolation and comments, "Jesus, but it's taken you a long time!" (278).

But it is Helen Chalmers who is at the center of the novel. It is Waters's narrative technique to convey the mystery of her character not only through her interactions with other characters, but also through the compressed imagery of her mystical experiences, through the counterpointing of life and death forces, through her own words as expressed in a *Secret Journal*, through the symbolism of her death scene, and through the perceptions given by a Chorus, as I call it, of major and minor characters after her death. Out of this narrative complexity we finally perceive Helen's experience in the perspective of myth, the paradigm for humankind.

The novel highlights five mystical experiences of which three are incidents frozen in time and two are dreams. The first experience is one of totality:

> Then suddenly it happened.
>
> A cataclysmic explosion that burst asunder the shell of the world around her, revealing its inner reality with its brilliant flash. In its blinding brightness all mortal appearances dissolved into eternal meanings, great shimmering waves of pure feeling which had no other expression than this, and these were so closely entwined and harmonized they formed one indivisible unity. A selfhood that embraced her, the totality of the universe, and all space and all time in one immortal existence that had never had a beginning nor would ever have an end. [21]

This vision of the interpenetration of space and time in which an infinite, timeless, and yet dynamic present is experienced instead of a linear succession of instants is the basis of Helen's emergence, but it is also a basis of theoretical physics and of pueblo ceremonialism. Little wonder, then, that Helen comes to be admired by the Indians of San Ildefonso Pueblo. After telling Facundo about a strange dream, he takes her to a kiva, and the meaning of her dream is revealed by its symbolic architecture:

> In a flash she saw it all. The kiva, the whole multiworld universe, was at the same time the body of man. The whole of Creation already existed in him, and what he called an Emergence or a round of evolution was but his own expanded awareness of it. Once again with ecstatic intuition she glimpsed what

she really was. Constellations ringed her head and waist; planets and stars gleamed on her fingers; the womb-worlds of all life pulsed within her. [62]

Since a kiva reconciles all opposites (see *Masked Gods*, 421), Helen's precognitive dream of it connotes her participation in the reconciliation to the point of a mutual embodiment of all parts of the universe. The dream reinforces her original experience of totality, and the bowl incident, the next of her psychic experiences to be dramatized, both consolidates her sense of a timeless reality and brings into focus the redemptive nature of Emergence.

In one of the most powerful passages in the novel, Helen moves through three-dimensional time of past, present, and future to atonement with eternity. She has unearthed a piece of pottery on which is the thumb print of a Navawi'i woman (i.e., a woman from a local tribe of perhaps a thousand years ago) at the same time that wild geese in a V-formation fly overhead. A psychic experience results:

At that instant it happened again: the strange sensation as of a cataclysmic faulting of her body, a fissioning of her spirit, and with it the instantaneous fusion of everything about her into one undivided, living whole. In unbroken continuity the microscopic life-patterns in the seeds of fallen cones unfolded into great pines. Her fingers closed over the splotch of clay on the bowl in her arms just as the Navawi'i woman released her own, without their separation of centuries. She could feel the enduring mist cooling and moistening a thousand dry summers. The mountain peaks stood firm against time. Eternity flowed in the river below.... And all this jelling of life and time into a composite *now* took place in that single instant when the wedge of wild geese hurtled past her—hurtled so swiftly that centuries of southward migrations, generations of flocks, were condensed into a single plumed serpent with its flat reptilian head outstretched, feet drawn back up, and a solitary body feather displaced by the wind, which seemed to be hanging immobile above her against the gray palimpsest of the sky. [124-25]

While the passage glances only figuratively at the fission-fusion experiments of nuclear technology, the allusion to the plumed serpent, Quetzalcoatl, underscores Helen's experience of timelessness as the principle of all Creation and the theme of all world religions. In Waters's interpretation, that is "the agonizing redemption of matter by spirituality" and "the transfiguration of man into god" (*Mexico Mystique*, 126). As the feather is arriving as a symbolic annunciation of the way of redemption for humankind, the mythic Woman at Otowi Crossing assumes the role of the Plumed Serpent, that of a Redeemer.[19] From this moment, the nature of Helen's visions is shifted out of its initiating and consolidating phase into an apocalyptic and synchronistic phase, and she, herself, is authorized, in the fullness of achieved identity, to suffer the anguish of the forces of death and destruction in order to light the way to rebirth.

The mushroom incident and the candle nightmare illustrate this trend. Once, while Helen and Jack are walking in the woods, they find a monstrous mushroom, and Jack boots it into the air as Helen screams:

At that instant it happened. With all the minutely registered detail of a slow-motion camera, and in a preternatural silence, she saw the huge and ugly mushroom cap rise slowly in the air. Unfolding gently apart, its torn and crumpled blades opening like the gills of a fish, the fragmented pieces revolved as if in a slow boil revealing a glimpse of chlorine yellow, a splotch of brown and delicate pink. Deliberately it rose straight into the air above the walls of the canyon, its amorphous parts ballooning into a huge mass of porous gray. The stem below seemed to rise to rejoin it; then, shattered and splintered, it settled slowly back to earth.... Now again she screamed. Crouching down in terror, she vainly covered her head with her arms against the rain of its malignant spores. Countless millions, billions of spores invisibly small as bacteria radiated down around her. They whitened the blades of grass, shrivelled the pine needles, contaminated the clear stream, sank into the earth. Nor was this the end of the destruction and death they spread. For this malignant downpour of spores was also a rain of venomous sperm which rooted itself in still living seed cells to distort and pervert their natural, inherent life forms. There was no escape, now or ever, save by the miracle of a touch. [173]

Helen registers this experience while she is still ignorant of its synchronistic, deadly equivalent as atomic mushroom cloud. Similarly, she is prescient but untutored when her dream of a candle visits her just before the bombing of Hiroshima:

Then one night she had awakened screaming. It was as if everything, house, mountains, the world, the heavens, was enveloped in one brilliant apocalyptic burst of fire.... How horrible it was! That long narrow candle with a wick on top casting a tiny radiance. Then the wick suddenly erupted into flame, touching off a monstrous explosion that enveloped earth and sky, the whole world in a fiery flame.... Her dream had been more than a hellish illusion, but not another breakthrough like the first she'd experienced so long ago. That had opened to her the one creative wholeness with all its peace and plenitude. This last ghastly dream-vision, for all its overpowering bril-

>liance, had been impacted with something negative,
>destructive, evil. [204]

Her visions of creative wholeness now countered by visions
of apocalyptic destruction, Helen becomes the scale in which
the forces of life and death are weighed in precarious balance.

The narrative art of *Otowi* tilts that balance in favor of life.
It is of the utmost interest to observe how Waters goes about the
business of validating the authenticity of Helen's emergence.
For Waters knows exactly how large a stone he is casting into
the shallow pond of modern civilization. In raising Helen to the
Woman, to the level of transfiguring myth, he is also, as I have
previously noted, careful to raise the possible objections. Just
as in *Romeo and Juliet*, for example, we are convinced about
love's beauty because we are given the cynical Nurse and
Mercutio to set our threshold doubts at rest, so in *Otowi* our
conviction of Helen's health and wisdom is heightened because
we are given a cast that includes "tough-minded" characters
who measure her for us but in the final analysis are themselves
measured and usually found wanting. Emily Chalmers is one of
these. Always guided by the rational and scientific assumptions
of archaeology and anthropology, Emily disdainfully recalls her
mother as having "come from a middle-class family distinctly
commonplace compared to the Chalmers" and as having "had
no advantages and little education" (36). But this certified
expert on the Indians is frightened by the primitivism of naked
Navajos during a fire ceremony, is disturbed by the hoofbeats
of a wild stallion, and considers the Indian myth of Emergence
not as a parable of the evolutionary journey of mankind but as
the literal record of ancient migratory routes. In a fit of narcis-
sistic rage, Emily aborts her child, and the sterility of her life
thus subverts her opinions about Helen.

Another and tougher character is Jack Turner. This honest
newspaper editor and reporter loves Helen and is himself lovable, so when he scouts her mystical experiences as the result
of a mental breakdown, he clearly represents a majority opin-

ion in American culture and is doing the "right" thing by trying to lure Helen to the couch of a Freudian analyst. But Turner's limitations are revealed in a number of ways: his love of Western Americana is tainted with nostalgia, symptomatic of his addiction to thinking in terms of linear time (the Chile Line railroad a symbol here); he has a habit of doing harm through good intentions, such as when he helps Emily to find an abortionist; and he lugs around his own repressed guilt for having fathered an illegitimate daughter with an Indian woman. At the end of the novel he confesses to Meru, an investigator of psychic phenomena, that he has considered destroying Helen's *Secret Journal* because he feared it was the "product of an unbalanced mind" (312). Even though he has made some amends in life by setting up his daughter in a New York apartment, Turner's interest in promoting Helen's legend makes it doubtful that he ever understood her at all, for she has no wish for celebrity status or to impose her will on others. Of those closest to her, then, only Facundo initially and Gaylord finally comprehend her and feel compassion for a person visited by all the joys and terrors of the unseen life. One might think that an old Indian cacique and an atomic physicist would present the most formidable obstacles to acceptance of a mystic who is a white woman. Accept her they do, however, because each in his own way considers as valid Helen's emergence.

Further validation is accomplished through techniques of counterpointing and of witness bearing.

In American literature, structural, symbolic, and thematic counterpointing traditionally leads to simplistic juxtapositions of individual and society, nature and civilization, intuition and reason, timelessness and temporality, and the like. *Huckleberry Finn* and *Go Down, Moses*, for example, are developed by counterpointing, and the characters of Huck Finn and Ike McCaslin, once exposed to experience of absolutes, are isolated in the ideal. But Huck's idyll on the river and Ike's initiating encounters with wilderness and the bear represent nostalgic and negative reinforcements of American pastoralism; that is, the dream of a better way of life is seen by Twain and by Faulkner as doomed, as powerless to link past with present, individual with society. *The Woman at Otowi Crossing* breaks with this tradition by means of a reconciliation of opposites at "the still point of the turning world," as Eliot in his *Four Quartets* famously described this interplay.[20] Living at the "crossing" between counterpointed territories (Los Alamos versus San Ildefonso Pueblo), cultures (modern-scientific versus primal-mythopoetic), psychic polarities (rational consciousness versus unconscious), values (materialistic versus humanistic-ecological), and rituals (science with laboratory rituals enforced by a priesthood of intellectuals versus mysticism with tribal rituals enforced by a priesthood of hierophants), Helen dissolves differences by superseding them, in herself, in a higher state of awareness. She seems to be isolated, like the classic American boy-man protagonists. Unlike them, however, as a Chorus figure remarks, she is at the hub of time:

> "She had it all right, a glimpse of the universal whole. "What a spot she was in to receive it! At the birth place of the oldest civilization in America and the newest. Probably in no other area in the world were juxtaposed so closely the Indian drum and the atom smasher, all the values of the prehistoric past and the atomic future. A lonely woman in a remote spot with few friends, she felt herself at the hub of time." [179]

Instead of being an outcast, exile, or rebel, Helen becomes an open individual, and her openness will, through its power, open society to transformation.

Counterpointing is a valid way of seeing opposites as two sides of the same coin, *if* contrasting images and symbols are meaningfully connected. They are in *Otowi* through the myth of Emergence. The reader of this novel not only has to question his or her habit of categorizing situations as either-or, but also has to participate in the myth of the Woman in order to perceive that it is *our* myth and that in judging her in her mythic role we are in effect evaluating life and death forces in our own spheres of being. We can understand well enough the contrast of a kiva and a nuclear reactor, though it's unlikely we've actually seen either one, but once we've synthesized these images as representing energies, we are no longer ignoring the esoteric and unconscious forces but *admitting* these to consciousness. And that is a pointer to Emergence. On the one hand, the sun is associated with creativity, fertility, Facundo (as sun-priest), the face of Gaylord's mother, the temple at Mesa Verde, the plumed serpent and rhythmic order; on the other hand, the sun is associated with atomic and thermonuclear destruction, the power of the sun having been usurped. Once we recognize that the sun has both constructive and destructive power, we have increased our moral awareness of the necessity of controlling excessive human intervention in the processes of a primal source. And that is a pointer to Emergence, too. Chronological time imagery links the Chile Line's whistle, Turner's guilty memories, and nuclear-test countdowns, whereas the imagery of eternity links stones, mountains, pools, circles, kachina forces, magnetic fields, a cooking pot, Earth, ancient America, and the Mother Goddess in her archetypal aspect as the Woman. When we perceive spiritual reality, it is then possible for us to be aware of living in a world of linear time, yet capable of experiencing the timelessness of an eternal reality of which we are a part. Our consciousness is then experienced as moving, rather than fixed.[21] And that is also a pointer to Emergence. In sum, life and death forces in *Otowi* both oppose each other and interact, and our "explanation" of the interaction turns out to be a mode of mythic consciousness.

Otowi has the power—and *power* is an oft-repeated word at the heart of this novel—to unsettle our sense of the self in its relationship to an "external" world and to recall us to a deeper mode of awareness beneath this self-consciousness that remains mythic in its overall patterns. The dualism of subjectivity and objectivity is not given with the human condition.

What *is* given with the human condition, in the words of Falck, "may be an integrated mode of vision which comprises both the perceptual and the subjective or spiritual, and which we can recapture from the viewpoint of a later cultural stage only through a unifying and metaphorical effort of poetic imagination."[22] There is, so to speak, a mode of vision that accommodates as self-validating the emergence of Helen Chalmers.

Helen, herself, bears witness to her experience in the excerpts from her *Secret Journal* (1, 145-46, 250, 314) that frame the novel as prologue and epilogue and also appear at the novel's approximate midpoint, like a fulcrum by means of which vital powers are exercised. The myth she reveals is not dogmatically privileged, as would occur in the approach of traditional religion, and the questions of truth have not been pre-judged. Like a piece of music, the novel gives us an immediate presence and presentation of ontological meaning, and the truth or satisfyingness of myth remains open to critical question. Helen questions it, too. The fragments of her journal are not reiterations of her mystical experiences (though by implication these form part of an undisplayed journal), but philosophical reflections upon the meaning of the experiences. The reflections, moreover, are addressed to Turner in a spirit of love and bewilderment ("*I don't know, Jack. I don't know why this happened to me when it did,*" 1, italics in original). To her, Emergence is "*a normal, natural experience that eventually comes to every one of us,*" the import of which is that "*we're not separate and alone*" but "*part of one vast interconnected, living, conscious whole*" (146, italics in original). Moreover, psychic forces, "vast projections from the soul of humanity," have "the cosmic authority" (250) to deter nuclear war. The key passage of the journal, however, is not conveyed in the style of argumentation but in that of exaltation:

> *So all these scribbled pages, Jack, are to help you understand that an awakening or Emergence, as the Indians call it, is more than a single momentary experience. It*

requires a slow painful process of realization and orientation. Just like a newborn child, you get it all and instantaneously in the blinding flash of that first breakthrough—the shattering impact of light after darkness, of freedom after confinement. Then the rub comes. The learning how to live in this vast new world of awareness. The old rules of our cramped little world of appearances won't work. You have to learn new ones. The hard way, too, because everything you've known takes on new dimensions and meanings. This process of awakening with new awareness, a new perspective on everything about you, of perceiving the 'spherical geometry of the complete rounded moment' as Gaylord once called it— this is the wonderful experience I've been going through.... So when your turn comes, Jack, don't be afraid. Be glad! It's our greatest experience, our mysterious voyage of discovery into the last unknown, man's only true adventure.... [314, italics in original]

The passage is a summation of the process already dramatized in the novel as a whole: realization and orientation of the inner self are the dynamics of characterization in a novel that must break with conventional form in order to be a disclosure or revelation of the true nature of the world in which we live, or at least of a meaningful world. It has been meaningful to Helen Chalmers, and her hard-won exultation is the song of life.

We are also given the testimony of ten individuals who have a wide range of responses to Helen. Most of these individuals are interviewed by an unidentified omniscient narrator. The interviews, interspersed throughout the present time of the novel, are "flashforwards"[23] (most take place in the future) effecting a sense that three-dimensional time (past, present, future) is an illusion from which few escape. Some of those interviewed are major characters in the novel—Emily (35-38; also author of a letter, 152-53), Turner (58-59), and Gaylord (73-

74, 269-72; also author of reminiscences, 309-311)—while some are characters whose roles are minor or whose only appearance in the novel is through the interview—Dr. Gottman, Freudian psychologist in California, who rejects Jungian ideas as occult and considers Helen's "case" to be abnormal and morbid (132-34); Kaminsky or Kerenski, New York bookseller specializing in mysticism, who believes in the authenticity of Helen's experience (179-80); Alice Person, conventional Chicago matron once resident at Los Alamos, who is offended by Helen's lack of vanity as a "psychic" (207-9); Verna Taylor, shopkeeper in Cuernavaca, who discredits Emily's character and academic pretensions (241-43); Guy Alvord, big-time media reporter, who has popularized Helen's legend and who reveals Turner's self-interest in the same promotion (272-74); Milton P. Jasper, former political campaign manager now a Washington executive, who attests to Helen's power in transforming Throckmorton from a dangerous demagogue to a philanthropist (293-96); and M. Meru, New York authority on psychic phenomena, who accepts Helen's *Secret Journal* as the most complete record of a valid mystical experience in modern times (312-14).

Taken together, these ten characters form a Chorus with differing viewpoints. Emily, Turner, Gottman, and Alvord are dubious witnesses; Person, Taylor, and Jasper are a mixed lot; Kaminsky, Gaylord, and Meru are authoritative, Gaylord because he has mystical experiences of his own, including a telepathic "witnessing" of Helen's "death and transfiguration" (311), Meru because he has the privileged last word about her in the epilogue, understands the significance of myth, and is himself mythical. M. Meru, as his name implies, signifies Mt. Meru in Hindu and Buddhist cosmography, a metaphysical hub of the universe whose final judgment of Helen's spirituality is clearly to be heeded. Frances M. Malpezzi summarizes Meru's authority:

> Standing at his office window in his blue serge suit, enhaloed by fluttering white birds, bearing the name

of a sacred mountain of Eastern mythology, Meru represents the amalgamation of reason, Christian mysticism, harmony with nature, Eastern mysticism. He is a synthesis of the sacred and the profane. As the *axis mundi* connecting the secular world with the divine, he authenticates the Emergence of Helen Chalmers.[24]

Malpezzi believes that Meru is central to *Otowi*. I believe that he should more properly be considered as a coda to the novel, introduced after the natural conclusion to its movement. I agree to the extent that Meru joins Gaylord in placing Helen's experience in the perspective of myth. For it is Gaylord, we recall, who, at the instant of a thermonuclear explosion over the Pacific, knows that Helen has become assimilated to indescribable light, her life energy suddenly liberated as a symbol of absolute inner unassailability and of life that survives death—a resurrection like a new sunrise.[25]

There is no actual death scene (though I have called it that); rather, there is a quiet vigil, a tableau, in which Emily, Turner, and Facundo wait for Helen's death. The focus is on Facundo, who is outside in the chill of night. Suddenly a band of seven deer becomes visible beyond the fence. To Facundo, the deer are her emblem, their celestial counterparts in the Pleiades, and this symbolic amalgamation of a living universe provides an eerie sensation of an Absolute Consciousness interpenetrating time and space. When Facundo taps a drum and sings a death song, the deer bound away, then slowly turn about, "and with quick delicate steps" (306) come back to wait at the fence. This tableau of the deer calls up various associations, all with the same meaning. As the Pleiades, they are glimpsed as the highest stage beyond the ascendent architecture of the kiva. Buddhism postulates seven stages for evolutionary development, the seventh stage ending the Road of Life, with man now divine and perfected. Whereas Western medical science recognizes seven physical centers ascending upward from the base of the spine to the brain, Eastern mysticism postulates seven centers (chakras) of psychic energy, with the seventh and most important chakra lying just below the crown of the head and regarded as the seat of universal consciousness. In Kundalini yoga the serpent power rises from the lowest physical center to the highest psychic center, pictured on Buddhist temples as the horned antelope. What all these representations of seven have in common is emergence to divinity.[26] But it is the superb feeling and decorum of the tableau with Facundo and the deer that may surpass its esoteric meaning and accomplish in one powerful image more than the reflective testimony of characters accomplishes. Waters approaches the mystery of death as John Donne does the mystery of love in "A Valediction: Forbidding Mourning":

> Our two souls therefore, which are one,
> Though I must go, endure not yet
> A breach, but an expansion,
> Like gold to airy thinness beat.[27]

The quick delicate steps of Helen's deer foretell a death that will not bring about a separation from life but a triumphant expansion of her essential spirit into the golden radiance of a larger sky.

The SELF AS A FORCE FOR HUMAN SURVIVAL

Literary scholars, in popular belief, are quite useless when it comes to discussion of reality. I shall approach with moderation the august subject of war and peace. But, as Oscar Wilde said, one should not carry moderation to extremes. There is a great deal of literature about war, and once in a while some literary chap has contributed a world-shaking idea. For example, Goldsworthy Lowes Dickinson, a reclusive Cambridge don and poet, was first to propose the League of Nations. The study of letters, in fact, need not be narrowly circumscribed. Not only does it poach upon such related disciplines as philosophy, psychology, and sociology, it also proceeds along lines of inquiry associated with the mathematical and physical sciences. Furthermore, because literary study necessarily involves investigation of verbal signs and symbols, some of us find ourselves pondering the meaning of myths, their nature, development, and influence in human cultures. Mythology, as it turns out, has very much to do with war and peace. It has even been said that all wars are holy wars. Whether true or not, the statement suggests the complicity between aggression and culture and opens the possibility, from a humanistic perspective at least, of understanding the problem of human survival—a very real problem indeed.

Mythology has been seriously studied only in recent years. We mark its progress from the publication in 1890 of Sir James Frazer's *The Golden Bough: A Study in Magic and Religion*, through the depth psychology of Freud and especially of Jung whose theory of a Collective Unconscious burst the crust of rationalistic dogma, and to, in our own time, the monumental works on mythology of Joseph Campbell. My indebtedness to Campbell will be apparent to anyone familiar with such books as *The Hero With a Thousand Faces* (1949), *The Masks of God* (in four volumes, 1959-1968), and *Myths to Live By* (1972).[1] The latter work contains a chapter entitled "Mythologies of War and Peace," and from this I shall borrow extensively, though occasionally elaborating upon its insights. We need a grandstand view of the subject in order to evaluate calmly our present condition in the Atomic Age.

Campbell discerns, as the basic idea of practically every war mythology, that the enemy is a monster and that in killing him one is protecting the only truly valuable order of human life on earth, which is that, of course, of one's own people. The Orient and tropical zones aside, the two most important war mythologies in the West have been Homer's *Iliad* and the Old Testament. Let us examine these stories as myths, calling the Greek epic an example of the myth of heroic war and the Hebrew epic an example of the myth of holy war.

Though steeped in gore, the *Iliad* is irradiated by moments of humanity. In Book VI the Trojan hero Hector, soon to be slain in battle by the Greek hero Achilles, bids farewell to Andromache, his wife, and their little son Astyanax. Their fate is all but certain: Hector, slain, will have his corpse dishonored by Achilles, and Andromache and Astyanax will be put to the sword or enslaved. Hector, we are told, smiled in silence as he looked on his son, but Andromache, letting her tears fall, spoke to him:

> Dearest, your own great strength will be your death, and you have no pity on your little son, nor on me, ill-starred, who soon must be your widow; for presently the Achaians, gathering together, will set upon you and kill you; and for me it would be far better to sink into the earth when I have lost you, for there is no other consolation for me after you have gone to your destiny—only grief.

And Hector answered:

> Poor Andromache! Why does your heart sorrow so

much for me? No man is going to hurl me to Hades, unless it is fated, but as for fate, I think that no man yet has escaped it once it has taken its first form, neither brave man nor coward.

Little Astyanax, we are told, shrank in fear from his father's gleaming helmet, but Hector removed it, kissed his son and prayed for him to Zeus before departing. Although Hector is fighting for his family as much as for Troy, he expects everyone he holds dearest to remain unflinchingly faithful in all circumstances and to share with him that heroic spirit fretting at the limitations set on human effort and striving to break through them by some prodigious exertion and achievement. In refusing to surrender his manliness and decency, Hector appears as morally superior to the Greeks.

Campbell makes the point about Homer's humanity, that it shows with what respect and great capacity for empathy the ancient Greeks could regard their enemies. Moreover, they could regard the heroic spirit, when put to the test of war, as of dubious value. The motive for the sack of Troy is vengeance: Helen deserted her dull husband for a Trojan prince, so some of the Greek gods, we are told, favored war to get her back, though other gods supported Troy. When we move from the *Iliad* to the *Odyssey*, the myth of heroic war collides with a narrative about values of home and peace. Heroes like Achilles, dead for twenty years, report from Hades that perhaps life would have been better, after all, in a quiet cottage in the countryside. Agamemnon, co-leader of the Greeks at Troy, has been murdered by a faithless wife; his brother Menelaos, though alive in Lacedemon, has *his* faithless wife home again, but Helen is a sulky vixen who expresses little remorse for the past. Odysseus himself, whose intelligence has frustrated his own ends, has become a bit of a veteran bore who weeps to hear his own exploits recounted and really has nothing to do save flex his aging muscles and dream of slaughtering his wife's suitors, over a hundred of them. Even Odysseus's dog dies on a dungheap at sight of him as if to reproach the master for having left home to fight a war "for a whore" (as Daniel Defoe summarizes the affair).

The Greek playwrights Aeschylus (525-456 B.C.) and Sophocles (497-406 B.C.) continue the tradition of depicting enemies as human. Aeschylus himself fought the invading Persians at Salamis yet humanized them in his tragedy, *The Persians.* In *Agamemnon* his uncompromising conception of human responsibility comes close to a virtual condemnation of war as a cultural aberration: the goddess Artemis, protectress of the innocent and unborn, will not allow Zeus, an Olympian tyrant, to get away with the sacrifice of Agamemnon's daughter (a pretext for war) or with the destruction of Troy, and, when Queen Clytemnestra, having murdered her husband, announces that war crimes are expiated and utopian peace has arrived, it is clear from the play's tragic irony that historical justice has not been accomplished. Sophocles, like Aeschylus, also explores the ambiguities of violence but emphasizes that sacred view of life which alone may preserve mankind and the earth we inhabit. For example, *Antigone* begins after a fratricidal war in which one of the heroine's brothers has been slain, his body thrown out to rot and be eaten by wild dogs. The tyrant Creon then forbids anyone on pain of death from offering burial rites to the fallen enemy. Antigone defies his authority, buries her brother, and is entombed and driven to suicide. So one of the themes of the play is that rituals are needed to prevent the increase of the killing mania. Burial of a warrior, notably an enemy of state, carries the life principle back to Mother Earth for rebirth.

However, it would be a mistake to believe that the Greeks, in general, ever thought it desirable or even possible to love their enemies. Greek civilization centered itself in legends about heroic wars of the late Bronze and early Iron Age masters of the Aegean. Consider the marble friezes taken from the Parthenon by Lord Elgin and now displayed in the British Museum: they depict a mythical battle between Lapiths, whose figures are human, and Centaurs, whose bodies are half human, half animal. In other words, the conflict of civilization and barbarism is in the nature of necessity, and the banner of civilization is necessarily Greek. It is *our* fully human people overcoming *those* less-than-human, more or less monstrous people. Meanwhile on Mount Olympus, divinities quarrel among themselves while directing human quarrels below. A polytheistic pantheon of gods could thus favor both sides of a war simultaneously, and therefore the barbarians like Trojans and Persians could sometimes be comprehended in their humanity. Most of the time, the myth of heroic war merely perpetuates the idea of the superior order of one's own tribe.

Among the Greeks' approximately contemporaneous neighbors in the ancient Near East were some tribes overrunning Canaan, one of them the earliest Hebrews. Their god is singular, Yahweh, and His sympathies are forever on one side. Accordingly, the enemy depicted in the Old Testament is not even half-human, but subhuman, a monster to be wasted by Yahweh's chosen people. We are in the mythological ambiance of holy war.

Just how holy, one may judge from some typically brutal passages from the Mosaic or Deuteronomic traditions:

> When the Lord your God brings you into the land which you are entering to occupy and drives out many nations before you—Hittites, Giggashites, Amorites, Canaanites, Perizzites, Hivites, and Jebusites, seven nations more numerous and powerful than you—when the Lord your God delivers them into your power and you defeat them, you must put them to death. You must not make a treaty with them or spare them. You must not intermarry with them, neither giving your daughters to their sons nor taking their daughters for your sons; if you do, they will draw your sons away from the Lord and make them worship other gods. Then the Lord will be angry with

you and will quickly destroy you. But this is what you must do to them: pull down their altars, break their sacred pillars, hack down their sacred poles and destroy their idols by fire, for you are a people holy to the Lord your God; the Lord your God chose you out of all nations on earth to be his special possession. (Deut. 7:1-6)

When you advance on a city to attack it, make an offer of peace. If the city accepts the offer and opens its gates to you, then all the people in it shall be put to forced labor and shall serve you. If it does not make peace with you but offers battle, you shall besiege it, and the Lord your God will deliver it into your hands. You shall put all its males to the sword, but you may take the women, the dependents, and the cattle for yourselves, and plunder everything else in the city. You may enjoy the use of the spoil of your enemies which the Lord your God gives you. That is what you shall do to cities at a great distance, as opposed to those which belong to nations near at hand. In the cities of these nations whose land the Lord your God is giving you as a patrimony, you shall not leave any creature alive. You shall annihilate them—Hittites, Amorites, Canaanites, Perizzites, Hivites, Jebusites—as the Lord your God commanded you, so that they may not teach you to imitate all the abominable things that they have done for their gods and so cause you to sin against the Lord your God. (Deut. 20:10-18)

Is this the same Yahweh who commanded, "Thou shalt not kill"? The myth of holy war continues in the Book of Joshua. After the trumpets and the fall of Jericho, as we read: "they destroyed everything in the city; they put everyone to the sword, men and women, young and old, and also cattle, sheep, and asses." (Joshua 6:21). On and on the holy massacres are accomplished in the name of the local deity until Jerusalem, itself, is besieged and taken by the King of Babylon, Nebuchadnezzar, in the year 586 B.C. (II Kings 25), beginning the so-called period of exile.

Campbell notes that the Old Testament may beguile us with a vision of peace such as that in Isaiah 65:22-25 which echoes that of Isaiah 11:6-9 (the so-called First Isaiah who lived before the exilic period):

> My people shall live the long life of a tree,
> and my chosen shall enjoy the fruit of their labour.
> They shall not toil in vain or raise children for misfortune.
> For they are the offspring of the blessed of the Lord
> and their issue after them;
> before they call to me, I will answer,
> and while they are still speaking I will listen.
> The wolf and the lamb shall feed together
> and the lion shall eat straw like cattle.
> They shall not hurt or destroy in all my holy mountain
> says the Lord.

This beautiful passage from the post-exilic Third Isaiah is unfortunately preceded by the usual call for a bloodbath: "The nation or kingdom which refuses to serve you shall perish, and wide regions shall be laid utterly waste" (Isaiah 60:12).

The Old Testament is not our only literature about divinely authorized war. The Arabs have the Koran that reveals Mohammed as the ultimate prophet. From him, since the seventh century A.D., has been derived a fanatic mythology of unrelenting war in God's name, the jihad or Holy War. According to this concept, it is the duty of every Moslem male who is free, of full age, in full possession of his intellectual powers, and physically fit for service to fight in the cause of Truth and to conquer all lands not belonging to the territory of Islam.

Our Western world has its own version of the myth of holy war—the crusade ("bearing of the cross")—for the message conveyed by Christendom has often been governed by sentiments of hatred, with love reserved for the elected communicants. At the height of the Middle Ages, under Pope Innocent III (1198-1216), the Church authorized the genocide of a million people in the south of France, yet the victims of this Albigensian Crusade had, like Jesus, explicitly rejected the sword for lives of ascetic purity in peace. The crusading mania accounts for the slaughter of, among other peoples, the native inhabitants of Hispanic America and of North America where Christianized Euro-Americans have sought for centuries to stamp out "heathen"—and peaceful—Indian beliefs and ceremonies.

The myth of heroic war and the myth of holy war have in common a belief in divine authorization for the dehumanizing of the enemy and for the glorifying of the homefolks. Closely related to these myths is the myth of terminal war—the Apocalypse. The basic idea is that there will be a series of wars followed by the end of historic time and the subsequent restoration of the right people to a universal reign of peace under a King of Kings. We encounter here the idea of the Messiah, first envisioned by the pre-exilic prophets as simply an ideal king on David's throne but then in the post-exilic period as a King of Kings who, at the end of time, should be given everlasting dominion over all peoples. Where did this post-exilic idea come from? Not, according to Campbell, from the Hebrews but from the Persians, for whom the first King of Kings was Cyrus the Great. When Babylon fell to him in 539 B.C., he restored peoples to their homelands and governed them through subordinate kings of their own races and traditions. It is Cyrus who is celebrated in Isaiah 45 as a virtual Messiah—but *now* the servant of Yahweh doing Yahweh's work so that it would ultimately not be the Persians but the people of Yahweh who would reign over the world. As we know, the myth of terminal war, allied with the idea of a Messiah who will resurrect the dead and rule the guiltless, has been in vogue among Christians for two thousand years. The anticipated savior, of course, is Christ, even though the original savior was Persian.

The names for the combatants in terminal war were also adopted from Persian mythology, specifically from Zoroaster or Zarathustra, a Persian prophet of the sixth century B.C.: the powers of Light would achieve victory over the powers of Darkness after a season of general wars and the arrival of an ultimate savior whose name was Saoshyant. Surely it is no coincidence that the Dead Sea Scrolls of the last century B.C predict a terminal war to be fought between "the Sons of Light" and "the Sons of Darkness." The Essenes seem to have been a community preparing itself for an imminent Apocalyse that they were elected to survive for all eternity. Whether John the Baptist and Jesus were members of the Essene sect or influenced by it, we may only speculate, but it is clear that Jesus delivered his own version of the apocalyptic message and that Christianity came to birth in an atmosphere of widespread despair (caused by the Roman occupation of Palestine) and of panic (caused by belief in the end of the world). Christian eschatology (i.e., concern with ultimate things such as a Day of Judgment) has continued to make a powerful appeal for two thousand years. For example—and the spectacle is indeed touching—there are good people right now preparing to sit on deck-chairs on a rooftop in Brooklyn Heights, there to witness the destruction of New York City, one of the places evidently designated for the wrath of God. In banalized form this eschatological concern with war between light and dark forces can be discovered in a movie like *Star Wars* and its sequels. The point here is that all end-of-the-world thinking is based on the apocalyptic premise of terminal war, its survivors an elect people. The exception to this rule is nuclear annihilation in which there would be no survivors. More about that presently.

Although the teachings of Jesus have their apocalyptic drift, they represent our best-known mythology of peace. Now the sentiment of love is to prevail according to laws of God. Instead of affirming that life is war, we are to renounce war as well as other concerns of the flesh. Consider Matthew 10:34-36: "You must not think that I have come to bring peace to the earth; I have not come to bring peace, but a sword. I have come to set a man against his father, a daughter against her mother, a son's wife against her mother-in-law; and a man will find his enemies under his own roof." What Jesus meant by reference to a sword seems to be clarified in Matthew 26:50-52 in the scene of his arrest in the Garden of Gethsemane: "They then came forward, seized Jesus, and held him fast. At that moment one of those with Jesus reached for his sword and drew it, and he struck at the High Priest's servant and cut off his ear. But Jesus said to him, 'Put up your sword. All who take the sword die by the sword.'" Clearly, a very special if not impossible discipline is being called for: absolute abandonment of all the concerns of normal secular life such as family ties and community *and* a renunciation of violence, by which, however, the human species has lived and will continue to live. I, speaking only for myself and not attributing the opinion to Campbell (though I believe he shares it), consider ascetic renunciation of the world as a *negative* aspect of the mythology of peace. Its negativeness need not be construed as a criticism of Christian sacrifice or of the achievements, via nonviolence, of Gandhi or a Martin Luther King. But we sometimes overlook the marvelously *positive* aspect of Jesus's peace teaching—it is the teaching that cost him his life—and that is atonement. Here the emphasis shifts from penal atonement for sins to an at-one-ment, a universal confraternity based upon the simple, radical, world-transforming theological doctrine that God the Father has come down, so to say, is joined with the Son and through the Son is conjoint with all humanity. Jesus transforms myths of war and the apocalyptic theme from a historical future to, as Campbell perceives, a psychological present. The battle of good and evil has, as it were, already been resolved, and we are to love our enemies because the Kingdom of God is here and now, though we see it not.

We must ask, again presently, whether this positive at-one-ment is merely a wish-fulfilling ideal or a moral and psychological reality irrespective of its originally theological, hence mythic conception. If the human, individual Self is the source of wonder and is naturally equipped with the power to be "at one" with mankind, we have a gospel, if not a guarantee, of survival.

The ancient myths of war that we have surveyed and summarized with Joseph Campbell as guide, and that I have classified as myths of heroic, holy, and terminal war, are very much alive in today's world. Even heroic war, though seemingly a dinosaur, has been usurped for revolutionary purposes as "the people's heroic struggle" and all that. But at least since the seventeenth century in the modern West there has evolved a realization that it is men, not divinities, who authorize war and wage it. Men also authorize peace and make it. We live, in part, in a *de-mythologized* world.

There is at least one modern myth of war, that of the just war, which is mythical precisely because it elevates to absolute status the relative abstractions of thought, such as "rights," "humanity," "reason," "history" and "nature," all spelled with initial capital letters and all variously appealed to as if they embodied universal ethical laws. An early example is Hugo Grotius's treatise, *The Rights of War and Peace*, published in 1625 during the Thirty Years War that was devastating Europe. Beginning with the idea that there is a kinship among humanity established by nature, Grotius sees in this bond a community of rights. The society of nations, including as it does the whole human race, needs recognition of these rights, nor do the accidents of geographic boundary obliterate a human demand for justice that springs from the nature of man as a moral being. There is, therefore, his argument goes, a Natural Law that, when properly apprehended, is perceived to be the expression and dictate of Right Reason. Moreover, this Law of Nations is also based upon a system of consent, of practically recognized rules of procedure. In sum, war and peace issues involve ethical principles and can be enforced by rational, mutual interest. One can wage a just war because it is the expression of sovereignty.

The myth of just war lives today deeply in our thinking and remembrance. To name a few "just" wars, we have the American Revolution, the American Civil War, and the Second World War (in its anti-totalitarian, anti-racist aspect). So-called wars of liberation are usually considered justifiable, although those who have suffered liberation Communist-style, which is to say totalitarian, discover that the revolution has yet to be decided in terms of justice and freedom. Still, Communists have justified aggression on the basis of capital-H History just as fascists have justified theirs on the basis of capital-N Nature. Like other myths of war, the myth of just war assumes that *our* tribe, nation, or people are enlightened and the *other* people, their leaders at least, are monsters.[ii]

War mythologies ancient and modern affirm war as life and life as war. Our roles in the social realm are those of murder's perpetrators or of its victims. Either way, we are accustomed to believe in a future when blood-guilt can be expiated, the pious elected and redeemed, the biological and cultural heritage transmitted to future generations. True, we think, war is a disaster—but no more than the sum of fallen cities, killed and injured people, mourning survivors. Which is to say the sum is never the total of living things converted to corpses. Even when totalitarianism attempts to erase the factual record of past and present, counterforces have hitherto existed to preserve the record in human remembrance lest we forget the death-camps and Gulags, the "disappearances" and genocides. It seems possible to go on holding life as sacred and invoking divinities and moral absolutes of somebody's tribe, somewhere (we always think it is ours).

Suddenly, since 1945, we can imagine—we *must* imagine—a world in which no one survives nuclear war and all life has been foreclosed where any future is concerned. In that event, life is not only not sacred but worthless. Moreover, the extinction of the species cannot, save by a perversion of religion, be attributed to God's will when it is we ourselves who possess the means to unleash the utterly meaningless, completely unjustified weapons of annihilation. This would not be a Day of Judgment in which God destroys the world but raises the dead and metes out perfect justice to everyone who has ever lived. The complete destruction of mankind by men is an apocalyptic premise without apocalyptic promise.

Surprisingly, the author of *The Fate of the Earth* (1982), Jonathan Schell, has been attacked as arrogant and pretentious for his eloquent and grimly passionate description of the apocalyptic premise. Yet it is scientifically accurate, and the fact that it has not been scientifically validated—exactly Schell's point—does not amount to pretense. We do indeed have weapons of such character and magnitude that they could annihilate the species and contaminate the earth. Scientific knowledge, Schell writes, has brought us face to face with "the death of mankind" and in doing so has "caused a basic change in the circumstances in which life was given to us, which is to say that we have altered the human condition."[iii] The fact is, for the first time in history, we live in a *post*-war posture, or we don't live at all. Our only probable peace arrives *this* side of *one* nuclear war and makes of the whole earth a new common kingdom founded upon ethical and ecological principles.

Although our choice is probably between peace and total annihilation, the most terrible reality mankind has ever faced may still be graced with enough time for us to deal with it. Schell wants instant relief from peril, meaning abolition of nuclear arms, abolition of sovereignty, and abolition, somehow, of aggressive instinct. I hope he has oversimplified the nature of the dangers we face. Although they are frightening, unreasoning fear of them can lead to unwise and destructive behavior. Do nuclear weapons make nuclear war inevitable? Does nuclear war mean the end of the human race? Even to allow logical probability to these questions does not mean that nuclear weapons will be abolished all at once, sovereignty surrendered all at once to a nebulous world order, and violence extirpated from human nature.

Few, I think, still believe the earth is flat. Or that the earth is the center of the cosmos instead of a blip on the tail of one galaxy among billions of galaxies. Or believe that a mountain called Purgatory rises in the South Atlantic toward a heavenly mansion presided over by a gender-coded anthropomorphic deity originally seated there by Babylonian priest-mathematicians. Yet not so long ago, historically considered, these mythic images constituted a cosmology for various clergies, and woe to the seers and stargazers who experienced something else and said so! Put simply: mythologies, as they lose support, undergo change and may do so again under pressure of a technological reality of nuclear-arms potential. Our heritage of war myths can be discarded and the authorities behind the myths unmasked until we see the warmakers for what they always were—ourselves. We have never abolished war before, so let's make a start by abolishing the myths of war.

Demythologizing has already, I assume, been in progress for untold centuries. The myth of heroic war, encouraging the valorous to assert their vitality and individuality and to earn values from struggle, itself, belongs by definition to heroic culture, an anachronism like Don Quixote. The myth of holy war has also lost cultural support, especially in the modern West; and in the nuclear age there is no local, tribalized aim or ideal worthy of any people whatsoever. Now we peer down from the moon and see our global village as she is, a small, lonely oasis lost amidst infinities of dark space. The only truly valuable order of life on earth is that of all people everywhere. And the myth of terminal war should surely be relegated to the nursery where the evangelicals and fundamentalists play. There is no *human* basis, let alone a scientific one, for postulating an end-of-the-world kingdom of peace to be ruled for all eternity by a savior, unless one is not disconsolated to imagine a few survivors of the nuclear holocaust. Although men of good will serve us well by spreading gospel, we would be better off if we devoted our energies and thoughts to the postponement of terminal war rather than to its certainty. Apocalyptic pronouncements panic us from thought of authentic survival, the high goal for all mankind that requires consideration of the best ideas that lead to the best ways.

The modern myth of just war is the problematic one. That war and peace are issues to be decided by an international law based upon ethical principles and enforced by rational self-interest is an enlightened concept. It is, in fact, the one we try to live by in what is clearly not the best of all possible worlds. The problematic aspect is precisely the mythical: divine authority has dwindled to philosophical abstractions and these, in turn, have become absolute authority for the totalitarian state. The Kingdom of God, which in Jesus's teachings is a here-and-now spiritual (we might say psychological) reality, has become a monolithic secular kingdom that promises peace, but "peace" without justice or freedom, the "peace" of the police-state. For peoples in historically despotic regions such as the Orient, including the greater part of the former Soviet Union, the idea of total state authority is customary, so the tyranny of rationalism tends to preempt reason, itself. Since the break-up of the medieval synthesis under the impact of science, capital-ism, and mass civilization, even individuals of the western world have sometimes experienced such a sense of powerless-ness that "fear of freedom" has prepared a way for Big Brother.[4] As we know, the slogans of Orwell's 1984—"Peace is War" and "Freedom is Slavery"—reveal insanity at the core of purely log-ical formulations.

Although the concept of the *un*-conscious mind—related to spontaneity, intuition, and creative imagination—has been available since ancient times, Descartes thrust it down in favor of the alpine air of logic and deductive reasoning.

Now, the rediscovery of the unconscious mind is of the high-est interest in our consideration of the problem of human sur-vival. The human "mind" is evidently prepared to wrap the whole planet in a shroud, and the exercise of all our best efforts and ingenuity has produced no assurance that it will be deterred from that end. Moreover, the prolonged failure of conscious means in dealing with world crisis simply points to their inadequacy, to the need for transcending them in a fresh approach. This is the promise of the creative spirit; it has power to effect alteration of our inner life and of the outer forms in which life finds expression and support. Creativity can break up too rigid patterns of thought and feeling and shape them to meet the needs of life. Creativity, an image-making capacity, is present in the Self; imagery gives psychological presence to the absent, which can be the not-self, even the mass of the earth's inhabitants. Imagery, when externalized as a creative product, is changed to relate to reality by means of a conceptualizing component. Our ability to conceptualize exposes us to an unending organization of cognitive elements, an unending variety of emotions, and the possibility of moral choice. *The human Self is thus a force for human survival.* The endlessness of man can now be recognized. Man is a product not simply of nature, but also of his own making.

A friend of mine who taught briefly at a university in the former Soviet Union summed up his impressions in three words: "Skinnerism. No fun." Depressing as that picture is, we might lift—and lengthen—our gaze to envision ourselves not as doomed automatons, but as creatures in a stage of evolving World Culture. For the creative Self contains vast social implications. A creative society uncovers, selects, reshuffles, combines, and synthesizes already existing facts, ideas, faculties, and skills. By contrast, a closed society will decay for lack of exchanges with an unceasing expansion of reality. In the monotonous environment of a closed society, responses will become stereotyped, flexible skills will degenerate into rigid patterns, and the person will more and more resemble an automaton governed by fixed habits.

The spiritual determinant of World Culture has been and can be the individual Self. If I read correctly the teachings of Jesus, world peace begins with personal peace—the radical transformation of atonement. The technological determinant of World Culture has been, at an accelerating pace since the twelfth century A.D., the methods of science, and so we can put our knowledge to use in a responsible way with human experience, not mythological authorities, as the actual center of awe and hope.

As I began with the wisdom of Joseph Campbell, so I shall conclude. In the long view, we see a gradual amplification of the group from the early tribal cluster to the modern concept of a single World Culture. Against the amplitude of this concept, the various national, racial, religious or class mythologies that may once have had their reason are now out of date. In the recent past it may have been possible for intelligent men of good will honestly to believe that their own society was the only good, that beyond its bounds were the enemies of God, and that they were called upon, consequently, to project the principle of hatred outward upon the world, while cultivating love within, toward those whose system of belief was of God. Today, however, physical facts have made closed horizons illusory. The old god of little, closed societies is dead. "There are today no horizons, no mythogenetic zones," Campbell writes. "Or rather, the mythogenetic zone is the individual heart ...each the creative center of authority for himself."[V] Our task is to awaken within each of us the principle of love as it was mythologically wakened in God. Mythology, too, functions to initiate the individual into the order of realities of his own psyche, guiding him toward his own spiritual enrichment and realization. Formerly—but in archaic cultures still—the way was to subordinate all individual judgment, will, and capacities to the social order. Gradually in Europe, the principle of individual judgment and responsibility was developed in relation not to a fixed order of supposed divine laws, but to a changing context of human activities, rationally governed. This humanistic individualism has released powers of creativity that have revolutionized the world and set the task for each of us to quest within for those creative values by which cultural sterility is redeemed.

The full emergence of Self[vi] upon the world scene is yet to come, but it is already so far advanced as to give us hope for survival. Our laws are from ourselves, not from the gods or from the universe; they are conventional, not absolute; and in breaking them we offend our fellow human beings and our fragile planet. We, ourselves, elicit the sense of awe before the mystery of being, and we support that sense with a cosmology based upon the discoveries of the arts and sciences in the depths of both the psyche and the galaxies of space. We join all mankind in our Self's spiritual becoming, having by nature essentially and by the accident of nuclear technology necessarily the power to be at-one with all others. Man, of course, is not an end in himself in an absolute sense. He has not created the universe or himself. He has, however, created culture and, pretending otherwise, authorized war. He no longer has that self-appointed authority because war, as an expression of culture, no longer functions mythologically. In order to abolish war and to survive, he emphatically does not need, as is sometimes argued, to change human nature. He needs to change the bad habits of his culture. He needs the circles of his love to expand, like the ever-widening ripples on a pond, to include the mutual humanity of all the other selves here and now and to come, in each and all. And he will, I think, fulfill those needs, given patience and fortitude to persevere and vigilance to protect his ever-larger sky from the last trumpets of his own folly.

PEACE STARS

Few people, I surmise, really believe in the possibility of peace, though most would profess an abhorrence of war and assert that they, themselves, are pacific with but occasional outbursts of aggressive behavior, usually justified on the basis that human beings are, after all, animals. Peace is a dream, an ideal, whereas war seems the natural state for the species, consequently inevitable and unavoidable. Pointing to history, we observe the violent rise and fall of civilizations. We conclude that our own civilization is also doomed, and with it, all mankind. If anything is to save us, it is technology; we spend hundreds of billions of dollars on so-called defense, not only here on earth, but also in space where the latest system, "Star Wars," is a wish-fulfillment that will no more shield us now than the Maginot Line protected France from invading German armies in 1940. We need to open our eyes and see, not Star Wars but Peace Stars—the omens of hope and human possibility.

Our awareness of peaceful possibility is, to borrow an analogy, a little like our ability to see stars in daytime. The sun is so bright that the stars are invisible, despite the fact that they are just as present in our sky in the daytime as at night. When the sun sets, we are able to perceive the stars. In the same way, the brilliance of our most recent evolutionary accretion, the analytical, verbal, and "scientific" abilities of human consciousness, obscures our awareness of the cognitive functions of the intuitive, integrative, and holistic abilities of human consciousness, which in our ancestors must have been the principal means of perceiving the world.[1] In fact, when it is a question of human survival, intuition may actually be the most competent mode of awareness, with our highly prized rational and analytical abilities quite ineffective, unless collaborating with intuition, to solve complex problems. We already possess, in other words, the Peace Stars that can save us and our plundered planet. They do not sparkle in outer space. Instead, the new world of the future lies in the interstellar spaces within ourselves where the creative spirit dwells.

How, we might well ask, did we get into our daytime blindness? The ideology of the modern world, by which I mean chiefly Western civilization, has been derived from some crucial misconceptions about the nature of the mind, itself. Since the rise of modern science in the seventeenth century and as a consequence of Cartesian and Lockean theories of rationalism, "mind" has been regarded as synonymous with reason, and all other effects and processes of thinking have been relegated to a distasteful, demonic, and useless black box, the unconscious. Even psychology, which began as the science of consciousness, whether waking or dreamlike, is, as psychologist Robert Ornstein reminds us, often reduced to behaviorism that stimulates research in the realms of learning and of the motivation of behavior, but ignores the existence of phenomena that do not fit in the dominant scheme.[2] Given such narrow scope, psychology is blind to stars. As Abraham Maslow, commenting on the effects of a strict behaviorism in psychology, said, "If the only tool you have is a hammer, you tend to treat everything as if it were a nail."[3]

But rationalism—or, to be more precise, *over*-rationalism— has not been the only fallacious assumption in the civilization of the recent West. Materialism is another. Under the materialistic assumption, mind and matter are essentially separated, so that the material universe, be it seas, forests, or atomic particles, exists for our "property," our personal use, exploitation, and enrichment without any social regard for such emotional and spiritual sentiments as the sanctity of an environment that nourishes life. That both rationalism and materialism, for all their advances, have brought us to the brink of catastrophe, we in our blindness are still not quite ready to admit. We forget that John Locke made reason the only permitted source of spiritual being in individuals and thus severed any organic relation which makes an individual dependent upon the existence of other persons. Because, for Locke, there are no social laws prescribed, either by God or by nature, the sole authority for government rests in the private, introspectively given opinions of atomized individuals and their joint majority consent. Locke gave low status to emotions and passions. People exhibiting these and proclaiming the priority of human rights over property rights are, in a tendency of Western ideology, regarded as inferior and unrealistic. This category of the ideologically weak thus includes poets, artists, women, and most of the world's so-called primitive and nonscientific populations. Businessmen and engineers have the highest status in our ideology.[4] They are the ones with the largest stake in Star Wars.

Still, there is hope in stars. Just as nearly 2,000 years ago a new star appeared to wise men and led them to the manifested spirit of a new urge within man to recognize the godhead in persons, today, it would seem, we have come to the historical verge when a new star must appear. Its name, according to prophecy of the Hopi Indians, is the Blue Star, Sasquasohuh, far off and invisible but to appear soon. But, as Frank Waters warns us, we do not need to read what is probably a mythical parable as an astronomical or historical event. The roots of faith lie in the unconscious. Their unfoldment in consciousness comes by way of evolution, and evolution by way of meeting a crisis in the strategies of survival. In other words, there is a coming world of consciousness, and, according to Waters, its symbolic stars are not far off.[5]

But *is* there a coming world of consciousness? Will it be a consciousness expanded into the form of world understanding, ecological preservation, and peace? There is a remarkable and increasing amount of evidence that the answers to these fundamental questions are in the affirmative. Accordingly, it is my purpose in what follows to summarize the speculations and findings about consciousness as these appear in recent perspectives.

Let us begin with Waters, a philosophical writer who has devoted most of his life to studies of Amerindian and ancient Mesoamerican civilization, to Jungian psychology, to Eastern religious mysticism, and to modern science, including Einstein's revolutionary concept of a space-time continuum in the physical universe. As a resident of New Mexico, too, and formerly Information Director for Los Alamos Scientific Laboratory, Waters had close personal acquaintance with the Atomic Age from its terrifying inception.

The sun is our ultimate source of life. It gives out matter in electronic state—light, heat, radiation—that travels at some 186,000 miles per second and combines to produce matter in a cellular state, or organic life, on the surface of the earth. Because the total amount of light received from the sun is exactly the same at a distance of a million miles as at ten yards, so that the process of diffusion of light without loss goes on indefinitely, light is undiminishable, omnipresent, and eternal. This fact leads Waters, as it did our ancestors, to conclude that the energy transmitted from the sun to the earth, where it becomes organic life, must be reconverted into light when the organic bodies incorporating this energy die. The body of man, then, has an organic relationship with the cosmos. Cosmic effects, on a superlative scale of space-time movement, must be postulated for the evolution of life in all its forms and stages. Of course, when we observe things in a mineral, seemingly inert state, we may imagine that matter exists. But it does not. Modern science, in its reduction of material units to ever-smaller size, now knows that matter consists only of electrical fields unified by the attraction of their opposite polarities. Therefore, the difference between a star, a planet, a rock, a tree, a bird, a chimpanzee, and a human brain is not absolute. Energy links us all, though we obviously differ in degrees of evolutionary ascent.

If we approach our relationship to the cosmos from a *cosmic* viewpoint, moreover, it is clear that time is not a medium of linear measurement but a deep, still pool of an ever-living *now*, not a motion but a duration, and not, as some socio-religious-political doctrines would insist, a clock ticking away toward Apocalypse but an element in which power is stored up and held over into later events. It follows that what we call time is really a sense of ever *becoming* within a duration of immovable time. Over millions of years, the human species has been in process of becoming until we are now conscious of our existence in three-dimensional space (length, breadth, height) and in three-dimensional time (past, present, future). However, this three-dimensional sense of time is expanding into a fourth dimension, an "apperception" released from the unconscious psychic forces to unite us with eternity. As we perceive ourselves as part of the mysterious unity and continuity of life, our encounter with timelessness may evoke beneficent psychical energy. We will remain, as humans, dualistic and can be polarized, according to the prevailing philosophy, either to destructive or constructive ends. What happens in the psyche can occur in the cosmos. If the happening is destructive, as in thermonuclear cataclysm, the very energies of the cosmos can be warped. If, conversely, we maintain our psyche's balance with the evolutionary way that the Indians have always mythologized as Emergence on the Road of Life, we will emerge to a stage of increased awareness with an ethic of earthly preservation and of human solidarity.

As we are just beginning to comprehend the world-catastrophe that may attend modern science's usurpation of the power of the sun for the sake of military expediency, we are probably better able to see the sanity of Waters's ideas now than when he first enlarged upon them in 1950 in *Masked Gods*. He writes in that study of Navaho and Pueblo ceremonialism, the "problem of humanity at various stages of its development is the same as for the individual during his growth to maturity: relief from the ruthless tyranny of the instincts, or from the exclusive domination of the conscious ego" (409-410). Following Jung, Waters believes that the best way to thwart the psychic forces that impel nations to war is through a "reconciling symbol" that arises from the collective unconscious and has power to transform "the dynamic forces of millions of people to flow into new channels of collective ethics and morality toward a new

Emergence" (411). Since the power of some archetypes such as the cross, the sun, the lotus, and the square has deteriorated through centuries of deployment in doctrine, he proposes the ancient symbol of the circle or mandala as a reconciling symbol for our time, a metaphysical meaning implicit in the very Einsteinian equation that led to the Bomb – $E = MC^2$ (energy is but mass multiplied by the square of the velocity of light). The synonimity of matter and energy, with energy as boundless and infinite, applies both to the universe, where the large part of physical energy is locked inside the atom, and to consciousness, where the large part of psychic energy is locked within the psyche. With the "fusion" of primal dual forces of all life, atomic and psychic, a tremendous conflict takes place and from it is released "a new birth of energy" (442). We already know that the Bomb is one form, but the form of a new faith could be the circle. Einstein, himself, in the Relativity Theory established that the light energy travelling from the sun at 186,000 miles per second will describe a great cosmic circle and return to its source after 2,000-million terrestrial years. Modern science hereby defines the cosmos by the ancient symbol of the circle. The coming world of consciousness, then, is already here-and-now for a few individuals aware of our existence in a space-time continuum that finds its end in its beginning. We can emerge, fulfilling ourselves and civilization, to a beneficent new state, "returning to and merging with the eternal source, undifferentiated from the complete cosmos" (436-37).

The myth of Emergence is essentially a revolutionary philosophy of something so mysterious that we still have not fully defined it, human consciousness. William James had argued in 1890 in *Principles of Psychology* that phenomena of consciousness have a direct bearing on behavior, and the subsequent Freudian and Jungian talk about the *un*conscious mind as a cause of behavior has made the assumption seem obvious. To James, consciousness might be biologically significant in the struggle for survival. He called attention to a common belief of the 1880s that the complexity and intensity of consciousness increase with advances in evolutionary development. As James suggested, each act of consciousness appears to express a "teleological function" in the sense that it has ends to realize or purposes to accomplish.[6] Just *how* the consciousness exercises control, James granted, was an unsolved problem, nor have introspective psychological theories, Freud's and Jung's as based on the study of dreams, succeeded in opening the black box. As we shall see, the box has now been opened by neurophysiologists, and the new synthesis called *neuropsychology*, combining studies of brain function with those of behavior, is indeed showing how the consciousness exercises control. We are on the threshold of one of the greatest of all scientific revolutions, one that connects the creative spirit to life.

Before we enter the black box and name some of the Peace Stars becoming visible in the interstellar spaces of the brain, I wish to emphasize that the ancient idea of *duality* (reason/intuition, conscious/unconscious, male/female and so forth) is indeed applicable to world understanding. One road to peace lies through the mutual supplementation of global polarities as between the civilizations of East and West. So argued F.S.C. Northrop, Professor of Philosophy and Law at Yale University, in *The Meeting of East and West* (1946). Northrop traced to their fundamental assumptions the two civilizations, finding that of the West polarized to science, the male rationalistic component, and that of the East polarized to art, the female intuitive component. Could the twain ever meet? According to Northrop, there was already evidence in at least one culture, that of the United States, of an initiating shift to new philosophical foundations in which intuitive, indeterminate knowledge is complementing rational, determinate knowledge, both forms united by a common base. Northrop believed that Western civilization was beginning to learn that intuitional and emotional knowledge is "as primary and hence as justified as a criterion of trustworthy knowledge and of the good and the divine in culture" (311) as rational knowledge, thus affirming the basic insight of eastern civilization. For in the East, consciousness is the very stuff of an "emotional, all-embracing ineffability" (398) of reality. As the West becomes more polarized to the intuitive and the East becomes more polarized to the rationalistic, we can raise to a worldwide level both "the primitive intuition of the past" and "the sophisticated science of the present" (459). Northrop's argument is attractive and convincing. In fact, it was influential in the establishment of the United Nations and its economic and cultural spearhead, Unesco.

Northrop's mistake, however, was to confuse the notion of mutual supplementation of polarized civilizations with the notion of a world order. To envisage world understanding is one thing, to impose it is another. Even though the possibility of nuclear annihilation seems to make paramount the establishment of a world political order, the emergence of a new world of consciousness remains the prior event. First, as we have seen in discussion of Waters's ideas, the contents of the unconscious mind must spontaneously rise to awareness and heighten it, enforcing an acceptance of life through natural process. Even then, at the stage of increased awareness, the establishment of a world political order, which will necessarily be hierarchical with authority coming down on a vertical plane, is of highly dubious value. As we shall see, the architecture of human consciousness is not itself hierarchical. World order systems would seem to be contrary to nature.

Biologist Carl Sagan affirms individuality as a mark of the human species. The human brain, he tells us in *The Dragons of Eden* (1978), is characterized by some 10^{13} synapses.[7] Thus the number of different states of a human brain is 2 raised to this power—i.e., multiplied by itself ten trillion times. It is because of this immense number of functionally different configurations of the human brain that no two humans, even identical twins raised together, can ever be really very much alike. "From this perspective," he concludes, "each human being is truly rare and different, and the sanctity of individual human lives is a plausible ethical consequence" (44). Equally astonishing from the biologist's point of view are the physiological changes accompanying intellectual experience. Sagan cites a remarkable series of experiments performed by the American psychologist Mark Rosenzweig and his colleagues at the University of California, Berkeley. They maintained two different populations of laboratory rats, one in a dull, repetitive, impoverished environment, the other in a variegated, lively, enriched environment. The latter group displayed a striking increase in the mass and thickness of the cerebral cortex, as well as accompanying changes in brain chemistry. "This would mean," Sagan writes, "that new learning corresponds to the generation of new synapses or the activation of moribund old ones" (46-47). Clearly, the capacity for new learning will greatly enhance the chances of survival of the human species. The emergence of a global culture just as we have acquired the means for self-destruction of the species seems to evince biological inspiration. As we confront complexity, our brain follows the standard evolutionary practice of increasing the amount of genetic information "by doubling part of the genetic material and then allowing the slow specialization of function of the redundant set" (183). The point I am making here is that Carl Sagan, a biologist, would have no quarrel with Waters or with Northrop, philosophers, about our having two different, accurate, and complementary modes of thinking, or about the brain's capacity for creating collaboration between reason and intuition and for adapting to new environmental circumstances.

Although Sagan is skeptical about the pace of salvation—can we wait for evolution to create the correct mind?—the psychologist Robert Ornstein of the Institute for the Study of Human Consciousness believes that we can assist nature in construction of consciousness. In *The Psychology of Consciousness* (1972) Ornstein argues that conventional "textbook" psychology erroneously equates our "personal consciousness" (a mixture of thoughts, fantasies, ideas, and sensations of the external world) with all of so-called "objective" reality, whereas in fact we have experience of "events and objects that are totally produced by ourselves, as in dreams" and "unconscious experience of such processes as X-rays, even the air we breathe" (17). What we do is "select the sensory modalities of personal consciousness from the mass of information reaching us, then we construct a stable consciousness from the filtered input" (17). But if consciousness is a personal construction, "then each person can change his consciousness simply by changing the way he constructs it" (18). This active mode, necessary to survival, is conscious of events enduring in time, in sequence, of causes and effects, is essential in the development of culture, and is necessary for planning into the future, for taking the past lessons of history into account. The problem with this active, analytic mode is that we have almost forgotten that other constructions of individual consciousness are even possible. The solution to the problem, long known to the so-called "esoteric" psychologies of the Orient, is to cease our screening out of constancies in the external environment, a proceeding Ornstein calls "a deautomatization of consciousness" (183) through "exercises in attentional deployment" (138). It is as if all we need do is give ourselves personal permission to shift from an analytic world containing separate, discrete objects and persons to a second mode, an experience of unity. Here we perceive, for example, that our efforts to locate a scientific point of departure for time experience have been foolishly based on belief that a real linear time exists somewhere outside of man, whereas time is merely a dimension of the consciousness, existing in itself, not in how it relates to hours. All action occurs in an infinite present, and all events occur simultaneously. By opening ourselves to the intuitive, holistic side of consciousness, we become more receptive to a sense of being within time and at-one with all peoples on earth, past, present, and to come.

Ornstein's advocacy of a comprehensive psychology has already been anticipated by Waters's description of a coming world of consciousness, both the philosopher and the psychologist basing their views on what Ornstein calls a "fundamental duality of our consciousness" (58). Both, I infer, would agree that the analytic mode of consciousness, which disconnects us from objects and persons, must result in war unless we bring that mode into balance with the intuitive mode, which reveals the connectedness of life. If a key to peace is recognition that the analytic mode is no longer as necessary to biological survival as it was when beasts pounced out of the jungle, then we should give intuitive processes back their dignity, especially in education where we deemphasize and even devalue the arational, nonverbal modes of consciousness and are taught little about our emotions, our bodies, and our intuitive capabilities. Evidently we are just starting to come out of our Cartesian-Lockean swoon and to learn that we are future-oriented beings who, early in life, can make automatic and habitual the actions that serve peace through unity of mind and brain.

The automatism of habit as a derivative of consciousness has dynamic implications. Psychologist David Klein gives a simple illustration of how balked habits reinstate alertness to the conditions responsible for their frustration.

> The experienced driver can be absorbed in conversation with a passenger while the automatism of habit permits him to act as a quasi-mechanical chauffeur. He gives focal attention to the ideas being exchanged and only peripheral or subliminal attention to the engine and the road. This holds true as long as the situation is routine, but there is immediate and drastic reversal in the face of engine failure or hazardous road conditions, which precipitate maximum attention to the business of driving. If the engine fails, a veteran driver will stop the car at the side of the highway, as he will do if he hears a fire siren or sees an ambulance approaching. This is a commonplace maneuver for experienced drivers and becomes an inherent component of their entrenched driving habits, executed through *force* of habit.[8]

What is especially striking about the dynamics of persistent motivation, Klein concludes, is their ethical implications for the development of desirable traits of character and the reaping of the destiny of nations from the sowing of such traits. The nervous system can be our ally instead of our enemy.

Such conclusions from the field of psychology become compelling when we move to the field of neuropsychology to study neurons, the highly specialized cells that comprise the elementary units of the central nervous system.[9] Unlike other cells in the body, neurons—and this is their magic—are modifiable. They change as the result of growth during development and maturation—and they change as the result of experience.

Let us now peer in to the black box.

As our eyes become accustomed to the dark and our metaphorical telescope is trained on the interstellar spaces of the brain, we discern—of course figuratively speaking—a constellation of marvelous stars becoming ever brighter in our time and bearing auspicious tidings of the mind's ability to understand itself. These are, let us say, Peace Stars, and the wonder aroused by discovery prompts me, a nonscientist, to alter their abstract names into strange, poetic ones, like powers of a galactic allegory: Triunus is one, Hemisphaeria is another and brighter, Callosum is brighter still, Cognon is absolutely brilliant, and Heterarkia, with its satellites of Imaginationem, Memoria, and Rationem, may yet prove most radiant of all.

Triunus is the three basic, intermeshed formations of the brain, the "reptilian" (the most ancient part of the brain), the "paleomammalian" (old mammalian brain), and the "neo-mammalian" (the cerebral cortex). This triune brain communicates vertically and horizontally, but the important thing to observe is that the self-preserving drives of the reptilian brain do not dominate the neocortex, which serves to express and comprehend rich emotional meanings as well as to formulate altruistic, futuristic concern for others and to broaden the expanse of space, time, and habitat. Undoubtedly, human actions are influenced by the reptilian brain. It plays an important role in aggressive behavior and territoriality, but this role, contrary to some popular beliefs, is not imperative. The neocortex represents about 85% of the brain. Our long human childhood gives us plasticity to prevent slavish adherence to genetically programmed behavior. What the star *Triunus* tells us is that we can resist surrender to every impulse of the reptilian brain. The neocortex, enveloping the old brain structures with massive folds of neural tissues, is a *cognitive* brain containing billions of single neural units, any one of which has the power to decide whether to initiate an act or not.

Hemisphaeria, the star that has been known since ancient times in the concept of duality, loomed into recent view with discovery by Nobel Prize-winning psychologist-physiologist Roger W. Sperry of right and left hemispheres of the brain, with lateral specialization of function to each hemisphere but also with some doubling of conscious awareness. At first, the powerful evidence that our left brian is specialized for language led investigators to call this the "dominant" hemisphere, implying that the right side of the brain was subordinate, minor, and inferior. But such one-sided emphasis on language, perhaps our most distinctive human characteristic, allowed us to overlook the extremely important spatial, attentional, emotional, and musical abilities that are possessed by the nontalking half of the human brain. The mistake was to concentrate on cognitive functions related to intelligence, perception, language, verbal learning, and memory, and to pay little attention to expressive and receptive aspects of emotion. Not until it was realized that emotions and feelings are also localizable has the mistake been rectified. Now there is dramatic proof that affective aspects of language are localized in specific parts of the right hemisphere of the brain. As Alberta Gilinsky of the University of Bridgeport reports in *Mind and Brain*, "the findings on emotional processes do not support the idea that one side of the brain is rational, intellectual, or cognitive, in contrast to an impulsive, affective, or emotional side. Instead, both hemispheres possess affective aspects, but the right and left hemispheres have different emotional response patterns" (84). Still, the idea of mental duality, of two brains that influence development, is a striking one and explains some of our inner conflicts. For example, we may believe strongly in peace, ecological preservation, and equality for all, yet thrill to war, to the slaughter of whales, and to exclusion of women and minorities from the economic and political arena. Evidently, we need two brains, each hemisphere providing space for increasing specializations of functions, but we also need a fusion to take place at the midline to knit the two hemispheres together and, by uniting them, actually increase our powers of mind.

The star *Collosum* does exactly this. It is, of course, the Corpus Collosum, the bundle of nerve fibers which is the principal cabling between left and right hemispheres of the cerebral cortex. When Carl Sagan declares that "The path to the future lies through the corpus callosum" (*Dragons of Eden*, 191), he is certainly not overstating the case any more than Frank Waters is being esoteric and "mystical" in foreseeing a coming world of consciousness. As *mind is what the brain does*, and as we now know that the brain has evolved to the point of connecting its two hemispheres, it is clear that we possess the capacity for combining critical thinking with creative and intuitive insights in a coordinated search for new patterns. We have simply underestimated this capacity and doomed ourselves to sterility and possible annihilation.

I have said that the star *Cognon* is absolutely brilliant. Here's why. In 1972 a group of investigators at Princeton University were studying the cortex in macaque monkeys when a particularly stubborn neuron was encountered from which the investigators were unable to elicit any response, no matter what stimulus they tried. Finally one of them began to wave his hand in front of one monkey's eyes. Immediately the reluctant neuron sprang into an excited burst of activity. What was the cell responding to? For the next twelve hours, the investigators tested the cell's response to one silhouette after another—symmetrical patterns, five-pointed stars, leaf patterns, cutout of the human hand, and, finally, a cardboard model of the monkey's own paw. That stimulus evoked the most vigorous response. Thus it was deduced that a biologically meaningful stimulus object is importantly represented in the cognitive field of the monkey's brain. Hence we can postulate what Gilinsky, synthesizing psychology and neurophysiology into a unified field of neuropsychology, calls the "cognon," an elementary unit of thought derived from perceptual learning but constrained by the prewired cellular structure of the brain. As our brains have developed by superimposing on primitive layers the new layers of cortical integration, multiple new cognons have formed in minicolumns (about five million of them in turn composed of about 60-billion nerve cells) to represent all experienced objects and patterns and to provide the serial order in thought and action. The most fascinating aspect of the cognon is its ability to "call up" an image in anticipation of an expected event. As we undergo new experiences, cognons form to represent them. The mind has the capacity for permanently changing its structure by interacting with the environment. As we learn new patterns of behavior, we can retain the change permanently and irreversibly. *Cognon's* star quality is precisely this: "As cognons are formed in the cognitive centers of the brian, they ...take part in providing the stimuli for still higher-order cognons." (Gilinsky, *Mind and Brain*, 446)

Gilinsky illustrates the role that mind may play in changing our notions of reality by asking us to consider the word "grandfather." A grandfather is simply the father of a parent. Yet he must be old, bent, bespectacled, bearded, of beaming wrinkles and gentle ways. So it comes as a shock to you to learn that your car-racing friend with his smooth young face is a grandfather. Does your image of grandfather change? Not at all. What is most likely to change is that your grandfather stereotype remains in one set of cognons just as before, but now you make room for a new set of cognons representing youthful, daring grandfathers. The new set does not replace the old set. Instead, you now have two sets of related but independent cognons in place of one (*Mind and Brain*, 170).

Certainly some such process is currently changing our notions of "feminine" and "masculine" behavior as we cling to old sex stereotypes. This process must be awakening us to the notion, an ancient primitive one, of Earth as our nurturing Mother who must be preserved, even as we cling to stereotypes of Earth as exploitable matter. Some such process can change our notions of enemies, as recently happened with the collapse of the empire of the Soviet Union. The basic notion underlying all war is that our group, our tribe, our nation, our civilization is superior to any other, which group, tribe, nation, or civilization is considered monstrous—the "enemy." Yet we know that the human species is its own enemy. We are developing a new set of cognons representing "enemies" as friends, people like ourselves with the common goal of survival. Because the old set of cognons remains as before, we are not likely to embrace enemies in a permanent gush of the sentiment of brotherhood. However, in the interest of the protection and preservation of the self and the species, a drive can be said to be evolving to bring pressure to bear in support of the behavior that serves the chief goals of the human brain. The drive toward power can be replaced by an antidrive that inhibits destructive tendencies and leads us toward the constructive ones. Evolution has given the mammalian brain its competitive edge by introducing into its activity a flexible, integrative thrust, with lower-level cognons forming higher-order cognons.

Here coming into astonishing, unexpected focus of our metaphorical telescope is the great star *Heterarkia*, which represents the flexibility of organization that explains the superiority of the human brain. We have, according to Gilinsky, three pictures of the mind's architecture. One is that programs are combined serially, data from one program taken over by the next in line—always a linear, assembly-line progression of neural reactions. Another picture is that the combination occurs hierarchically, with one program having overall control and the flow of control moving from top down. Neither system has flexibility, for both assembly-line and hierarchy suffer from the fixed progression of responsibility through successive levels of the system. The heterarchical arrangement offers equal distribution of responsibility for control throughout the system. As Margaret Boden writes in *Artificial Intelligence and Natural Man* (1977), "the human analogy is a group of intercommunicating specialists contributing their several skills to a cooperative enterprise, rather than a troop of servants each unquestioningly obeying their mistress."[10] Gilinsky, who compares the brain's architecture to a smoothly functioning football team, concludes:

> Our heterarchical brain is a dynamically organized, interconnected set of systems and subsystems that can pass control from one to another in many different directions. Earlier units in a heterarchy can be modified by the activity of the later ones, later units can undo mistakes, and units at any point can forestall adverse contingencies. This is the power of intelligence responsible for the higher reaches of human thought. (*Mind and Brain*, 460)

This image of the central nervous system as a heterarchy should give pause to those whose model for world order is a hierarchy. A heterarchy achieves orderliness by having many autonomous units serving in specialized capacities on different levels of the system and brings all units to work toward common goals through harmony, mutual respect, and unity of purpose.

We have gazed at Peace Stars but have not named the constellation of which they are part—*Consciousness*. As it happens, no line can be drawn between conscious and unconscious "sides" of the brain: all neural structures are involved in the programming and guidance of behavior. In carrying out the survival-function of the nervous system, evolution must have favored the development of consciousness, allowing us, when we are confronted with increasingly complex, changing environments, to call for radically different adaptations and for selection of appropriate actions. Consciousness plays a causal role in brain function and behavior. Gilinsky sums up this role of consciousness, as follows:

> Complex work involving millions of neurons and billions of synapses takes place at a level that proceeds effectively without our conscious intervention. Consciousness is thus freed to concentrate on the priorities of the moment, and by its selective emphasis can direct our behavior to our self-selected ends. (*Mind and Brain*, 478)

Such a view of consciousness represents to the neuropsychologist a revolution in our conception of the nature of intelligence, a revolution no less profound than the Darwinian conception of our origins or the Einsteinian conception of the physical world.

As we stand on the threshold of a new epoch, there are indeed signs betokening the emergence from the unconscious of those contents that, unified with conscious elements, will lead to a union of the opposite polarities. Already we are psychically beginning our transition to a new world of consciousness in which we may find, in Waters's words, "That all life itself is but a series of stages of cosmic evolution" (*Mexico Mystique*, 283). If world-crisis prompts us, as seems possible, to recover spiritual wholeness, our creative spirit will of itself control the Atomic Age. Wisdom is not out of reach. The mental equipment is there, but unused. One day, perhaps not too far off, an allegorical Blue Star will appear, the Peace Star in the light of whose radiance we shall have learned to lift the gaze of our hearts—our minds—to mysterious, measureless worlds without end.

A THEODICY OF HUMAN LOVE

Doris Betts, *Souls Raised from the Dead*. New York: Alfred A. Knopf, 1994. 339 pp.

Doris Betts lives with her husband on a horse farm in Pittsboro, not far from Chapel Hill, where she recently retired as Alumni Distinguished Professor of English at the University of North Carolina. For more than forty years she has been writing plaintively and wittily about everyday people in a realistic "new" South. She has several collections of short stories in addition to her five novels, one of which, *Heading West* (1981) was a main selection of the Book-of-the-Month Club. Her fifth novel, *Souls Raised from the Dead*, confirms her reputation as one of our most accomplished writers, and in it there is fresh evidence that she works at imaginative depth. When she speaks of a character, that "She wanted the explanations Job had wanted" (315), Betts speaks of herself as well—and for all of us in an age that demands images of its almost unimaginable catastrophes. *Souls Raised from the Dead* is one of those rare, powerfully envisioned works of fictional art that inscribe reality in the face of the potent and alien forces of chaos.

The novel's pivotal figure is a young girl who sickens and dies of kidney disease, Mary Grace Thompson. She lives with her father, Frank Thompson, in Carrboro, North Carolina, a wrong-side-of-the-tracks suburb of Chapel Hill (population 45,000, not counting students). Mary's beautiful, selfish, and feckless mother, Christine, has abandoned the family three years earlier and is now divorced from Frank, who is left to raise Mary as best he can with what he earns as a sergeant with the highway patrol. Fortunately, his love, as well as that of his parents, Tacey and Dandy Thompson, has succeeded in saving Mary from bouts of sleepwalking and self-doubt. At age twelve, on the verge of puberty, Mary is blossoming into a self-confident person armed with intelligence and fortitude and potentials of the heart. Then disaster strikes. As she gradually becomes aware of her mortal illness, she accepts it with an equanimity that members of her family lack. She is not at all like Ivan Ilyich in Tolstoy's famous novella about dying. She doesn't cry about helplessness, about terrible loneliness, about the cruelty of people, about the cruelty of God, about the absence of God.[1] She simply grants the idea of her death the strength of her intelligence. Not so, the others. Frank desperately seeks a cure and, to add to his frustrations, is denied the opportunity to donate one of his kidneys. Tacey's religious faith is tested and lost. Christine, who denies the crisis and any responsibility for its outcome, gets comeuppance in the form of guilt-ridden hysteria.

We do not see in Mary's plight the judgment of fate. She is just unlucky—significantly, she owns a horse named Chancy. But, like her own middle name, she embodies grace and exhibits an elegant style of behavior that confers dignity upon the proceedings and, in a sense, upon her world. She is the calm center of stability in this novel, the eye of the hurricane.

The main focus of the novel is on her father, Frank. When the story begins on June 1, 1990, he is present, in his capacity as an officer, as an overturned poultry truck is spewing panicked chickens to fatal accidents on a highway. These "7,500 capons, fed on chemicals, raised for slaughter in houses heated and lit by electric current," have never before set foot on ground and must test it "to be the actual birds they almost remembered" (3). Frank's life, we are told, "included moments of bravery, others of dignity; but often he had been required to impose order on a chaos less criminal than ridiculous" (3-4). Perhaps there is irony in this word, impose. Frank would like to believe, as would any rational being, that he is in control of events even while uncontrollable elements are breaking out all of the time. He indulges the wishful thinking that pretends to establish order as a social form. Actually, however, Frank is all too aware of human vulnerability to violence. He is aware, too, of how seldom we are prepared for it, as if we were just so many chickens unnaturally nurtured on technology. He dreads, with good contemporary reason, that his own world may at any moment be invaded and violated. After the chicken incident, he returns home, the patrolman become over-protective single parent:

> Frank stood motionless in the foyer and for the ritual moment allowed fear to cover him in flood, since he was constantly fearful, on entry, unreasonably fearful, of discovering that fire, disease, murder, or rape had on this day found his house at last. (5)

By the end of the novel such disasters have "found" him indeed: Lila Torrido, the next-door neighbor alleged to be the illegitimate daughter of Al Capone's brother, has been horribly molested and murdered, and disease has claimed Mary not long after her thirteenth birthday on August 12, 1990.

In the last scene of the novel, Frank is again present at a wreck, this time an automobile accident in which a mother is killed, a father is flung out, and a teenaged daughter is injured and trapped. Subconsciously he sees the resemblance between this family situation and his own, the difference being that *this* girl is still alive, as Mary no longer is. Accordingly, he bounces back from his emotional dead end, supervises the rescue of the girl, and plans to make a personal call to her father. Order is no longer something to be imposed, as it were, from external authority; it is, rather, the effect of an internalized authority, one that offers rituals of compassion in the knowledge that no space, no person is inviolable. In other words, Frank has worked out a personal salvation and brings it to his community.

The body of the novel plays out two related scenarios, Mary's case history from diagnosis through dialysis treatment to kidney transplant and pneumonia, and the reactions to her illness of the other characters whose moral fitness is tested, so to speak, before the bar of fate. Such is the effect of Betts's technique of using multiple points of view, we experience the lives of characters as they exist in isolation from one another. Their expressive habits are insightfully described, their attitudes respectfully considered, but their isolation is consistently pegged as a violation of the human position. Although Frank is deeply bonded to Mary and hence the human being par excellence, other characters seem less than fully human. Christine, the spineless mother, is so insensitive that she uses the occasion of a family reunion to take orders for the cosmetics she peddles. Her mother Georgia is a palm reader with a trashy past and a violent temper. The Thompsons are well-meaning grandparents who have long ago moved from the land and have apparently lost some of the values therein accrued. Dandy is a joker ("The Broomes thought Beethoven's Fifth was a bourbon," 77) who has spent his working life as manager of the shoe department at Belk's store and who refuses to go to church even though he'd like to keep churches around as a bulwark against secularization. Tacey has never wanted to be touched by life ("With rumors so widespread, there must be something to this orgasm business, but the most Tacey had ever felt was some brief internal reflex, as if her womb had sneezed," 173). If anybody seems to have the old-time religion for our comfort, it is Tacey. But after Mary's death, the moral usefulness of that religion comes a cropper when, "full of dread, nauseated," she recognizes it as "all a lie" (316). That the moral limitations of the family members as a whole are those of society in general is a function of Frank's girlfriends, Cindy Scofield and Jill Peters. Their female chauvinism leaves them lost when it comes to genuine relationships and commitments to others.

Here is a society, the society of this novel, that is composed of individuals living without faith and, except for Frank, without purpose. Any fundamental order in terms of which they may make sense of life and recognize their own identities is in process of disintegration. They are exposed to a violent world, and they are unable to cope. Not only have these individuals lost some of their moral bearings, with disastrous psychological consequences (Frank's despair, Tacey's disillusionment,

Christine's breakdown), but also they are left uncertain about their cognitive bearings ("It all felt like a movie, a TV show," Frank reflects, "with the director temporarily off the set for coffee break," 56).

Nor is history, the history of this novel, a sanctuary for a living and concrete reality. Frank has had some past loyalty to the old Thompson farmplace. He, we are told,

> had meant to grow up, grow rich, and reclaim this land, build himself a white-columned house and set purebred dogs to guard each door with purebred horses posed like statues down the hill. (16)

But little remains to absorb Frank's longing: most of the land has been converted into a shopping center with paved parking lots, and what remains is remote to present needs. When Jill comes upon the family burial plot, she dreads "these shrunken, sunken, country graves with unlikely markers and dragonflies drinking some invisible vapor off their names" (128). Everything that might have historical staying power, like Chapel Hill, itself, and its university, has succumbed to the intrusion of modern civilization (and intrusiveness and violation are basic metaphors for Betts). Thus Dandy reflects:

> At thirty-five miles per hour he entered green Chapel Hill, a university town he loved but could not understand. Most of the time its neighborhoods were chock-full of friendly, likable people whose ideas he disapproved of: liberals favoring abortion, welfare, eminent domain, peace at any cost, fornication, homosexual weddings, and the secularization of American public life. (73)

History is, like society, no longer a basis for stability and order.

The situation isn't new nor is it unique to Doris Betts. Like many writers of the "new" South who grew up in the 1930s and 1940s and began writing fiction in the years after the Second World War, Betts belongs to a generation that is further removed than her ancestors from—to quote Louis D. Rubin, Jr.'s *The Faraway Country: Writers of the Modern South* (1963)—"the concepts of a particular kind of community, of man as a creature of a particular history, and as a creature whose life is ordered by a particular scheme of theological belief." But, he continues, "the general attitudes, the general ways of looking at human experience remain real." What we ought to expect from these writers "is a literature that involves the examination of these attitudes as they survive, or fail to survive ...a literary exploration of the potentialities of certain surviving attitudes for imparting meaning and order to modern human experience, an experience that by no means is identical with traditional Southern life as described and assumed in the work of the earlier writers."[2] As I read Betts's novel, its vision of reality, I see an attitude carried over from tradition: the protagonist of *Souls Raised from the Dead*, Frank Thompson, is tested for his capacities for responsibility, courage, and above all, for love and gains personal salvation—a "soul." He knows and perhaps cares little about historical and social links with his past, but he creates his own salvation and becomes emblematic of order in values. His love for Mary represents a constant. He is the one who makes sacrifices for her, of his kidney (if he could), of his relationships with Cindy and Jill, and finally, almost, of his sanity.

Although this novel may make its initial appeal through a style that is humorous, even droll, vivid, perceptive and great-hearted, the power it generates through 339 pages of dramatically organized text—a spell unrelieved except by double-line breaks and by switching viewpoints—derives not from style but from the effect of envisioning its world. This effect is the magnificent achievement of novels as art, and Tolstoy was a master—so to work that the reader does not feel he is reading the work of a particular author at all, but feels that he is, simply, there, in an actual world.[3] Betts achieves this effect. In rendering the sense of life, she also frees herself to make manifest the particular way of conducting life that has supreme value for her. She conjures fictional "souls" out of the "dead" state of uncreated life and projects these souls into the forefront of created life. Here they could become, but only Frank fully becomes, a shield against terror, projecting a theodicy of human love.[4]

Souls Raised from the Dead engenders Job-like questions without accepting traditional answers to them and without flinching before the abyss. But Betts's world still carries redeeming assurance of faith in the potential of man as a moral and spiritual being capable, when pressed, of integrity, responsibility, and the measures of devotion. This world is not structured as a tragedy, but it sustains a tragic vision throughout. The problem of theodicy—how the extraordinary power of a transcendent unitary god may be reconciled with death and suffering in the world that "He" has created and rules over—is touched upon more than once before it is reconstituted in terms of the creative spirit. If we cannot be reconciled to the Judeo-Christian mythology, we can try to be reconciled to ourselves. The need for salvation remains. At no time in human history is this truth more apparent than it is now, with a nuclear peril that threatens not just each person's life on the planet but the very meaning of our lives. It is a great intellectual task of our time to recast the image of man and the values by which he lives and to rediscover the humanity that is becoming lost and frustrated in our technological civilization. The world of Doris Betts's novel grants us no peace. But it evokes–as Thomas Mann, after the Second World War, put it in *Last Essays*, in "Nietzsche's Philosophy in the Light of Recent History," in proposing the role that a man of letters in the Atomic Age plays–"a new feeling for the difficulty and the nobility of being human."[5]

NOTES

A Writer's Quest for Knowledge

1 John Atkins calls Orwell a "social saint" and Irving Howe calls him a "revolutionary personality," views disputed by Richard H. Rovere, "Introduction," *The Orwell Reader: Fiction, Essays, and Reportage by George Orwell* (New York: Harcourt, Brace & World, Inc., 1956), xix.

2 The conversion of Blair into Orwell is the subject of Peter Stansky and William Abrahams, *The Unknown Orwell*, New York: Alfred A. Knopf, 1972.

3 George Orwell, "A Hanging," in *The Orwell Reader*, 11.

4 Leo Tolstoy, *What Is Art?* (Indianapolis: Bobbs-Merrill, 1960), 51-52.

5 On changing interpretations of Ulysses, see W.B. Stanford and J.V. Luce, *The Quest for Ulysses*, New York: Praeger, 1974.

6 George E. Dimock, Jr., "The Name of Odysseus," in *Homer: A Collection of Critical Essays*, edited by George Steiner and Robert Fagles (Englewood Cliffs, N.J.: Prentice-Hall, 1962), 107.

7 On Pound in the persona of Odysseus and on the robust, Homeric quality of Canto XLVII, in which the poet seeks knowledge of life renewed, see George Dekker, *Sailing After Knowledge: The Cantos of Ezra Pound* (London: Routledge & Kegan Paul, 1963), 37-38.

8 R.W.B. Lewis, The *Picaresque Saint: Representative Figures in Contemporary Fiction* (Philadelphia & New York: J.B. Lippincott Company, 1959), 19. See also Frederick J. Hoffman, *The Mortal No: Death and the Modern Imagination*, Princeton: Princeton University Press, 1964.

9 James Joyce, *A Portrait of the Artist as a Young Man* (Harmondsworth: Penguin Books, 1969), 171-72.

10 On motivations of a revolutionist, see Eric Hoffer, *The True Believer: Thoughts on the Nature of Mass Movements*, New York: Harper & Row, 1951.

11 From Robert Lowell, "Waking Early Sunday Morning," in Robert Lowell, *Near the Ocean* (London: Faber & Faber, 1967), 16. The poet resigns himself to seeking knowledge in the wreck of human life and of experience. Patrick Cosgrave sees the poem as Lowell's greatest work "and one of the greatest as well as the most important for the future of contemporary poems," in *The Public Poetry of Robert Lowell* (London: Victor Gollancz, 1970), 10.

Experience, Imagination, and Revolt

1 Wallace Stegner, *The Sound of Mountain Water: The Changing American West* (Garden City, N.Y.: Doubleday & Company, 1969), 176.

2 From William Faulkner, *Absalom, Absalom!*, cited in this context in David Minter, *William Faulkner: His Life and Work* (Baltimore and London: The Johns Hopkins University Press, 1980), 20.

3 Ibid., 95-97.

4 Eudora Welty, *The Eye of the Story: Selected Essays and Reviews* (New York: Random House, 1977), 121-22.

5 See Denis Donoghue, *The Sovereign Ghost: Studies in Imagination* (Berkeley and Los Angeles: University of California Press, 1976), 7-10, 27-28, 68-70, 78-81.

6 Richard Poirier, *A World Elsewhere: The Place of Style in American Literature* (New York: Oxford University Press, 1966), 6.

The Long Habit of Living

1 "Writing Schools," *The Times Literary Supplement*, Thursday, April 8, 1965, p. 275.

2 Initial paragraphs of this essay were published in my entry, "William Maxwell Blackburn," in *Dictionary of North Carolina Biography*, vol. I (Chapel Hill: The University of North Carolina Press, 1979), 165-66.

3 William Blackburn, *The Architecture of Duke University* (Durham: Duke University Press, 1939), 25.

4 William M. Blackburn, "Sketches for a Memoir," *Duke Alumni Register*, 58 (1973): 18-21.

5 Robert W. White, *The Abnormal Personality*, New York: Ronald Press, 1948. In this book in my possession, Elizabeth Blackburn annotated passages relevant, she believed, to her former husband's personality.

6 *Joseph Conrad: Letters to William Blackwood and David S. Meldrum*, edited by William Blackburn (Durham: Duke University Press, 1958), 27, 88.

7 Letters from William Blackburn to Elizabeth Blackburn, 2, 3, 4, 5, 7 October 1927, in Duke University Library archives. Not trusting Durham doctors during the final weeks of her pregnancy, Tris had gone to New York to be under the care of her uncle, Dr. Alexander Lambert, though she had visited briefly in Connecticut with her mother, Mrs. Helen Cheney Bayne, and with her sister, Mrs. Helen Knapp. Blackburn was committed to teaching his classes at Duke. Although he was dismayed by his bride's absence, he was elated at the prospect of fatherhood and would join Tris in New York for the birth of Mary April on 16 November 1927. For a couple who sometimes played the parts of Robert and Elizabeth Barrett Browning, the separation afforded an opportunity to show off their literary skills.

8 Letter from Elizabeth Blackburn to her mother-in-law, Mrs. Charles S. (Amy) Blackburn, 11 September 1935, in Duke University Library archives. Once a tiny village on the Atlantic coast above Myrtle Beach, South Carolina, Cherry Grove is now North Myrtle Beach.

9 Letter by Fred Chappell, quoted in Marguerite Hays, "William Blackburn: Teacher of Writers," *The Furman Magazine*, 19 (Spring 1972), 29.

10 Reynolds Price, quoted in Earl Wolslagel," Mentor of Authors Succumbs at Duke," *Durham Herald*, 10 December 1972.

11 William Styron, "William Blackburn," in William Styron, *This Quiet Dust and Other Writings* (New York: Random House, 1982), 253, 254, 256. The Blackburn-Styron relationship is explored at length in James L. W. West III's *William Styron: A Life*, New York: Random House, 1998, especially in the chapter entitled "Duke and William Blackburn," pp. 93-108.

On Teaching Creative Writing

1 Richard Hofstadter, *Anti-intellectualism in American Life* (New York: Vintage Books, 1963), 3.

2 Ross Lockridge's novel, *Raintree County*, and Thomas Heggen's play, *Mr. Roberts*, were enormously successful. In spite of their successes (and in part because of them) these authors committed suicide. See John Leggett, *Ross and Tom: Two American Tragedies* New York: Simon and Schuster, 1974.

3 Richard Hofstadter, *Anti-intellectualism in American Life*, 51.

4 Ronald Sukenick, quoted in the University of Colorado *Silver & Gold Record*, 2 September 1975.

5 George Garrett's remarks were made at the Denver Conference of Associated Writing Programs, 30 January 1975, and remain relevant in the 1990s.

6 Playing roles and being hip make the Holy Barbarian very nearly the same as the Organization Man, according to Paul Goodman, *Growing Up Absurd: Problems of Youth in the Organized Society* (New York: Vintage Books, 1960), 170-190.

7 I studied creative writing under John J. Maloney in 1954 at the New School for Social Research in New York. According to a mutual friend in the publishing business, Maloney was a writer, but he had destroyed the manuscript of his only novel because, in his opinion, it wasn't as good as *Ulysses*! William Blackburn, my mentor, wrote beautifully, but not in the forms of imaginative literature.

8 Betty Shiflett, "Story Workshop as a Method of Teaching Writing," *College English* 35:2 (November 1973): 144, 146, 147.

9 Quoted by permission of Paul L. Robins.

10 Yusef Komunyakaa, "The Way the Cards Fall," *Writers' Forum*, 2 (1975): 11-12. Komunyakaa's extraordinary promise as a poet when he was an undergraduate proved decisive for him. Instead of pointing toward a career as a psychologist, he continued to study creative writing in graduate schools at Colorado State University and at University of California at Irvine.

Character as Style

1 Frank Waters, novelist and philosopher born in Colorado Springs in 1902, lived in Arroyo Seco, near Taos, New Mexico, with his wife Barbara until his death on 3 June 1995.

2 Francisco Vásquez de Coronado explored what is now the southwestern United States in 1540-1542, "hacking his way into one pueblo after another, looting, raping and spitting their inhabitants on lances," says Frank Waters in *The Colorado* (Athens, Ohio: Swallow Press, 1984), 141. A segment of Coronado's trail to Taos Valley is preserved in Carson National Forest in the high country between Taos and Peñasco.

3 Frank Waters, *Flight from Fiesta* (Athens, Ohio, and London: Swallow Press/Ohio University Press, 1987), 101-102.

4 Marshall Sprague, "Frank Waters: Narrator of the Region," *Colorado Springs Gazette Telegraph*, 2 February 1954.

5 Frank Waters, unpublished letter addressed to the people of Colorado Springs, 27 April 1991. The letter was read aloud to the public gathered for the dedication of Frank Waters Park.

6 Cited in F.L. Lucas, *Style*, 2d ed. (London: Cassell, 1974), 51. Lucas's book, originally published in 1955, has been a source and a guide for some of the observations on style in this essay.

7 Ibid., 112.

8 Ibid., 113.

9 Frank Waters, *The Man Who Killed the Deer* (Athens: Swallow Press/Ohio University Press, 1970), 164. Originally published in 1942, this novel is about a Taos Pueblo Indian named Martiniano.

10 Jack Shaefer, *Shane*, the Critical Edition edited by James C. Work (Lincoln and London: University of Nebraska Press, 1984), 61. This novel was originally published in 1949. Thomas J. Lyon's remarks appear in *Writers' Forum*, 11 (1985): 180-194.

11 Frank Waters, *People of the Valley* (Chicago: The Swallow Press, 1969), 68. This novel was originally published in 1941.

12 *The Essential Hemingway* (Harmondsworth: Penguin Books, 1967), 237.

13 Hervey Allen, *Anthony Adverse*, Limited Edition (Mount Vernon, N.Y., 1937), I, 84-85.

14 Frank Waters, *People of the Valley*, 40-41.

15 Cited in F.L. Lucas, *Style*, 159.

16 Ralph Waldo Emerson, *The Complete Essays* (New York: Modern Library, 1950), 262.

17 William Faulkner, *Go Down, Moses* (New York: Vintage Books, 1973), 208-209.

18 Frank Waters, *Mountain Dialogues* (Athens, Ohio: Swallow Press, 1981), 27-28.

Myth and the Picaresque Novel

1 Cited by Palmer Bovie, "Foreword," *The Age of Fable or Beauties of Mythology*, by Thomas Bulfinch (New York: Mentor Books, 1962), xi.

2 Arthur Koestler, *The Act of Creation* (New York: Macmillan, 1964), 147-48, 154.

3 Tamas Aczel, "The Mythology of Full Consciousness," in *Ten Years After: The Hungarian Revolution in the Perspective of History*, edited by Tamas Aczel (New York, Chicago, San Francisco: Holt, Rinehart, and Winston, 1967), 193.

4 Albert Camus, *The Rebel (L'Homme revolté)*, translated by Anthony Bower (Harmondsworth: Peregrine Books, 1962), 28.

5 Joseph Campbell, *The Masks of God: Creative Mythology* (London: Secker & Warburg, 1968), 609.

6 Cited by G.S. Kirk, *Myth: Its Functions in Ancient and Other Culture* (Berkeley and Los Angeles: University of California Press, 1970), 48.

7 Henry Adams, *The Education of Henry Adams* (Boston: Houghton Mifflin, 1981), 381-82.

8 Sure foundations for critical analysis of picaresque fiction have been laid since 1927 when F. Courtney Tarr discerned the artistic unity in and continuity of *Lazarillo de Tormes*. Since then, a solid structure for its understanding has steadily risen from the insights of, among many others, Américo Castro, Claudio Guillén, Fernando Lázaro Carreter, Francisco Rico, Stephen

Gilman, Alan D. Deyermond, Joseph V. Ricapito, and George A. Shipley. For a detailed scholarly guide to the novel, see Robert L. Fiore, *Lazarillo de Tormes*, Boston: Twayne, 1984. For a summary of the new view of the picaresque novels in Spain, see Peter N. Dunn, *Spanish Picaresque Fiction: A New Literary History*, Ithaca: Cornell University Press, 1993. For studies of picaresque fiction both in and outside of Spain, the reader is referred to Richard Bjornson, *The Picaresque Hero in European Fiction*, Madison: The University of Wisconsin Press, 1977; to my *The Myth of the Pícaro: Continuity and Transformation of the Picaresque Novel, 1554-1954*, Chapel Hill: The University of North Carolina Press, 1979; and to Edward H. Friedman, *The Antiheroine's Voice: Narrative Discourse and Transformations of the Picaresque*, Columbia: University of Missouri Press, 1987.

The Pícaro in American Literature

[1] Folklorists point to the existence of an indigenous American trickster hero; see, for example, Richard M. Dorson, *American Folklore*, Chicago: University of Chicago Press, 1959. On the development in American humor of a popular antihero, the Yankee, see Walter Blair, *Native American Humor*, San Francisco: Chandler, 1960, and Constance Rourke, *American Humor: A Study of the National Character*, New York: Harcourt, Brace, 1931. On picarism as a cultural outlook of the American people, see Warwick Wadlington, *The Confidence Game in American Literature*, Princeton: Princeton University Press, 1975, and Gary Lindberg, *The Confidence Man in American Literature*, New York: Oxford University Press, 1982.

[2] See R.W.B. Lewis, *The American Adam: Innocence, Tragedy and Tradition in the Nineteenth Century*, Chicago: University of Chicago Press, 1955.

[3] See Victor L. Chittick, *Thomas Chandler Haliburton*, New York: Columbia University Press, 1983.

4 The *Spirit of the Times*, edited by William T. Porter, appeared from 1831 to 1860. It began as a sporting paper, and the stories of backwoods life tended to grow organically out of factual sporting narratives. See Norris W. Yates, *William T. Porter and the 'Spirit of the Times': A Study of the Big Bear School of Humor*, Baton Rouge: Louisiana State University Press, 1957.

5 On Hooper, see Kenneth Lynn, *Mark Twain and Southwestern Humor* (Boston: Little, Brown, 1960), 46-99.

6 Twain's determinism is studied in Roger B. Salomon, *Twain and the Image of History*, New Haven: Yale University Press, 1961.

The Interior Country

1 Theodore Roethke, "The Rose," in Theodore Roethke, *The Far Field* (Garden City, N.Y.: Doubleday & Company Anchor Books, 1971), 31.

2 Frank Waters's novel, *Pike's Peak* (1971), is a revision of a trilogy of his novels, *The Wild Earth's Nobility* (1935), *Below Grass Roots* (1937), and *The Dust Within the Rock* (1940).

3 See Thomas J. Lyon, *"The Man Who Killed the Deer,"* Writers' Forum, 11 (1985): 180-194.

4 A psychological theme of rightness with the land is dramatized in many of the novels of Frank Waters but especially in *People of the Valley* (1941*)*, *The Man Who Killed the Deer* (1942), and *Pike's Peak* (1971).

5 Wallace Stegner, *The Sound of Mountain Water: The Changing American West* (Garden City, N.Y.: Doubleday &Company, Inc., 1969), 10.

6 Gerald W. Haslam, "Western Writers and the National Fantasy," in *Western Writing*, edited by Gerald W. Haslam (Albuquerque: University of New Mexico Pres, 1974), 4.

7 Genocide defined as the forced relocation of native peoples is studied in Jerry Kammer, *The Second Long Walk: The Navajo-Hopi Land Dispute*, Albuquerque: University of New Mexico Press, 1980.

8 For this summary view of tragedy I am indebted to John Wain, *The Living World of Shakespeare* (Harmondsworth: Penguin Books, 1966), 163-64, 167.

9 See Peter Wiley and Robert Gottlieb, *Empires in the Sun: The Rise of the New American West*, Tucson: University of Arizona Press, 1985.

10 Frederick Jackson Turner, *The Frontier in American History* (New York: Holt, Rinehart and Winston, 1962), 212-13. Turner introduced his thesis at a meeting in Chicago in 1893, just three years after Hotchkiss guns, firing a shell a second, massacred a group of Indians at Wounded Knee (a fact never mentioned by Turner). According to the thesis, the American character was formed on the frontier over a period of hundreds of years of in-migration, by people motivated by the existence of "free" lands. By 1893, however, free lands no longer existed in the West to give individuals a chance to improve their lot in life. Retiring from Harvard in 1924, Turner moved to Pasadena, California, where he died in 1932, just a few years before completion of Hoover Dam—symbol both of the marriage of public money with free enterprise and of the rise of a metropolitan West that has destroyed the frontier.

11 On the relevance of Ancient America to Modern America, see Frank Waters, *Masked Gods: Navaho and Pueblo Ceremonialism*, Albuquerque: University of New Mexico Press, 1950.

12 Theodore Roethke, "The Far Field," in Theodore Roethke, *The Far Field*, 28.

13 Will Gatlin is the soul-searching protagonist in Edward Abbey's novel, *Black Sun* (1971).

14 Barry Lopez, "Winter Count 1973," in *The Interior Country: Stories of the Modern West*, edited by Alexander Blackburn with Craig Lesley and Jill Landem (Athens, Ohio: Swallow Press/Ohio University Press, 1987), 205.

A Western Renaissance

1 See A. Carl Bredahl, Jr., *New Ground: Western American Narrative and the Literary Canon*, Chapel Hill and London: The University of North Carolina Press, 1989.

2 See Richard H. King, *A Southern Renaissance: The Cultural Awakening of the American South, 1930-1955*, New York: Oxford University Press, 1980, and his essay, "Framework of a Renaissance," in *Faulkner and the Southern Renaissance*, edited by Doreen Fowler and Ann Abadie (Jackson: University Press of Mississippi, 1982), 3-21.

3 Frank Waters, *The Wild Earth's Nobility* (New York: Liveright, 1935), 3.

Faulkner and Continuance of the Southern Renaissance

1 C. Vann Woodward, *The Burden of Southern History*, rev. ed. (Baton Rouge: Louisiana State University Press, 1970), 24.

2 See Cleanth Brooks, *William Faulkner: The Yoknapatawpha Country*, New Haven: Yale University Press, 1963, and Louis D. Rubin, Jr., *The Faraway Country: Writers of the Modern South*, Seattle: University of Washington Press, 1963.

3 All quotations from William Styron's novels are from the first editions as published by Random House, New York.

4 Malcolm Cowley's review of *Lie Down in Darkness*—"The Faulkner Pattern," *New Republic*, 125 (8 October 1951), 19-20—concentrated attention upon the novel's apparent similarities to *The Sound and the Fury*. Such comparisons thereafter became a sort of mandatory exercise, to the point of irrelevance in John W. Aldridge's chapter called "William Styron and the Derivative Imagination," in *Time to Murder and Create: The Contemporary Novel in Crisis* (New York: David McKay, 1966), 30-51. A sensible approach becomes evident in Louis D. Rubin, Jr., *The Faraway Country*, 185-230, and in Jonathan Baumbach, *The Landscape of Nightmare: Studies in the Contemporary American Novel* (New York: New York University Press, 1965), 123-37, and thereafter in Marc L. Ratner, *William Styron*, New York: Twayne, 1972, who emphasizes Styron's talents as a satirist. Styron's indebtedness to Faulkner is of little moment in the essays printed in *The Achievement of William Styron*, edited by Robert K. Morris and Irving Malin, Athens: University of Georgia Press, 1975.

5 Rubin, *The Faraway Country*, 201.

6 Styron's statement in a *Paris Review* interview—"I don't consider myself in the Southern school"—is cited as evidence that he doesn't belong to a "new mode" of southern writing, in Willard Thorp, "The Southern Mode," *South Atlantic Quarterly*, 63 (1964): 576-82.

7 C. Vann Woodward, *The Burden of Southern History*, 230.

8 American pastoralism in general has been studied by Leo Marx, *The Machine in the Garden: Technology and the Pastoral Ideal in America*, New York: Oxford University Press, 1964. It should be noted that regional art becomes pastoral only when the contrast between past and present, simplicity and complexity, is taken seriously by a writer.

9 Reynolds Price, "Speaking of Books: A Question of Influence," *New York Times Book Review* (29 May 1966): 2.

10 Reynolds Price in *Conversations: Reynolds Price and William Ray* (Memphis: Memphis State University Press, 1976), 24. Although Price has successfully fended off the claim that his own fiction, especially *A Long and Happy Life* (1962), is shaped by Faulkner's, he writes generously of Faulkner's art in an introduction to the

Signet edition of *Pylon* and has reprinted this essay in *Things Themselves: Essays & Scenes* (New York: Atheneum, 1972), 91-108.

11 Flannery O'Connor, from an unpublished lecture, cited in Stanley Edgar Hyman, *Flannery O'Connor* (Minneapolis: University of Minnesota Press, 1966), 44. Similar remarks about misunderstanding of "gothicism" and "grotesque" may be found in Flannery O'Connor, "The Fiction Writer and His Country," in *The Living Novel: A Symposium*, edited by Granville Hicks (New York: Macmillan, 1957), 157-64.

12 Stanley Edgar Hyman, *Flannery O'Connor*, 43.

13 Wright Morris, "The Territory Ahead," in *The Living Novel*, edited by Granville Hicks, 145.

14 William Styron, "My Generation," *Esquire*, 70 (October 1968), 123.

15 One critic suggests that Styron's whole procedure in *Lie Down in Darkness* is "elaborate literary pastiche," a kind of sympathetic mockery of Faulkner's techniques. See Melvin J. Friedman, *William Styron* (Bowling Green, Ohio: Bowling Green Popular Press, 1974), 29-30.

16 Alexander Blackburn, *The Cold War of Kitty Pentecost*, Chicago: Swallow Press, 1979.

17 Denis Donoghue, *The Third Voice: Modern British and American Verse Drama* (Princeton: Princeton University Press, 1959), 10.

18 Ibid., 260.

19 Albert J. Guerard, *The Triumph of the Novel: Dickens, Dostoevsky, Faulkner* (New York: Oxford University Press, 1976), 323.

20 William Faulkner, *Absalom, Absalom!* (New York: Vintage Books, 1972), 89.

21 I have adopted and enlarged upon the approach to structure taken by Lawrence Thompson, "A Defense of Difficulties in William Faulkner's Art," *The Carrell* (University of Miami), 4 (December 1963): 7-19. Thompson discusses dramatic structure in *Absalom, Absalom!* and in *Go Down, Moses.*

22 Faulkner's inspiration of García Márquez is explored in Mario Vargas Llosa, *Gabriel García Márquez: Historia de un deicidio* (Barcelona: Barral, 1971), 140-50. Vargas Llosa stresses Faulkner's creation of Yoknapatawpha, a unified world, as model for Macondo and Aracataca in the fiction of García Márquez.

On Reading Frank Waters

1 Frank Waters, *Pumpkin Seed Point* (Chicago: Swallow Press, 1969), 69.

2 Ibid., 72.

3 Essays and commentaries by those who consider Waters as the primary voice for western America are gathered in *Frank Waters: Man and Mystic*, edited by Vine Deloria, Jr., Athens, Ohio: Swallow Press/Ohio University Press, 1993.

4 No on-screen or off-screen credits for the film, *Wyatt Earp*, have been given to Waters, nor can one be sure that they were necessary, nor can I say that Waters would have welcomed them. Waters's original research on the Earps, and his story-telling powers in *The Earp Brothers of Tombstone: The Story of Mrs. Virgil Earp*, Lincoln and London: University of Nebraska Press, 1976, are open to anyone's discovery.

5 Faulkner's behavior remains mystifying. As guest of the University of Virginia, he was usually open, honest, and painstaking in his handling of conferences. See *Faulkner in the University: Class Conferences at the University of Virginia, 1957-1958*, edited by Frederick L. Gwynn and Joseph L. Blotner, Charlottesville: The University of Virginia Press, 1959.

6 Quay Grigg, review of *A Sunrise Brighter Still*, *American Literature*, 64:3 (September 1992): 619-620.

Waters and Modern Fiction

1 Henry James, *Essays in London and Elsewhere* (New York: Harper & Brothers, 1893), 138. Having just finished reading Flaubert's *Correspondence*, James began to see Flaubert as a tragic idealist and perfectionist.

2 Henry James, *Notes on Novelists with Some Other Notes* (New York: Charles Scribner's Sons, 1914), 108. The essay on Flaubert was originally written in 1902.

3 Mark Schorer, "Technique as Discovery," in *Critiques and Essays on Modern Fiction, 1920-1951*, selected by John W. Aldridge (New York: The Ronald Press Company, 1952), 68.

4 Ibid., 82.

5 Gustave Flaubert, *Correspondence*, 9 vols. (Paris: Louis Conard, 1926-33), III, 61. This famous observation, quoted by James in his 1893 essay, turns up again in Joyce's *Portrait of the Artist as a Young Man.*

6 Ibid., VIII, 374.

7 Ibid., III, 74.

8 Ibid., 149.

9 Henry James, "Preface to 'The Ambassadors'," in *The Art of the Novel: Critical Prefaces*, by Henry James (New York: Charles Scribner's Sons, 1934), 308.

10 Percy Lubbock, *The Craft of Fiction* (New York: Charles Scribner's Sons, 1921), 164.

11 Frank Waters's "Relationships and the Novel" was published in *The Writer* 56:4 (April 1943), 105-07. "Visions of the Good" (a title not chosen by Waters) is an unpublished 12-page typescript dated 16 July 1986.

12 Gustave Flaubert, *Correspondence*, III, 322-23.

13 Denis Donoghue, *The Sovereign Ghost: Studies in Imagination* (Berkeley and Los Angeles: University of California Press, 1976), 175.

14 Colin Falck, *Myth, Truth and Literature: Towards a True Post-Modernism* (Cambridge, New York, New Rochelle, Melbourne, Sydney: Cambridge University Press, 1989), xii.

15 C.G. Jung, *Modern Man in Search of a Soul*, translated by W.S. Dell and Cary F. Baynes (New York: Harcourt, Brace & World, Inc., 1953), 162.

16 Joseph Campbell, *The Masks of God: Creative Mythology* (London: Secker & Warburg, 1968), 3, 6-8, 40, 94, 646.

17 G. Wilson Knight, *The Wheel of Fire*, rev. and enl. ed. (London: Methuen & Co., Ltd., 1949), 11.

18 Joseph Campbell, *Creative Mythology*, 25.

19 Frank Waters, "Mysticism and Witchcraft," *South Dakota Review*, 15:3 (Autumn 1977): 70.

20 See John R. Milton, "Symbolic Space and Mysticism in the Novels of Frank Waters," *Studies in Frank Waters*, 5 (1982): 12-27.

21 Quay Grigg, "Frank Waters and the Mountain Spirit," *South Dakota Review*, 15:3 (Autumn 1977): 45.

Archetypal Promise from Apocalyptic Premise

1 Page references are to the revised edition of *The Woman at Otowi Crossing*, Athens: Swallow Press/Ohio University Press, 1987.

2 The "discovery" of psychic energy has only recently been accredited. For instance, Dr. Joseph Banks Rhine and his wife Dr. Louisa E. Rhine spent some fifty years at Duke University trailblazing and then doing the work of establishing the scientific foundation for parapsychology, but final respectability was not granted to parapsychology by the scientific establishment until 1969. At that time, the prestigious American Association for the Advancement of Science accepted, after rejecting two previous applications, the Parapsychological Association as a member organization.

3 See Arthur Koestler, *The Act of Creation*, New York: Macmillan, 1964; Fritjof Capra, *The Tao of Physics: An Exploration of the Parallels Between Modern Physics and Eastern Mysticism*, 2d ed., rev., Boulder, Colo.: Shambhala, 1983; and F. David Peat, *Synchronicity: The Bridge Between Mind and Matter*, Toronto: Bantam, New Age Books, 1987.

4 The concept is surveyed in Ernest W. Lefever and E. Stephen Hunt, eds., *The Apocalyptic Premise*, Washington, D.C.: Ethics and Public Policy Center, 1982.

5 In "Prelude to Change," Waters's commencement address at the University of Nevada, Las Vegas, on 23 May 1981, he reviews the Hopi prophecy about world destruction and then rejects the view that cataclysmic changes will overtake the planet.

6 References to editions of Frank Waters's works are as follows: *Masked Gods: Navaho and Pueblo Ceremonialism*, Chicago: Swallow Press, 1969; *Mexico Mystique: The Coming Sixth World of Consciousness*, Chicago: Swallow Press, 1975; *Pumpkin Seed Point*, Chicago: Swallow Press, 1969; *Mountain Dialogues*, Athens: Swallow Press/Ohio University Press, 1981.

7 M. Esther Harding, *Psychic Energy: Its Source and Goal* (New York: Pantheon Books, 1947), 8.

8 Jonathan Schell, *The Fate of the Earth* (New York: Alfred A. Knopf, 1982), 115. Scientific knowledge, Schell argues, has brought us face to face with the "death of mankind" and in doing so has "caused a basic change in the circumstances in which life was given to us, which is to say that we have altered the human condition."

9 In summarizing some conclusions about motivation, I have consulted Arthur Koestler, *The Act of Creation*, 495-508.

10 Joseph Campbell, *The Power of Myth*, with Bill Moyers, edited by Betty Sue Flowers (New York: Doubleday, 1988), 67.

11 Synchronicity was a concept long incubated. In 1930, Jung introduced the "synchronistic principle" in a memorial address to his friend Richard Wilhelm. The best-known references are Jung's Foreword to the *I Ching* (1950), "On Synchronicity" (1951), and "Synchronicity: An Acausal Connecting Principle" (1952).

12 F. David Peat, *Synchronicity*, 27.

13 In a letter to Dr. Selig dated 25 February 1953, Jung wrote, "It was Einstein who first started me off thinking about a possible relativity of time as well as space, and their psychic synchronicity." See June Singer, *Boundaries of the Soul: The Practice of Jung's Psychology* (Garden City, N.Y.: Doubleday, Anchor Books, 1973), 398.

14 Peat, *Synchronicity*, 186-87.

15 Erich Neumann, *Creative Man: Five Essays*, translated by Eugene Rolfe (Princeton: Princeton University Press, 1979), 254.

16 Jean Shinoda Bolen, *The Tao of Psychology: Synchronicity and the Self* (New York: Harper & Row, 1979), 84, italics in original.

17 Fritjof Capra, *The Tao of Physics*, 104-5.

18 An incidental source for the characterization of Helen Chalmers is the life of Edith Warner, who befriended J. Robert Oppenheimer and other physicists from Los Alamos. Waters himself was acquainted with Warner, and he began composition of *Otowi* in 1953. Therefore, he is not directly indebted to a book by Peggy Pond Church, *The House at Otowi Bridge* (1959). On Waters's use of details from Warner's life, see Frances M.

Malpezzi, "The Emergence of Helen Chalmers," in *Women in Western American Literature*, edited by Helen Stauffer (Troy, N.Y.: Whitson Publishing, 1982): 100-113.

19 Waters consistently views Quetzalcoatl as a Redeemer in *Pumpkin Seed Point* (101, 161-63, 167), in *Mexico Mystique* (57-59, 124-26, 133, 139, 193), and in *Mountain Dialogues* (143) and believes that the original transcendental myth was distorted by the Aztecs into a secular, materialistic ideology. It was this Aztec vulgarization of Quetzalcoatl that D.H. Lawrence fictionally restored to Mexico in his novel, *The Plumed Serpent*, according to Waters in an article, "Quetzalcoatl versus D.H. Lawrence's *Plumed Serpent*," *Western American Literature*, 3 (Summer 1968): 103-113.

20 In any edition of "Burnt Norton" this is part of line 64.

21 This point is made by Jean Bolen, *The Tao of Psychology*, 9.

22 Colin Falck, *Myth, Truth and Literature: Towards a True Post-Modernism* (Cambridge, New York, New Rochelle, Melbourne, Sydney: Cambridge University Press, 1989), 121.

23 The term "flashforwards" for the interviews in *Otowi* is used by Thomas J. Lyon, *Frank Waters* (New York: Twayne Publishers, 1973), 128.

24 Frances M. Malpezzi, "Meru, the Voice of the Mountain," *South Dakota Review*, 27 (1989): 33.

25 The archetypal image of light as life energy suddenly liberated by the "explosion" of death is discussed in Marie-Louise von Franz, *On Dreams and Death: A Jungian Interpretation*, translated by Emmanuel Xipolitas Kennedy and Vernon Brooks (Boston: Shambhala, 1987), 84.

26 Waters discusses some representations of the number seven in *Masked Gods* (222-23), *Pumpkin Seed Point* (137-38), and *Mexico Mystique* (175, 191). There are allusions in *Otowi* to Amerindian myths of seven womb-caves (51, 95, 151), which Emily believes are references to the seven traditional kivas within a pueblo, but which Helen considers a parable of Emergence. The tableau with seven deer obviously supports Helen's interpretation.

27 In any edition of "A Valediction: Forbidding Mourning," these are lines 21-24.

The Self as a Force for Human Survival

1 Joseph Campbell, *Myths to Live By*, New York: Viking Press, 1972, offers some examples and argumentation that I have used throughout this essay. I have supplemented his examples with some of my own, have offered a classification of the myths of war, and have added a discussion of "just" war before focusing the essay on the Atomic Age.

2 In 1999, the NATO air war to save Kosovo was widely justified as the prevention of a humanitarian catastrophe. In the United States it was argued that "we" are debased collectively if we ignore genocidal assaults on people or refuse to make clear that the standards of human decency that we uphold aren't hollow. See especially "The Last No-Man's-Land of the Century," *The Washington Spectator* 25:10 (May 15, 1999), and "Saving People from Doom Becomes Western Policy," *ibid.*, 25:13 (July 1, 1999).

3 Jonathan Schell, *The Fate of the Earth* (New York: Alfred A. Knopf, 1982), 115.

4 See Erich Fromm, *The Fear of Freedom*, London: Routledge & Kegan Paul, 1942.

5 Joseph Campbell, *The Masks of God: Creative Mythology* (London: Secker & Warburg, 1968), 677.

6 I have capitalized the "s" in Self in order to suggest the revelation of the creative spirit in man.

Peace Stars

1 The analogy about consciousness appears in Robert E. Ornstein, *The Psychology of Consciousness* (San Francisco: W.H. Freeman, 1972), 11. The relationship of consciousness to survival concerns is eloquently discussed in his *The Evolution of Consciousness*, New York: Prentice Hall, 1991.

2 Ibid., 5.

3 Abraham Maslow, *The Psychology of Science*, cited in ibid., 7.

4 The Lockean ideology of the West is discussed at length in F.S.C. Northrop, *The Meeting of East and West: An Inquiry Concerning World Understanding*, New York: Collier Books, 1966.

5 Frank Waters develops in many of his books the myth of Emergence and the idea of a coming world of consciousness, but see particularly *Mexico Mystique: The Coming Sixth World of Consciousness*, Chicago: Swallow Press, 1975.

6 See David Ballin Klein, *The Concept of Consciousness: A Survey* (Lincoln: University of Nebraska Press, 1985), 82-83.

7 Carl Sagan, *The Dragons of Eden: Speculations on the Evolution of Human Intelligence*, New York: Ballantine Books, 1978.

8 David Ballin Klein, *The Concept of Consciousness*, 111.

9 In the remainder of this essay, I am especially indebted to Alberta Steinman Gilinsky, *Mind and Brain: Principles of Neuropsychology*, New York: Praeger, 1984.

10 Cited in ibid., 460.

A Theodicy of Human Love

1 Leo Tolstoy, *The Death of Ivan Ilyich*, first published in 1886.

2 Louis D. Rubin, Jr., *The Faraway Country: Writers of the Modern*

South (Seattle: University of Washington Press, 1963), 209.

3 This argument is developed in Arthur Mizener, *The Sense of Life in the Modern Novel* (Boston: Houghton Mifflin, 1964), 23.

4 A theodicy represents the attempt to make a pact with death and may carry no promise of "redemption" at all—except for the redeeming assurance of meaning, itself. For a discussion of these matters from a sociologist's viewpoint, see Peter L. Berger, *The Sacred Canopy: Elements of a Sociological Theory of Religion* (Garden City, N.Y.: Doubleday & Company, 1967), 56-80.

5 Thomas Mann, *Last Essays*, translated by Richard and Clare Winston and Tania and James Stern (New York: Alfred A. Knopf, 1959), 177.

ALEXANDER BLACKBURN is the author of numerous books, fiction and nonfiction, among them *The Myth of the Picaro*; *The Cold War of Kitty Pentecost*; *The Interior Country: Stories of the Modern West*; *A Sunrise Brighter Still: The Visionary Novels of Frank Waters*; *Higher Elevations: Stories from the West*; and *Suddenly a Mortal Splendor*.